Women Who Live Evil Lives

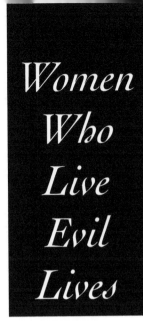

Women Who Live Evil Lives

Gender,
Religion,
and the
Politics of
Power in
Colonial
Guatemala

BY MARTHA FEW

University of Texas Press
Austin

Material from Martha Few, "Women, Religion, and Power: Gender and Resistance in Daily Life in Late-Seventeenth-Century Santiago de Guatemala," *Ethnohistory* 42:4 (Fall 1995), 627–637, is reprinted here with permission of the American Society for Ethnohistory.

Excerpts from Martha Few, " 'No es la palabra de Dios': acusaciones de enfermedad y las políticas culturales de poder en la Guatemala colonial, 1650–1720," *Mesoamérica* 20:38 (December 1999), 33–54, is reprinted here with permission of Plumsock Mesoamerican Studies.

"On Her Deathbed" by Martha Few, from *Colonial Lives: Documents on Latin American History 1550–1850*, edited by Richard Boyer & Geoffrey Spurling, copyright 2000 by Oxford University Press, Inc. Used by permission of Oxford University Press, Inc.

Library of Congress Cataloging-in-Publication Data

Few, Martha, 1964–
    Women who live evil lives : gender, religion, and the politics of power in colonial Guatemala / by Martha Few.
        p.   cm.
    Includes bibliographical references and index.
    ISBN 978-0-292-72549-2 (pbk. : alk. paper)
    1. Women—Guatemala—Antigua—Social conditions—17th century.
2. Women—Guatemala—Antigua—Social conditions—18th century.
3. Women healers—Guatemala—Antigua—History—17th century.
4. Women healers—Guatemala—Antigua—History—18th century.
5. Wizards—Guatemala—Antigua—History—17th century. 6. Wizards—Guatemala—Antigua—History—18th century. 7. Inquisition—Guatemala—Antigua. I. Title.
HQ1480.A58 F49   2002
305.42'097281—dc21   2002003572

For my parents

Contents

Preface

This project analyzes descriptions of the lives and practices of so-called *mujeres de mal vivir*, or women who live evil lives, in seventeenth- and eighteenth-century Santiago de Guatemala (now Antigua), the capital city of colonial Central America. Inquisition sources and other colonial-era documents contain this phrase and variations on it, such as *mujer-sillas de mal vivir* (worthless women who live evil lives), often used to identify female sorcerers, witches, magical healers, and leaders of clandestine religious devotions.

Scholars have employed Inquisition records as historical evidence in a wide variety of contexts and culture areas, from early modern Europe to colonial Mexico and Peru. The use of Inquisition sources and their interpretations remains controversial, however, in large part because of the ambiguous nature of the descriptions they contain of supernatural events and ritual power within community conflicts in daily life.

While working with Inquisition sources for colonial Guatemala, I have made a consistent effort to remain aware of how personal animosities and the racial, gender, and class hierarchies of colonial rule influenced the testimonies and to convey that in my analysis, both in the way Inquisition officials presented evidence and in the way men and women of different social and ethnic groups used and manipulated such descriptions and accusations in community conflicts. Colonial political and religious officials, along with community members themselves, strategically deployed characterizations of certain women as witches, sorcerers, and spell-casters in the social relations of power in Santiago de Guatemala. Women themselves also deployed the same terms in a variety of contexts, to attack or criticize the power of rivals and personal enemies, to enhance their own authority and reputations as magical specialists, and to attract more paying customers for the ritual services they offered, which included magical healing, sexual witchcraft, casting spells and curses, and protection from evil.

My goal, then, has been to critically assess the evidence presented and at the same time uncover and analyze the rich discourses and practices of ritual power found in women's cultural roles in colonial Santiago de Guatemala. Thus I use the phrase "women who live evil lives" in an attempt to capture this complicated and contested process. In this way, I wish to avoid exoticizing Guatemalan women as historical subjects, always a difficult endeavor because discourses and representations of African, indigenous, European, and *casta* (mixed-race) women found in Inquisition and other historical sources, especially in colonial contexts, specifically targeted and highlighted the exotic and the fantastic in prosecuting religious deviance.

Santiago de Guatemala, where this study takes place, was an important city in the seventeenth- and eighteenth-century Spanish colonial empire as the political and religious capital of the Audiencia of Guatemala, an area that encompassed what today is Chiapas, Guatemala, Honduras, El Salvador, Costa Rica, and Nicaragua. Yet despite Santiago's importance, historians working on colonial Spanish America have often overlooked it, focusing instead on central Mexico and the Andes, or on other regional histories, such as the Yucatán and Chiapas. This is in striking contrast to the field of anthropology, for which Guatemala has long been a central and significant area of scholarship. This work is in part an effort to address this gap.

In addition, Guatemala's continuing importance as an area of historical and anthropological study should not be underestimated. It has periodically become a prime focus of twentieth-century U.S. foreign policy and Cold War politics. Guatemalan military rule of the 1970s and 1980s, known as La Violencia, provides an important point of comparison with other Latin American countries that experienced military rule and state-directed violence against domestic populations. Furthermore, despite the legacies of colonialism, U.S. intervention, and the politics of La Violencia, Maya peoples in Guatemala and elsewhere continue an ongoing process of cultural resilience and revitalization.

In this work I have primarily relied on the colonial racial-ethnic designations used to describe those who appear in Inquisition records, such as "Indian" (*indio/a*); "Spaniard" (*español/a*); and "Black" (*negro/a*).

"Mestizo/a" referred to a person of mixed Spanish and Indian descent. In Central America, "Mulato/a" referred to a person of mixed African, Spanish, and/or Indian descent. To flesh out these crude and often imprecise categories, I offer more specific information wherever possible on race, ethnicity, place of origin, and language spoken. In addition, to enhance the readability of the text, I have modernized spellings and added accents to words and names used in the colonial-era documents that I consulted.

While completing this project, I benefited greatly from the generous help and support of family, friends, and colleagues. I wish first to thank my family: my parents, Dudley and Sue Ann Few, to whom I dedicate this book; my brother, John; and my husband, Keisuke Hirano. I could not have completed this without them. I would also like to thank my aunts, uncles, and cousins who invited me to stay with them during research trips and holidays far from home: the Ball family, Dan Few, Kathy Ledwith, the Powell families, and the McGrael family. Special thanks go to my aunt Lynda Smothers in Tucson.

I first began to study Latin America seriously when I was an undergraduate at the University of Chicago, and I benefited greatly from the faculty and my friends there. I also thank my fellow graduate students in the History Department at the University of Arizona, especially Michael Brescia, Donna Meyer-Hickel, Renee Obrecht-Como, Phyllis Smith, and Vicki Weinberg. I learned much from University of Arizona professors Maureen Fitzgerald, Donna Guy, Oscar Martínez, and Michael Meyer. I thank Karen Anderson, Laura Tabili, and especially Bert Barickman, who offered insightful comments at crucial points along the way. In Cambridge, I thank Guido Imbens and my fellow members of the Traymore Institute for all their help: Kate Baicker, Alan Durrel, Raymond Fisman, Scott Lasensky, Rory MacFarquhar, Peter Steinberg, and Nicholas Weiss. I also wish to thank Amanda Angel, Peter Guardino, Leonardo Hernández, Marcus Kurtz, Gregg Osborne, Matthew Restall, Christa Little-Siebold, and Todd Little-Siebold.

I have received financial support from the University of Arizona, the American Society for Ethnohistory, and the University of Miami's History Department and College of Arts and Sciences. I wish to thank the staffs at the Archivo General de Centro América, the Archivo Histórico Arquidiocesano "Francisco de Paula García Peláez" (both in Guatemala), the Archivo General de la Nación (Mexico), and the Archivo General de Indias (Spain). A Ruth and Lincoln Ekstrom Fellowship allowed me to spend a productive fall 1996 at the John Carter Brown

Library at Brown University. I would especially like to thank Norman Fiering and Daniel Slive for their help while I worked at the "JCB." Wendy Schiller gave me a place to stay and included me in her busy social life while I was in Providence. In August 1998 I presented a chapter of this work and received helpful feedback from Bernard Bailyn and the participants at Harvard University's International Seminar on the History of the Atlantic World.

I spent 1999–2000 in residence at the Newberry Library in Chicago revising my dissertation into a book with a Rockfeller Foundation Postdoctoral Fellowship. My formal and informal conversations with fellows and staff greatly enhanced my work, especially with James Grossman, Helen Tanner, Janaina Amado, Bruce Calder, Anne Cruz, Fran Dolan, Amy Froide, Peter Hulme, Janine Lanza, James Martin, Jean O'Brien, Susan Schroeder, Javier Villa Flores, Lisa Vollendorf, Michael Willrich, and Susan Wolverton. I also thank my colleagues in the History Department and the College of Arts and Sciences at the University of Miami. I thank Chris Lutz for his friendship and his skill at helping a young scholar enter the field of colonial Guatemalan history. Chris generously shared with me his enthusiasm, manuscript sources, and deep knowledge of the history of Guatemala. I am greatly indebted to Kevin Gosner, my graduate school adviser and friend, who patiently guided and encouraged me in my study of colonial Guatemala and who, in the end, stood back and let me find my own way.

Women Who Live Evil Lives

Contested Powers:
Gender, Culture, and the Process of Colonial Rule

Illustrious Sir: The roots of this evil are great, and have shamelessly spread throughout this city between *mujersillas de mal vivir* [worthless women who live evil lives].

—LETTER FROM JOSÉ DE BAÑOS Y SOTOMAYOR, *COMISARIO* OF GUATEMALA'S INQUISITION, TO THE MEXICAN OFFICE OF THE INQUISITION, 15 NOVEMBER 1695[1]

In 1704 Padre José de Quevedo denounced Lorenza de Molina and her sister-in-law, María de Santa Inéz, to the Inquisition *comisario* (commissioner; head of Guatemala's Inquisition) in Santiago de Guatemala, capital of colonial Central America.[2] Padre Quevedo asserted that the women entered his bedroom in the form of two bright lights, which then shape-changed into human form. One of the women ripped the rosary from the priest's neck and blindfolded him, and they both carried him to another room. There, they stripped him naked, tied him to a bench in the shape of a cross as if he were being crucified, and turned him upside down, so that his head pointed toward the floor and his feet pointed toward the ceiling. The women beat him severely over his body for the entire night and "shamefully wounded" his genitals. Padre Quevedo later claimed that in the middle of the beating, the women lit incense and made a pact with the devil, to which the priest responded with his own prayer, invoking the Virgin Mary and the Archangel Michael in an effort to save his life and his soul. The next morning, a neighbor found Padre Quevedo dazed and terrified, his body covered with infected wounds.[3] Lorenza de Molina, a mestiza immigrant from Peru, fled Santiago before Inquisition officials could arrest her. Authorities arrested and imprisoned her sister-in-law, María de Santa Inéz, a mulata street peddler who had a reputation for violence. María later escaped from jail, apparently with the help of some female friends.

Read in the broader context of the process of colonial rule in Latin America, Padre Quevedo's fantastic account of his beating illustrates the connections among gender, religion, and relations of power in con-

Gulf of
Mexico

Campeche

• Mérida

Yucatán
Peninsula

Salamanca •
de Bacalar

N

Caribbean

Sea

Ciudad Real
•
CHIAPA

SOCONUSCO

GUATEMALA

Santiago de
Guatemala •

Escuintla •

Trujillo

HONDURAS

Comayagua

Tegucigalpa

San •
Salvador

• Nueva Segovia

León •
• NICARAGUA

Granada •

Pacific Ocean

Nicoya •

COSTA

Cartago •
RICA

0   200 miles

0   300 kilometers

MAP 1. Audiencia de Guatemala. By John V. Cotter.

flicts and confrontations in daily life in a colonial Spanish American city.[4] This work analyzes the gender and ethnic dimensions of cultural authority and power within the process of colonial rule in Latin America. I focus on seventeenth- and eighteenth-century accounts of the lives and practices of so-called mujeres de mal vivir—female sorcerers, magical healers and midwives, and clandestine religious leaders— in Santiago de Guatemala. Community members from all segments of colonial society consulted these women in multiethnic urban communities such as Santiago and asked them to intervene in a variety of conflicts in daily life: in sexual and familial relations, in disputes between neighbors and rival shop owners, in instances of abuse by colonial officials, employers, and husbands, and in cases of bewildering and often bizarre illnesses. Women based their community authority on their knowledge of the body and the natural world, connected to Spanish, African, and Mayan ideas and practices of religion and the supernatural. Women maintained their power through reputation, public displays of healing, violence, and devotional acts, and the creation of informal social ties, which often crossed the ethnic, status, and rural/urban boundaries of colonial society.

Women's local practices of devotional acts, curing, and magic revealed opportunities for women's cultural authority and power in daily life in Santiago de Guatemala. On the one hand, women's use of ritual practices to intervene in community conflicts and earn money despite the dangers reveals the crucial but often overlooked gender dynamics of power within the broader framework of ethnic and cultural contestation of colonial rule. On the other hand, women's public roles in local religious cultures left them vulnerable to accusations of sorcery and became opportunities for the Spanish state to reinscribe colonial rule at the community level through institutions such as the Inquisition.

This work explores three broad historical processes and their interconnections, which have been central to the study of colonial Latin America. First, I analyze colonialism as a contested process, an idea that has characterized the last ten years of work in Latin American history and anthropology, spurred on by the Columbus quincentenary.[5] Analyses of daily life, as well as local and regional studies that address colonialism by considering the material and cultural history of the area under study, have shown that colonial rule was always mediated by precolonial indigenous practices as well as postconquest contestation by ethnic groups who challenged and reshaped colonial rule in Latin America.[6] Rethinking colonial rule as a contested process invites the integration of the actions of ethnically and economically marginalized groups into the analysis of state formation in colonial Guatemala.[7] Through the manipulation of institutions and the re-creation of cultural practices based on lived experiences in Spanish America, colonial peoples contested the terms of rule.

This study highlights the role of religion and the integration of Spanish, African, and Mayan ideas and practices in this process. Religious practices and beliefs became important not only through the formal, institutional practice of Catholicism but also through popular expressions of Catholic piety in daily life. The Catholic church and its repre-

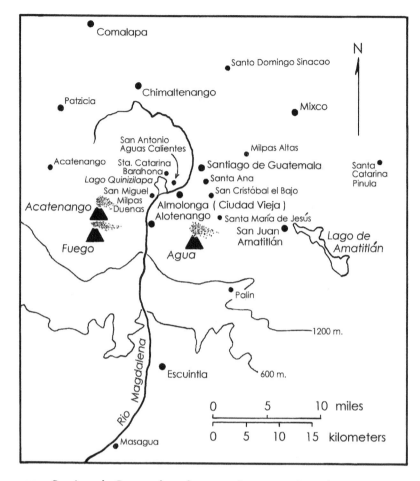

MAP 2. Santiago de Guatemala and surrounding towns. By John V. Cotter.

sentatives in the New World played an integral role in the violent process of Spanish conquest and the establishment of colonialism. Through
institutional mechanisms such as confession and the Inquisition and
through the vigilance of parish priests as well as members of Guatemala's religious orders—the Franciscans, the Mercedarians, the Dominicans, and the Jesuits—the Catholic church attempted to define and
monitor the social and cultural behavior of colonial peoples and outline normative gender roles for men and women.[8] Inquisition sources
such as those that recorded the violence used against Padre Quevedo
show how church officials became immediately concerned about such
shocking acts as an attack on a priest.[9]

In Guatemala and elsewhere in colonial Latin America, however, informal religious practices, in which ethnically and economically marginalized peoples drew on Spanish, African, and indigenous religious traditions, held the potential for symbolic and cultural contestation of colonial rule. There are numerous examples of nonelites using religious symbols and rituals to resist serious changes such as structural and political transformations of state power and outright rebellion against Spanish colonial rule.[10] Men and women also used religious symbols and rituals to legitimate their authority and power not just in larger revolts and rebellions but also in everyday social relations. Making this link between women and religion to analyze cultural authority and power under colonial rule reveals how women drew on ideas and practices of religion and the supernatural and reformulated them to assert their authority and power in the local community. Women then used this authority and power to overtly challenge gender, racial, and colonial hierarchies and intervene in conflicts and problems in daily life. As a result, the practices of female sorcerers, healers, and clandestine cult leaders informally linked women and men of different ethnic and social groups in colonial Santiago de Guatemala.

The second broad historical process that this study addresses is how women and men exercised authority and power in community social relations. I draw on the insights of social historians who integrated the lives of women, the poor, and other marginalized groups as historical actors.[11] Historians and anthropologists who have analyzed the connections between gender and state formation have argued that gender ideology formed an integral part of colonial power in the process of Spanish colonial state building.[12] These scholars maintained that colonial rule manipulated cultural systems of meaning and convincingly pointed to gender, along with ethnicity and status, as a site of contestation and negotiation.

All underline the importance of women's cultural roles and highlight women's use and re-creation of clandestine and illegal pre-Columbian religious practices to resist conquest and the ensuing restructuring of social relations, especially in rural settings.[13] Scholars of colonial Latin America have recently extended this analysis to urban histories, especially ethnic relations in colonial cities.[14] For the most part, however, women's cultural roles in social relations in urban life remain largely unexplored, despite the important although informal roles women played in political, economic, and social life. This work addresses this need and places women's social and cultural roles within the larger historical context of material bases for power and oppression in colonial Guatemala.[15]

Feminist and women's historians have critiqued frameworks that characterize the category "women" as a monolithic whole, in terms of ignoring important ethnic and status divisions and especially through characterizations of third world women, vis-à-vis first world women, as powerless victims of particular political or economic systems, such as colonialism.[16] To avoid this, I draw on Belinda Bozzoli's concept of a "patchwork of patriarchies" to analyze how women's lives and experiences under colonial rule differed by cultural context, ethnicity, and status.[17] While female sorcerers in seventeenth- and eighteenth-century Santiago de Guatemala did not attempt to overthrow colonial rule, neither were they simply passive victims of colonial political and patriarchal power. Instead, women played key roles in cultural relations in community life in Santiago, which took place on local, intimate, and face-to-face terms.

Female sorcerers, magical healers, and popular religious leaders based their authority and power on their knowledge of the human body and the natural world, derived from biological and social experiences of daily life: giving birth, lactation, preparing and distributing food, caring for the sick, and preparing the dead for burial. Furthermore, the human body became a site of power contestation in women's use of magical practices in daily life. For example, women seen as sorcerers used doctored food and drink that contained female body parts and fluids, supplemented with herbs, flowers, insects, and other ritual items, in attempts to control men's behavior. In the case of Padre Quevedo, the two women were said to have attacked the priest with the help of the devil and marked his body, including his genitals, with scars and wounds.

Michel Foucault and others have argued that the body is a site of power contestation and that the punishment of the body by the state is a political act.[18] This top-down view, however, focused on institutional power and ignored the gendered aspects of the body as a site of contestation. As early as 1941, Lois Paul noted in her ethnographic work on Zutuhil-Maya speakers on the shore of Lake Atitlán in Guatemala: "Ideas about the body are an important component of self-concept and can provide important clues to not only the individual but the social order as well."[19] By examining women's practices of magical authority and power in the community, based on knowledge of the body and the natural world and connected to religious beliefs and practices, this study places women's cultural roles within the larger historical context of unequal yet contested relations of power under colonial rule in Guatemala.[20]

The third major process that this study addresses is community formation. The construction of racial and ethnic identity has long been a focus of Latin American history and anthropology. Ethnohistorical studies of colonial Latin America, especially of Mesoamerica, have focused primarily on rural indigenous communities.[21] Recent ethnographic work by John Monaghan and John Watanabe, for example, has argued for a less structural view of communities and redefined them as "meaningfully bounded social places rather than institutionally delimited structures."[22] A dynamic view of community, wherein alliances and identities continuously re-form, can illuminate how and why women created multiethnic social networks given the conditions of their daily lives in colonial Guatemala.

Furthermore, by focusing mainly on indigenous rural communities, Latin Americanists have tended to overstate the dichotomy between city and countryside in colonial life and to gloss over the cultural, family, religious, and economic links between inhabitants of cities and the surrounding rural towns. Daily life in colonial cities entailed links to rural peoples in villages in the countryside, and this is certainly true in Santiago de Guatemala. This study seeks to illuminate the linkages between the two spheres rather than their separation. Historical records show the movement of people between city and countryside through religious pilgrimages, family ties, the activities of market vendors and traveling salespeople, sexual relationships, and the exchange of ritual items such as flowers, plants, and herbs. Women's popular religious practices, beliefs, and knowledge were continually reinforced by this movement of people, ideas, and ritual goods between the capital city and the countryside. This geographic mobility in daily life, in addition to migration in and out of the capital and the ease of flight from colonial authorities, made policies of social control difficult to enforce.[23] The social connections described in Padre Quevedo's testimony between Lorenza de Molina, a mestiza immigrant from Peru who became a resident of Santiago, with her sister-in-law María de Santa Inéz, a mulata from a primarily indigenous town close to the capital, is one example of ties between women that spanned urban-rural divisions.

I base my analysis on archival sources—Inquisition records, civil and ecclesiastical proceedings and correspondence, city council records—gathered in Guatemala, Mexico, and Spain. I supplement these sources with colonial Guatemalan and Mexican religious tracts, doctrinal manuals, relations of pious lives, and contemporary histories. Inquisition records typically contain information regarding living conditions, foods eaten and meals prepared, family life, ties to neighbors, personal conflicts, and the importance of religion and religious beliefs. They also contain detailed accounts of rituals and ritual objects used by women, as well as their ideas about the connections between religion and power. Accounts in Inquisition records show daily interactions between community members across gender, ethnic, and status lines, between people of different *barrios* (neighborhoods), and between urban and rural dwellers. These sources also offer evidence about how women claimed authority and power in multiethnic urban communities.

Accounts of women's roles in daily life contained in Inquisition sources, however, were structured through the bureaucratic procedures and practices of the Holy Office. These are historical sources from a Spanish institution, and the testimonies found there were shaped to some degree by the Inquisition. For example, many of the accounts are of seemingly fantastic occurrences, as in the case of Padre Quevedo, including pacts with the devil, strange illnesses, or miraculous healings, in which priests, colonial officials, neighbors, and family members attributed certain kinds of power and certain kinds of deviance to women. This included a knowledge of magical plants and herbs, the ability to communicate with the devil and other supernatural beings, and the ability to use sorcery to heal as well as to inflict harm and even death. Moreover, historians must take into account that Inquisition authorities used prescribed vocabularies during questioning and in the descriptions of testimonies in correspondence. These prescribed vocabularies, in turn, limited the possibilities and shaped the stories that emerged in the record.

Nevertheless, Inquisition sources capture firsthand accounts of women and the poor in colonial Guatemala at a time when most inhabitants could not sign their names to their Inquisition testimonies and left little in the way of written documents. What makes Guatemalan Inquisition sources particularly rich is that they were mostly unstructured and did not follow rigid lines of questioning. In addition, Inquisition officials themselves did not always follow the rules and sometimes took action that ignored or circumvented official procedures. As a result, historians can begin to uncover the lives of multiethnic populations to understand the issues that confronted women and men in colonial Latin America and the larger implications of these histories for the process of rule in colonial Latin America.[24] These sources reveal what people thought women could do, how they did it, and the reasons they did it, as well provide evidence regarding women's broader survival norms in Santiago de Guatemala. And, importantly for this study, these sources contain descriptions of religious rituals and beliefs that were both powerful and attractive to Black, indigenous, Spanish, and casta women and to their communities.

The Inquisition, as an institution, has received considerable scholarly attention in recent years in both Europe and the Americas. Some scholars have characterized supernatural manifestations, witch-hunts, and the role of the Inquisition as a conflict between the institutional church and popular religion, played out during the transition from a premodern to a modern era.[25] Others have analyzed the Inquisition as an institution exercising top-down social control and so characterized it as a colonial phenomenon in Spanish America.[26]

Sorcery and supernatural manifestations, however, can also be read as evidence of conflict within a culture, and that is where I focus my analysis. As a result, this is not an institutional study of the Inquisition in Guatemala. Instead, I use Inquisition records along with other historical sources as evidence regarding social relations of power within communities: the power of female sorcerers to intervene in community conflicts and difficulties and the power of the colonial state in general, and the Inquisition in particular, as an agent of colonial oppression or domination, to curb the activities of female sorcerers. Accounts of supernatural interventions described by women and men of all social groups provide evidence of how to understand and analyze the politics of power within communities under colonial rule.

These conflicting agencies—the agency of women in alliance with other women and men in local communities and the agency of the Inquisition in pursuit of illegal religious practices—enter the historical record through Inquisition documents. Within this field of power relations, men and women in Santiago de Guatemala at times chose to consult female sorcerers to resolve their conflicts and problems and at other times chose to cooperate with colonial officials and denounce the women. In many cases, however, the Inquisition and other colonial authorities were not brought into these kinds of conflicts until an extraordinary amount of agency was shown on the part of female sorcerers and their clients.

In the case of Padre Quevedo, the escalating conflict between the priest and the two women continued over a number of months. The women reportedly used intimidation, and the priest found suspicious leaves, herbs, and human bones in and around his home, evidence that he took to be ritual items associated with sorcery. At one point, fed up with the women's public disrespect toward him, Padre Quevedo beat Lorenza on the front doorstep of his home in full view of neighbors and passersby. Neither the women nor the priest called for the assistance of political or religious authorities until after the two women kidnapped the priest, beat him, and left him for dead.

The papal bulls of 1521 and 1522 initially established the Inquisition in New Spain. It was first directed by the regular orders and then by Mexican bishops, who were also sometimes friars.[27] In 1571 King Philip II formally established the Inquisition tribunal in Peru and Mexico. The Mexican Inquisition was centered in Mexico City and had jurisdiction over all of New Spain, an area that covered the southwestern United States, Mexico, the Philippines, and Central America. In 1571 Indians, deemed new converts, were exempted from the Inquisition, and a parallel institution, called the Proviserato, was established.

During the initial years of Inquisition activity in Spain and Spanish America, authorities focused on pursuing crimes of heresy, first against *conversos* (baptized Jews and their descendants) and later against suspected Protestants. In the New World, the focus on heresy extended to prosecuting crimes of idolatry among Indian populations. The early years of the Inquisition in Spain and colonial Spanish America were characterized by brutality and violence, including autos-da-fé in Spain and colonial Mexico.[28] The Mexican Inquisition's suppression of conversos peaked in the 1590s and again in the 1640s.[29]

The trials and punishments for heresy, especially in the early years of colonial rule, were among the most dramatic and severe examples of Inquisitional power. Nonetheless, the Mexican tribunal primarily policed less dramatic crimes of "superstitions," "sorcery," and "witchcraft."[30] According to Solange Alberro, heresy prosecutions made up only 11 percent of the *procesos* (lawsuits, proceedings) in colonial Mexico, while figures from peninsular tribunals indicate that approximately 40 percent of procesos dealt with heresy.[31] Thus much of the Inquisition's activity in New Spain, which included colonial Guatemala, targeted crimes other than heresy.[32]

Multiethnic networks of mainly poor Spanish, indigenous, Black, and casta women, described in Inquisition documents and discussed in civil and ecclesiastical correspondence, fed elite fears of the corruption of the larger society via *maestras*, female "masters" or "teachers" believed to have taught others practices of sorcery. Colonial officials did not express a similar concern for men's sorcery networks, nor were men's networks as such defined as deviant. In 1694, for example, the comisario of the Guatemalan Inquisition wrote to his superiors in Mexico City:

> I believe [this Indian woman] to be one of the evil roots of the tricks and curses that are being introduced among *mujersillas de mal vivir* in this city . . . and I am denouncing the women to cut short the cancer that has spread through the *gente ordinaria* [common people].[33]

Beneath this was the more general fear and repression of African, indigenous, and mixed-race populations under Spanish colonial rule in the Americas in the context of demographic and economic changes in Guatemala. These changes created an ambiguity of colonial authority within the specific historical context of the late-seventeenth- and early-eighteenth-century transformation of Santiago de Guatemala into a multiethnic city. This change, along with the revival of regional and local economies, opened up opportunities for women, in both economic and cultural life. I argue that an analysis of gender, ethnicity, and women's roles in supernatural activities in late-seventeenth-century Guatemala reveals how women became specifically vulnerable to sorcery accusations and at the same time had a wide range of opportunities opened to them.

Chapter 2 places the study in the historical and cultural context of the revival of the local economy and the emergence of Santiago de Guatemala as a multiethnic city. I argue that this period of flux created expanded opportunities for women's cultural authority and power in daily life, explored through rumors that a female mixed-race sorcerer bewitched the president of the Audiencia and other political and religious officials in the capital.

Chapter 3 analyzes the role that the physical body played in local social relations, as female sorcerers refashioned the body as a site of magical violence and women's power. Furthermore, female sorcerers and their clients used their own female body parts and fluids as magical weapons in practices of sexual witchcraft. Inhabitants of Santiago portrayed those female sorcerers as powerful and dangerous shape-changers, who used their ability to transform their bodies and the bodies of their enemies to enact magical violence.

Chapter 4 outlines women's authority and power in daily life through practices of magical healing and midwifery, an extension and re-creation of female domestic roles, connected to Mayan, African, and Spanish practices and beliefs about religion. I argue that men's and women's explanations for illness not only reflect intracommunity conflicts but also reveal opportunities for women's power, viewed through supernatural illness accusations against female healers and midwives.

Chapter 5 explores how women's sorcery practices intertwined with material concerns of daily life through economic witchcraft and highlights the formation of multiethnic social networks around supernatural strategies of community conflict resolution. Women reinforced their authority through public displays of power, spread through reputation and gossip, which, at the same time, attracted the attention of colonial officials and created opportunities for state intervention in community relations.

Society and Colonial Authority in Santiago de Guatemala

This woman . . . appears to be one of the common, shameless types of women in this city [who practice] frauds and mischief, and if we punished all of them, Illustrious Sir, there would not be enough jails to put them in. But I believe . . . that it is necessary to punish some of them, so that the others see it and are warned.

— LETTER FROM JOSÉ DE BAÑOS Y SOTOMAYOR, HEAD OF GUATEMALA'S INQUISITION, TO THE MEXICAN OFFICE OF THE INQUISITION, 14 MARCH 1695[1]

In 1523 Pedro de Alvarado, Hernán Cortés's second-in-command at Tenochtitlán, accompanied by his Spanish soldiers and Nahua-speaking allies, left Mexico and headed south toward what would later become colonial Guatemala. Even before Alvarado fought his first battle against the K'iche' Maya, European epidemic diseases, including pneumonic plague, smallpox, and typhus, killed large numbers of native peoples there.[2] In February 1524 Alvarado and his army defeated the K'iche' on the plains of Pinal outside Xelajuh (present-day Quetzaltenango). With Alvarado's victory in this battle and the subsequent destruction of the K'iche' capital of K'umarcaah, Spain began its effort to bring Guatemala under colonial control.[3]

Preliminary Spanish attempts to consolidate colonial rule originated with the construction of a capital city to represent, both literally and symbolically, the new political realities of conquest and the subjugation of indigenous peoples. Alvarado first established a military capital that functioned as the temporary center of Spanish rule in the defeated Kaqchikel city of Iximché. In 1527 Spanish authorities relocated the capital city to Santiago de Almolonga in the valley of Almolonga, on the lower slopes of Agua volcano. Fourteen years later, in 1541, after days of rain, a flood and mudslide, possibly triggered by an earthquake, swept down the slopes of the nearby volcano and destroyed the city. One contemporary observer wrote:

At two in the morning there was a great storm of water from the heights of the volcano that is above Guatemala, and it was so sudden that there

MAP 3. City of Santiago de Guatemala. By John V. Cotter.

was no place to help the dead and injured . . . and the storm of the earth was so great that it brought before it the water and rocks and trees.[4]

Some six hundred Indian slaves, one hundred Spanish colonists, and an unspecified number of African slaves died.

Colonial authorities then moved the capital city, Santiago de Guatemala, to the site occupied today by Antigua, in the nearby Valley of Panchoy, and construction began in late 1541.[5] On 10 March 1543, the new town council (*ayuntamiento*) met for the first time, and on 21 May of the same year, the city of Santiago officially celebrated the transfer of the capital with a religious procession on the day of Corpus Christi.[6] A royal directive (*real cédula*) established the diocese in Santiago as the bishopric capital. City officials assigned plots of land and Indian tribute goods and services to each of the three religious orders, the Dominicans, the Mercedarians, and the Franciscans, to aid in the construction of new parish churches, convents, and other religious buildings in the city. By 1542 the Franciscans finished construction on their church and convent, and in 1546 the Mercedarians completed the work on their convent, except for the main chapel.[7]

Colonial officials reaffirmed the link between secular and religious authority and power in colonial Guatemala when church officials and Santiago's town government together named San Sebastián patron saint and protector of the capital from earthquakes and established a yearly celebration in his name. The king of Spain sent a box containing the holy relics of San Sebastián to Santiago, and religious authorities deposited them in the parish church. The town government then distributed four keys to the box of relics to both secular and ecclesiastical officials: the Cathedral treasurer, the priest of the city council (*capellán*), and two unnamed royal officials.[8]

Catholicism and the Catholic church played an integral role in the conquest and the establishment of colonial rule in Spanish America. Mass baptisms of native peoples, using the conversion of Indian elites as examples to the rest of the community, characterized religious conversion in the aftermath of conquest. After Alvarado and his army defeated the K'iche' Maya, a K'iche' *título* (native-language land documents containing historical information) described the immediate religious conversion of the local male elite:

After battling with the Indians, the Spaniards returned to this town of Quetzaltenango to rest and eat. Then a *principal* [town elder] from Quetzaltenango came to see the Adelantado [Alvarado]. . . . [T]hen the

Adelantado don Pedro commanded that they [the *principales*] were to be baptized, and he gave each one a name.[9]

Religious authorities in Guatemala and the rest of Spanish America used violence and the threat of violence to suppress native religious beliefs and practices.[10]

The *Patronato Royal* (Royal Patronage), an agreement made between Rome and the Spanish monarchy, confirmed the Spanish crown's authority over the church in the Americas. This pact ceded to the crown royal control over ecclesiastical institutions, nominations, and the management of church revenues.[11] The Catholic church attempted to define and regulate the religious behavior of all colonial peoples, including the conversion of native peoples and the regulation of Indian life. In the Americas two main groups undertook this role, the regulars, who had the exclusive right to convert indigenous populations, and the seculars, who were concerned with enforcing Spanish and later casta orthodoxy mainly in towns and cities. In Guatemala, the regular orders of the Mercedarians, Franciscans, and Dominicans were charged with converting indigenous populations.[12]

Along with the official rituals and institutions of Catholicism, popular religious expressions by the faithful emerged outside of the institution of the church, among Indians and Spaniards alike. These included religious visions, such as that of the Virgin Mary, seen by community members of the Kaqchikel-Maya town of Sololá located near Lake Atitlán, west of the capital:

> Today, Saturday, June 16, [1600], or, that is, 9 Ymox, Mary and her beloved child were seen; she came to the table while they kneaded. It was the image of [the Virgin] Mary. Then they went to kneel before the image, and the children also knelt. We also knelt. On the following day, we told of the grace we had received. The heart would not let us speak when the child was in the arms of San Melchor. It was seven at night when our heart was comforted. I, Francisco Díaz. Twenty-one of us gathered to see [the Virgin] Mary.[13]

"Two Republics" in Santiago de Guatemala

Political, economic, and racial distinctions between the Spanish conquerors and the subject Indian populations, codified into law, structured colonial rule in sixteenth-century Guatemala. A series of royal

directives called for the creation of "two republics," Indian and Spanish, a policy at once designed to protect Indians from Spanish abuses
and to aid in the collection of tribute and forced labor. This policy applied to rural towns and urban communities. The division of society
into two republics reflected official Spanish racial and social hierarchies
of power and reinforced the political realities of daily life under colonial
rule.[14]

The two-republic system not only reinforced legal divisions in colonial society, it also shaped daily life in Santiago de Guatemala in important ways. For example, the structural layout of Santiago, named the
capital city of colonial Central America in 1570, reinforced the divisions
between Indian and Spaniard. El Sagrario parish, centered around the
main plaza (*plaza mayor*), formed the Spanish core of the city. Here,
Spanish officials located the most important institutions of colonial authority and power: the Cathedral, the offices of the city government,
the city jail, and the palaces of the bishop and the president of the Audiencia.[15] Major political and religious celebrations and rituals, such as
bullfights, public processions, and religious speeches, took place in the
central plaza. The plaza also served as the location of Santiago's daily
market.

Most of the Spanish inhabitants of the capital settled in large houses
near the plaza.[16] Indian barrios, legally recognized entities, ringed the
Spanish core. Indians who lived in these barrios had their own institutions of local government as well as religious brotherhoods (*cofradías*),
overseen by parish priests and other colonial officials. In return, Indian
officials ensured that the inhabitants of their barrios complied with tribute and forced labor requirements.[17]

As part of its broader effort to enforce Catholic orthodoxy in daily
life in Santiago and the rest of the Audiencia of Guatemala, the church
used institutions and practices such as religious brotherhoods and confession. The Holy Office of the Inquisition, established in New Spain
in 1571, along with other ecclesiastical institutions, enforced church-
defined religious and gender norms for acceptable behavior in colonial
society. On 18 January 1572, Santiago's town council received a letter from Mexico City that named Pedro Moya de Contreras Inquisitor
General of New Spain, with jurisdiction over the Audiencia of Guatemala.[18] The Holy Office sent letters of instruction to all the local heads
of the Inquisition in an attempt to regularize its policies and procedures
in New Spain. Inquisition comisarios in Guatemala heard complaints
of religious deviance, including witchcraft and sorcery accusations, de-

scriptions of strange and often incurable illnesses, pacts with the devil, solicitation in the confessional, and charges of bigamy, concubinage, and adultery. The Inquisition tried Indians for religious crimes in New Spain only from 1522 to 1571. In 1571 King Philip II formally removed Indians in Spanish America from the jurisdiction of the Holy Office. In Mexico, Spanish officials created the Proviserato to administer Indian religious orthodoxy.[19]

In addition to regular and secular male religious orders, Santiago de Guatemala also contained convents for nuns. In the late 1570s Santiago's town government gave permission for the establishment of the first convent in the capital. Church authorities requested that the archbishop of Mexico send a group of nuns from the convent of the Immaculate Conception of Mary in Mexico City to start a convent in Santiago. On 1 February 1578, four Conceptionist nuns, Juana de San Francisco, Catalina Bautista, Elena de la Cruz, and Inés de los Reyes, accompanied by two men appointed by Santiago's town council, arrived in the capital. The town council and the patron (*patrón*) of the convent, prepared a welcoming celebration with fireworks, one-act plays, and comedies. The first nun to profess in the convent was Sor María de la Concepción on 15 February 1579.[20]

Slavery and Forced Labor

In addition to religious conversion, the coercive practices of taxation and forced labor played a central role in the establishment of colonial rule in Guatemala. This played out in the aftermath of conquest through the institution of the *encomienda*, in which the crown rewarded individual Spaniards for their role in the conquest by giving them the rights to tribute and labor from Indian towns.[21] Indian tribute payments began almost immediately after conquest when Pedro de Alvarado distributed encomiendas to his soldiers from the Indian towns around the capital of Iximché.[22]

Colonial officials defined an Indian tributary as a married Indian male, his wife, and their children and collected tribute twice a year, on 24 June, the Feast of Saint John, and on 25 December, Christmas. Tribute goods included woven cloth, agricultural products such as maize, wheat, fodder (*sacate*), chickens, cotton, wool, and cacao. Indian community leaders usually collected the tribute goods and distributed them to Spanish *encomenderos* and colonial officials, who held them responsible when tribute payments fell short. Spanish officials also demanded that part of the tribute be paid in cash in the form of the *servicio del tostón,* an annual tax of one-half peso.²³

Spanish colonial tribute requirements also included labor. Indian slavery existed in and around Santiago de Guatemala until the 1550s. After the abolition of Indian slavery, colonial officials created other institutions of forced labor such as *servicio personal* and the *repartimiento de indios.* In Santiago and the surrounding valley towns, Spanish encomenderos and colonial political and religious officials used Indian labor for construction, repairs, and the maintenance of government and religious buildings, fountains, and bridges, street sweeping and grass cutting, and cleaning the presidential palace and the city jail. In addition, Indian men were used as soldiers in the wars against the Lacandón Maya in 1685 and 1695 and in the force sent to put down the 1712 Tzeltal Maya rebellion in Chiapas. Indian women were not exempted from forced labor; they served as wet nurses to Spanish children, household servants, and cloth spinners and, along with Indian men, acted as *tamemes,* carrying loads of maize firewood and water.

Specific taxes on Indian barrios and rural towns varied, however. In the 1570s the Indian settlement of Jocotenango, located on the northwest edge of the city, provided thirty Indians three times a week to clean the palace of the Audiencia, forty-six grass cutters and three wet nurses per week, and six men to clean the city jail.²⁴ Approximately one-fourth of the tributary Indian population worked in forced labor at any given time. This represented a high percentage, especially when compared to the valley of Mexico, where only one-tenth of the Indian populations performed agricultural tributary labor.²⁵ And while repartimiento labor was abandoned in the valley of Mexico by the 1630s, the institution continued in Guatemala until the end of the colonial period.²⁶

Naborías represented another form of forced Indian labor in colonial Guatemala. Often, these were migrant Indians who left their communities of origin to work for Spanish residents in Santiago. Naborías also could be orphaned Indian infants and children left on Spanish doorsteps, or young children contracted from Indian barrios and nearby towns. Naboría status conferred exemption from regular Indian tribute and thus drew many Indians to work in the capital to escape heavy tribute demands. After 1600 naborías gradually became independent from Spanish households and began to establish their own residences, working as artisans especially in the barrios of Sagrario and San Sebastián, located in the northwest section of the capital.²⁷

African slavery also played an integral role in the colonial economy and society. African slaves first came to Guatemala in 1524 with Alvarado's army. In 1543, one hundred fifty enslaved African adults arrived in colonial Guatemala via Santo Domingo. Thereafter, African slaves were regularly imported to the colony, though on a fairly small scale until the 1580s. Africans entered Guatemala on slave ships from Cartagena, various Honduran ports, and other parts of the Audiencia, as well as overland from New Spain and Panama. Symbols of high prestige, only the wealthiest Spanish families in Santiago de Guatemala could initially afford to own slaves.[28]

Historical evidence on the numbers and distribution of African slaves in Central America and Santiago de Guatemala is fragmented and incomplete. In the seventeenth century, approximately one hundred fifty African slaves per year officially entered Central America. Between 1635 and 1699, a period of economic depression, contracts for importing African slaves (*asientos*) showed that only a small number were legally imported. From 1700 to 1769, a period that coincided with the revival of the Central American economy and the rise of export agriculture, legal African slave imports increased. Most newly arrived African slaves, called *bozales*, worked in Guatemala's rural agricultural centers. More "hispanicized" slaves, including those who spoke Spanish, worked as servants in homes and religious institutions in the capital.[29]

Lack of documentation for Santiago's African slave population makes demographic estimates and ethnic breakdowns into percentages of Blacks and mulatos difficult.[30] Slave-buying patterns in the capital show that from the 1550s to the 1650s, almost 90 percent of slaves sold were defined as Black. In the second half of the seventeenth century, however, the pattern changed dramatically, with almost 70 percent defined as mulato. This suggests that slave importation to Central America declined in the seventeenth century and that there was increased miscegenation as a result of informal and formal unions. From 1660 to 1720 the Black slave population reached its peak, but by the late seventeenth century, mulato slaves outnumbered Black slaves. Mulata slave women and their children had higher rates of manumission than did Black women slaves and their children, a pattern reflected in other areas of the Americas.[31]

The Emergence of a Multiethnic Capital

In 1549, in an effort to assert royal authority over local political power, the first president of the Audiencia, Alfonso López de Cerrato, freed some three thousand to five thousand Indian slaves in and around Santiago. By enforcing the New Laws of 1542 freeing Indian slaves in Spanish America, ostensibly to protect them from violence and abuse, President Cerrato faced strong opposition from the Guatemalan elite, in particular, local encomenderos and political officials. The manumission of Indian slaves in the capital, as well as Alvarado's manumission of his Indian slaves in his will after his death in 1541, meant that control over the all-important Indian labor pool shifted from the local elite to crown officials and the religious orders.[32]

The bishop of Guatemala, Francisco Marroquín, resettled Indians freed in Alvarado's will in Jocotenango, northwest of the capital. The Franciscans, Dominicans, and Mercedarians resettled the Indians freed by Cerrato in Indian barrios around the Spanish core of the capital. The orders established the barrios close to their monasteries to more effectively convert and monitor them, and they also mixed different Indian ethnic groups in the same barrio. These new Indian barrios, described as *extramuros* (outside the walls), surrounded the Spanish core to the east, north, and west of the capital.

In 1549 colonial officials introduced Indian self-rule to barrios in the capital. The policy of Indian self-rule, along with forced resettlement and tribute and forced labor demands, became part of the crown's broader effort to hispanicize urban and rural Indian communities and draw them into the colonial economy. Indian self-rule nominally gave Indian communities the right to govern and police themselves, though they were monitored by Spanish authorities. At the same time, however, Spanish authorities gave Indian officials some measure of self-government and the right to police their own barrios through the use of Spanish institutions and legal practices.[33]

Each Indian barrio had a *cabildo* (municipal council) with its own building, most had a chapel or hermitage, and the barrios of Jocotenango, Santo Domingo, and San Francisco had their own jails. Indian elites and town elders usually filled the cabildo positions of *alcalde* (mayor; the chief barrio official), *regidor* (alderman), and *alguacil* (constable). Indian officials also policed their barrios but were restricted to only minor crimes and could not intervene in crimes that involved Spaniards.[34] Indian self-government along with other colonial institu-

tions such as the Inquisition played central roles in the Spanish colonial state's effort to capitalize on divisions within and between Indian
communities as a strategy to intervene at the local level and reassert
Spanish colonial rule of law.

Intracommunity conflicts and conflicts between colonial authorities
and female sorcerers that form the focus of this study emerged in the
context of important demographic and economic changes in late-
seventeenth-century Guatemala. A major social change of the seventeenth century was the emergence of a multiethnic population in Santiago by the 1650s. Although the Spanish crown issued a series of laws
designed to separate Spanish and Indian populations, such as a 1626
law that prohibited Indians in the neighborhood around the church of
San Francisco from selling their houses or land to non-Indians, the
two republic system began to break down almost immediately in Santiago. The rise of *mestizaje* (race mixture), which began to intensify in
the 1550s and accelerated over the course of the seventeenth century,
along with the introduction of African slaves, migration, and frequent
epidemic disease, gradually transformed the ethnic composition of the
capital, as poor Spaniards, castas, and free Blacks moved into Indian
neighborhoods.[35]

By the late seventeenth century, Santiago de Guatemala had approximately 39,000 inhabitants. Two-thirds of the population was defined as *gente ordinaria*, an ecclesiatical term meaning "common people"
that included mestizos, free and slave Blacks and mulatos, and nontributary Indians who no longer had formal ties to their communities
of origin. The gente ordinaria population almost doubled in size over
the previous century, from about 13,500 in the 1590s to almost 25,000
by the 1680s. Other urban areas in colonial Latin America, such as
Lima and Mexico City, experienced a similar emergence of multiethnic
populations.[36]

The remaining one-third of Santiago's population was split almost
equally between Spaniards and tributary Indians. Emerging class divisions within the Spanish population in the seventeenth century also
reflected changes in the larger society. Colonial authorities and inhabitants of Santiago used the term *español*, or Spaniard, to refer to those
at the top of the colonial ethnic-status social hierarchy. The term *Spaniard*, however, could also refer to the mestizo children of the Spanish
elite. In addition, there were divisions within Spanish society in Santiago de Guatemala between the wealthy elite, who lived in the Spanish
core as close to the central plaza as they could afford, and poorer espa-

ñoles, who, for reasons of economic necessity, moved into the more affordable Indian neighborhoods. These españoles tended to be of more
mixed origin, and they had a higher incidence of formal and informal
relationships with castas than did españoles from Sagrario parish.[37]
In addition to the profound demographic changes and the rise of a
multiethnic population in Santiago, the late seventeenth century signaled the gradual beginning of economic recovery from a decades-
long depression in Central America. From the 1630s to the 1680s, the
colonial Central American economy was characterized by economic
stagnation, a labor shortage, and a severe decline in the production
of cacao and other agricultural goods. Beginning in the 1680s, the
economy began to recover, fueled in part by the revival of trade with
Spain and Peru, a rise in clandestine trading, and increased commer-
cial crop production. Colonial officials struggled to adapt to the late-
seventeenth-century economic revival and the sweeping demographic
transformation of the capital. The changing order, in turn, created new
economic and cultural opportunities for Santiago's growing multiethnic
population.[38]

For example, with the increased commercialization of the local and
export economies in Guatemala during this period, casta economic participation mushroomed. Racial and ethnic divisions in the capital began
to blur as social mobility and mestizaje made it possible for some men
and women to become *nuevos españoles*, "new Spaniards." Some who
were considered "Spanish" by colonial authorities and who also defined
themselves as "Spanish" were actually castas who had been able to increase their social and economic status in the growing economy. The
new Spaniards, however, never quite made it to the upper levels of elite
Spanish society in Santiago, and they tended to live not in the Spanish
core but in the outer Indian neighborhoods.[39]

Nonelite Spanish and casta groups became active in the local market
economy, especially in illicit trading in and around Santiago, primarily
because the official economy did not provide much opportunity for legal
participation. By the late seventeenth century, castas, poor Spaniards,
nontributary Indians, and free Blacks gradually began to participate
in the local economy, displacing the tributary Indians who had dominated Santiago's market supply system since the 1550s. Many became
petty traders or worked in shops in their homes or in market stalls in
the city's plazas. Illicit economic participation continued to grow despite the attempts of colonial authorities to enact new laws and severe
punishments.[40]

In the seventeenth century, many poor Spanish, casta, Black, and Indian women legally and illegally participated in the local economy as peddlers, seamstresses, laundresses, market sellers, servants, and shop owners.[41] Women even dominated some trades, mostly those having to do with food distribution and preparation, such as *panaderas* (bakers), *tortilleras* (tortilla makers), and *revendedoras* (resellers of beef), running market stalls in the city's plazas, and managing small shops in their homes. By the 1690s, for example, Santiago's town council passed a series of laws that attempted to regulate female bakers, most of whom were poor Spaniards and mulatas living in the city's outer barrios. Santiago's town council set the weight and price of a loaf of bread at 11½ *onzas* (ounces) at one real. Bread consumption among Spaniards and wealthier casta groups had steadily increased, while at the same time wheat shortages in the second half of the seventeenth century became increasingly common, driving up costs. Although colonial authorities attempted to regulate the weight and cost of loaves of wheat bread, consumers repeatedly complained that the female bakers sold underweight loaves to unsuspecting customers, frequently adding cheaper corn flour, and that they increasingly sold bread clandestinely to avoid Audiencia taxes and controls. In 1693 the city council suspended ten female bakers for mixing corn flour into their loaves.[42]

Another problem group from the Audiencia's point of view were casta revendedoras, mostly female mixed-race beef vendors who bought meat from unlicensed butchers and cut it into smaller and more affordable pieces to resell in the plazas, in the streets of the outer barrios, and from small shops in their homes. The colonial government regulated the official beef supply, slaughter, and sales in Santiago. By the mid-seventeenth century, however, increased demand for beef, coupled with declining costs, led to the development of an extensive illegal beef trade on the outskirts of the capital, fueled primarily by casta cattle rustlers and clandestine vendors such as the casta revendedoras. Colonial authorities identified the majority of the illegal traders as mulatas, who had illegally sold beef in the capital since at least the mid-1650s.

In 1681 Audiencia officials attempted to revise the regulation of beef sales and granted female meat vendors the right to sell their beef in the market of the central plaza. The legalization of beef sales by market women opened the way for large numbers of casta women to legally enter the trade, provided that they bought beef only from government-licensed butcher shops and used scales regulated by colonial authorities. By the late seventeenth century, the female casta beef sellers had organized into a hereditary *gremio* (guild) in Santiago. Local officials, however, tried to put a stop to the licensing because of rumors that the women shortchanged buyers, and in 1699 again outlawed all revende-dora sales in Santiago. In 1703 all vendors were prohibited from selling meat in the streets. Local authorities continued to harass, arrest, and punish female beef vendors working in the central plaza into the early eighteenth century. At least one woman, a mestiza widow and mother of seven, was arrested and publicly whipped for flouting the ban.[43]

As Santiago's population swelled, the city limits extended in 1641 and again in 1697. Recurring destructive earthquakes that hit Santiago, especially in 1651 and 1680, revitalized the building and construction trades there. The city's architecture also became more formal and ornate, as permanent building materials, especially brick and terra-cotta roof tiles, began to be used regularly. The development of Indian brick manufacturers in the neighborhoods and towns of Jocotenango, Chimaltenango, and San Felipe, along with new stone quarries in the hills near the towns of San Felipe and San Cristóbal, spurred the development of a more sophisticated architectural style in Santiago. In addition, after 1650 the number of skilled builders and craftsmen increased as Indian, castas, and free Blacks entered the labor market.[44]

In the second half of the seventeenth century, Santiago's religious authorities began to construct more churches and convents. By 1690 Santiago contained twenty-four churches including the Cathedral, ten convents, three parish churches, five hermitages, and four churches belonging to *beaterios*. The elaborate reconstruction of Santiago's Cathedral represented the authority of colonial rule, reinforcing the link between secular and religious power. The construction of the Cathedral began in 1542 but proceeded slowly over the following decades. By the mid-seventeenth century, religious officials realized that the church had been poorly constructed. In 1668 Bishop Payo de Ribera decided to tear down the Cathedral to its foundations and reconstruct it in grand style. Completed in 1680, the interior of the Cathedral contained an elaborate high altar, and sixteen columns supported a dome with carved figures of the apostles. The Cathedral also contained an altar to Our Lady of Guadalupe that faced the central plaza, as well as sculptures of Jesús de Perdón, San Pedro, San José, Cristo de los Reyes, San Sebastián, and San Francisco de Paula.[45]

While on the surface the newly reconstructed Cathedral, located at the capital's Spanish core on the main plaza, represented the consolidation and stability of colonial authority and power, beneath the surface there was ambiguity about where casta women and men fit economically, socially, and culturally into late-seventeenth-century society in Santiago and the Audiencia of Guatemala. As the colonial state and the institutions of rule within the state attempted to redefine new colonial hierarchies and set them in motion through various political and religious institutions such as the Inquisition, new cultural, economic, and social opportunities opened for casta groups, including women.

Gender, Ethnicity, and Social Disorder in the Late Seventeenth Century

With the emergence of a multiethnic population and the rise of an extensive illegal economic trade network in the late seventeenth century, colonial officials and Spanish inhabitants of the capital expressed fears about the potential for rebellion among casta, Black, and Indian communities. In the 1680s Spaniards comprised only one-fifth of the capital's population. With the economic and physical expansion of the city, the growing population of multiethnic urban poor came together in plaza markets, public fountains, and neighborhood taverns. After 1690 abusive colonial officials faced increased numbers of protests, appeals to the Audiencia, refusals to pay tribute and taxes, and, in some cases, physical attacks from Indian communities.[46]

As a result, colonial authorities enacted a series of laws designed to control and contain growing casta, Black, Indian, and poor Spanish populations. Throughout the seventeenth century, colonial laws prohibited castas, Indians, or free Blacks from carrying and using weapons or guns of any kind, including swords, daggers, and machetes. A 1634 Audiencia judicial decree went so far as to outlaw castas from riding horses in the capital, at the risk of severe punishment. The town council also repeatedly passed laws that forbade "vagabondage," highway robbery, and cattle rustling. In 1698 three men were hanged in Santiago's central plaza for assaulting three Indian traders on the road to the capital, presumably in an attempt to rob them of the goods they brought to market. An Audiencia *auto* (judicial decree) enacted on 10 June 1693 prohibited Indians from marching and using arms and allowed them to use fireworks only at their *fiestas* (community celebrations). Mestizos, mulatos, and Blacks could ride mules only. Indians were exempt from this requirement.[47]

Colonial authorities attempted to enforce laws aimed at economically and ethnically marginalized populations through the intensification of Spanish-managed patrols (*rondas*) of mulato militias and Indian police forces headed by constables (*alguaciles*). The historian Christopher Lutz argued that the use of casta and Indian police forces in the capital, controlled by Spanish authorities, encouraged divisions and conflicts between subject groups:

The decision by Santiago's town fathers to intensify *rondas* (patrols) in the city was prompted by a growing fear that the Spanish would easily be surrounded and annihilated in any uprising by castas and Indians. . . . Establishing mulatto militias in the Indian barrios, recruiting non-mulattoes for other nominally Spanish infantry companies, using Indian justices to patrol predominately casta neighborhoods — all, they believed, would work to channel the hostility of the nonelites not against the Spanish who had devised these measures but against a diversity of fellow subjects who were obligated to implement and enforce them.[48]

Colonial authorities meted out punishments according to the ethnicity of the accused. Spaniards received the lightest punishments, such as fines, while castas, Blacks, and Indians tended to receive harsher, violent punishment. In December 1693 an Audiencia judicial decree authorized punishments for food hoarding depending on the ethnicity of the accused. Mixed-race peoples convicted of this crime received two hundred lashes, while a Spaniard convicted of the same crime paid a fine of two hundred pesos and spent two years in prison.

Spanish political and religious officials in Santiago became alarmed at the rise of the casta population, especially of free and freed mulatos who, by the late seventeenth century, formed the largest and most visibly distinct ethnic group in the capital. Colonial officials worried that free mulatos and Blacks might form alliances with *cimarrones* (runaway slaves) who established clandestine settlements between Santiago and the Caribbean coast and also along the Pacific coast, a fear that prompted them to periodically send military expeditions against them. Perhaps the greatest fear was that free and freed mulatos might join or "incite" Indians and African slaves to rebel. Francisco Ximénez, a colonial chronicler, wrote of the continued fears of potential Indian rebellion into the eighteenth century:

During the earthquake of 1717 in [Santiago de] Guatemala, the people of the barrio of Santo Domingo were the only ones who did not flee the city, leaving it unprotected, leaving it at the risk of being lost with the slightest invasion which the Indians, always enemies of the Spaniards, might have made.[49]

A September 1697 uprising in the barrio of San Gerónimo, located along the western edge of the Spanish core, probably heightened the racial tensions in the capital. The president of the Audiencia responded by sending one hundred militia troops to restore order, including twenty-five infantry and twenty-five cavalry.[50]

The breakdown of the "two republics" and the changing demographic makeup of the capital, along with the economic revival of the second half of the seventeenth century, put colonial structures and ideologies of rule in a state of flux. The demographic and economic changes created a context for developing new discourses of colonial rule, to address not only ethnic but also gendered social disorder. With the emergence of a multiethnic capital city, women, especially casta, Black, and Indian women, became particular targets of Spanish political and religious authorities concerned with their perceived tendency to cause disorder.[51] The changes in Santiago created a blurred social and cultural landscape that increased opportunities for women in families, the economy, and popular religious life. Some women took advantage of the opening to redefine their roles, despite the risks.

In addition to cracking down on women's illicit economic activities, secular and religious authorities began to redefine women's social and cultural behavior. In February 1676 Bishop Juan de Ortega arrived in Santiago de Guatemala and became scandalized over women's fashions there, especially *escotes*, low-cut dresses popular at the time. Later that year, on Easter Sunday, Bishop Ortega read an edict that prohibited women in Santiago from wearing escotes because they left the women "uncovered to their breasts." To enforce the ban on escotes, he directed parish priests not to confess or absolve any woman wearing the low-cut dresses.[52]

Colonial authorities in Santiago de Guatemala also expressed alarm at the inappropriate behavior of *damas de sociedad* (elite women) and their slaves and servants in church. The women apparently drank chocolate during Cathedral services, much to the consternation of Santiago's religious authorities. One priest complained that many of the women brought with them servants and slaves who carried cushion pads, chairs, prayer books, and jeweled boxes that contained fans for their mistresses to use during mass. In his eyes, however, the greatest abuse was that slaves and servants served the women steaming cups of chocolate *con gran lujo* (with great luxury), disrupting church services. In response, Santiago's city government enacted a law prohibiting chocolate consumption in church.[53] According to Pedro Rosuela, chaplain of the Cathedral, Santiago's nuns behaved just as scandalously. He denounced Madre Abessa María de San Pedro and Madre María de San Francisco for drinking chocolate in the confessional.[54]

In addition to increased policing of women by colonial secular and diocesan authorities, officials from the Guatemalan Inquisition became increasingly interested in pursuing cases targeting women's perceived cultural and religious deviancy. Inquisition authorities paid particular attention to so-called mujeres de mal vivir. As José de Baños y Sotomayor, head of Guatemala's Inquisition in the 1690s, put it, there were so many of these "shameless women" that there were not enough jails to put them in.[55]

As a result, the Inquisition pursued the strategy of investigating and punishing the most notorious of these women, "so that other [women] see it and are warned."[56] I located 44 Inquisition *legajos* (files) targeting women out of a total of 117 for the period 1650–1750. Twenty-six of these came from the period 1690–1705.[57] The overwhelming majority of the targeted women were free mulatas, often acting together with Indian, casta, Black, and even Spanish women. Though on the surface the number of legajos appears small, they represent hundreds of handwritten pages of testimony, letters, autos, and other kinds of information. I supplemented this with Inquisition proceedings targeting men and with criminal records involving men and women for the same period, sources that often contain information regarding men's ritual ties to various women, providing a broader comparative context for religious beliefs and practices in the capital.

In addition, many of the cases prosecuted in Santiago contained multiple denunciations of other women and men who were not pursued by Inquisition authorities for various reasons, including the death of the accused or flight from the capital. Inquisition judges could also refer such cases to other colonial authorities, such as ecclesiastical judges in cases of accused Indians (who did not fall under the jurisdiction of the Holy Office), and to *justicias reales* (royal justices).[58]

In 1572 the Holy Office in Mexico City named Diego de Carbajal the first head of the Guatemalan Inquisition. Officials in Mexico City sent out *cartas de instrucción* (letters of instruction) in an attempt to regularize their actions in the jurisdiction of New Spain. For example, Inquisition comisarios had to conduct proceedings in secret, and the instructions spelled out the processes for the confiscation of goods, imprisonment of the accused, and intent to flee, a common occurrence in Santiago de Guatemala.[59]

Indians were exempt from the jurisdiction of the Holy Office and had their cases referred to a *juez eclesiástico* (ecclesiastical judge). In some Inquisition documents, there was confusion over the process of ethnic definition, of how to decide just who was an Indian. In Santiago it appears that in practice Indians could be denounced to the Inquisition, but if they were classified by colonial authorities as *indios puros* ("pure" Indians), then the authorities referred their cases elsewhere.[60] The term "indio puro" probably described a tributary Indian, but this is not clear. The distinction between "types" of Indians in Santiago de Guatemala opens up the question of whether "hispanicized" Indians, sometimes called *indios ladinos*, could be tried by the Inquisition. These distinctions between Indians also suggest ways in which indigenous urban communities faced internal divisions based not only on ethnicity (such as Kaqchikel speaker or Nahuatl speaker) but also on community and institutionally perceived degrees of hispanicization. Nevertheless, though Inquisition judges often dropped such cases or referred them to ecclesiastical judges, Indians could and did appear as witnesses in Inquisition proceedings.[61]

Technically, the Inquisition in New Spain did not have jurisdiction over cases of *hechizos* (spells) and *maleficios* (spells, curses); these were supposed to be referred to justicias reales. And while many such cases can be found in Santiago's criminal records, the Guatemalan Inquisition did prosecute cases of curses, spells, and other magical-religious crimes such as pacts with the devil, miraculous healings, and religious visions.[62] Inquisition authorities intensified the prosecution of these cases during the period from 1680 to 1720 and particularly focused their efforts on women.

The Guatemalan historian Ernesto Chinchilla Aguilar noted that in the late sixteenth and early seventeenth century, Inquisition authorities were especially concerned with prosecuting crimes of blasphemy, bigamy, and cohabitation.[63] In the late seventeenth and early eighteenth century, Guatemala's Inquisition shared the secular authorities' concerns over the rising casta population and focused its prosecutorial efforts on casta women, especially free mulatas. The changing concerns of Inquisition authorities showed how Inquisition policy, including what kinds of cases were pursued, reflected the larger historical and social context of colonial Guatemala in general and Santiago de Guatemala in particular.

Parish priests were instrumental in the efforts to compel parishioners, especially women, to denounce others for illegal religious practices. While bishops read Inquisition edicts publicly and encouraged the faithful to denounce their neighbors and family members, parish priests attempted to push members of their flock to bring their accusations to Inquisition officials. Priests, acting on information described in their parishioners' confessions, including sickbed and deathbed confessions, withheld absolution until the parishioner went to the Inquisition to denounce the crime. In cases of deathbed confessions, priests sometimes refrained from giving the last rites until Inquisition officials visited the home and questioned the witnesses as they lay dying. In particular, priests used denial of absolution to persuade female servants and slaves, who were more vulnerable.

Some men and women in Santiago de Guatemala went of their own accord, without compulsion or being called, to the Inquisition tribunal. They denounced their neighbors, employers, and family members in the local community for illegal religious behavior for a wide range of reasons, including revenge, personal disagreements, the failure of sexual relationships, and the occurrence of strange illnesses and unexplained deaths.

Over the course of the seventeenth century, as women increasingly became targets for illegal economic and cultural activities, city officials built or expanded on a number of institutions that housed female prisoners and "women who live evil lives." Repeatedly in the 1680s, political and religious officials called for the establishment of more *casas de recogidas*, to effectively jail "lost women who live evil lives" and "female criminals who commit common crimes."[64] These institutions, usually run by female nuns, served multiple functions. Santiago's Colegio de Doncellas, also known as the Colegio de la Presentación de Nuestra Señora, served as an orphanage, a school for young girls, and a house of detention where civil and ecclesiastical authorities "deposited" women accused or convicted of criminal activities, including disobedience to their husbands and adultery.[65]

The Colegio de Doncellas de Nuestra Señora de la Asunción, also known as El Niñado, housed poor maidens (*doncellas*). Colonial authorities initially prohibited placing so-called women who live evil lives there, feeling that they would corrupt the young maidens. In 1643 the authorities changed their minds, perhaps because they needed more space to house female criminals. The women did prove troublesome, however: "on more than three occasions" they set the building on fire, broke out of El Niñado, and made their escape.[66]

Colonial officials also decided that they needed a women's jail in Santiago and completed construction in 1691. The women's jail was located next to the men's jail on the east side of the city council building, on the central plaza. Together, the men's and women's jails were called Cárcel de la Ciudad. Colonial authorities found it necessary to expand the jail in 1699 and again in 1701. Santiago's Inquisition authorities often imprisoned women accused of religious crimes in the women's jail or in a casa de recogidas until their cases were resolved.[67]

Bewitching the President: Gender, Ethnicity, and Challenges to Colonial Authority and Power

Accusations of sorcery in the changing historical context in Santiago transformed a personal conflict between husband and wife into a series of notorious Inquisition cases pursued against two casta women. In 1695 colonial authorities placed Cecilia de Arriola, a thirty-year-old married mulata, in a casa de recogidos for attempting to stab her mulato husband, Juan de Fuentes, with a knife during an argument. A few days after the argument, with his wife safely confined, Juan went directly to the home of José de Baños y Sotomayor, comisario of Santiago's Inquisition, to speak to him personally instead of presenting himself formally to the Inquisition court. Juan charged that Cecilia, under the direction of her comadre Gerónima de Barahona, a mulata meat vendor, had cast a spell on him "so that he could not be a man on all the occasions he desired," that the women "regularly used instruments for casting spells and curses," and that Cecilia was a sorcerer-witch (*hechicera-bruja*).

Ultimately, Juan's evidence that Cecilia had used sorcery to bewitch him centered on what he perceived as their inverted gender roles, shown by his inability to control his "unnatural" behavior of preparing the morning chocolate while his wife slept in:

His wife treats him not as a husband but as a servant. He lights the fire in the kitchen, he boils the water, he mixes the chocolate and heats the food . . . and he gets up very early every morning to do this while his wife stays in bed and sleeps until very late. And when his wife wakes, he brings her her chocolate so she can drink it after she dresses. And even though it is very late [in the morning], he has the water ready [and] he drinks chocolate with his wife. . . . [I]n this way his wife has turned him into a coward, and all this cannot be a natural thing.[68]

Baños y Sotomayor, alarmed at Juan's accusations, which he described in a letter to the Mexican Inquisition, ordered the Inquisition notary to search Juan and Cecilia's home for evidence of sorcery. There the notary found ritual items that cast suspicion on Cecilia and Gerónima: packets of dried roots, leaves, and sticks, various powders, a wooden "idol," a black clay toad, feathers, and amulets. As a result of the search, Baños y Sotomayor ordered that Cecilia be held indefinitely in the casa de recogidos known as El Niñado. He ordered the nun in charge, Madre doña Angela de Valdez, not to let any "suspicious" persons speak to Cecilia.

Gerónima de Barahona, the mulata meat vendor named by Cecilia's husband as the person directing Cecilia in her sorcery, somehow received word that Juan had denounced her to the Inquisition and that her arrest was imminent. The Inquisition notary and two of his mulato servants hurried to Gerónima's house to place her under arrest, but by the time they arrived, she had already fled. Neighbors speculated that she went to Las Salinas del Mar, one of many informal settlements on the Pacific coast, inhabited mainly by castas engaged in making salt.[69] Baños y Sotomayor described Las Salinas del Mar as a place "where most of the people have little fear of God and their custom is to hide criminals so they cannot be found."

The Inquisition, as one component of Spanish colonial power, was effectively set in motion in Guatemala and elsewhere in Latin America to reinscribe colonial authority in the face of various challenges and acts of resistance. The Inquisition in Guatemala, however, acted not only as a representative of colonial power. It also mediated local conflicts and cultural disorder in the capital and participated in what the historian David Sabean described as "face-to-face" social relations to carry on its policing activities, which, for example, allowed for a mulato who worked as a construction laborer to speak to the Inquisition judge personally and in his home.[70]

In the process, Gerónima de Barahona and Cecilia de Arriola, ethnically and economically marginalized, became notorious public figures in Santiago de Guatemala. What began as an intimate conflict between husband and wife gradually evolved into a showdown over the control of rival public spaces between the cultural authority and power of local and well-known women involved in sorcery, magical healing, and sexual witchcraft and the Inquisition, a religious representative of the colonial state.

In the aftermath of Juan de Fuentes's denunciation of Cecilia, Inquisition authorities felt the need to make an example of her and Gerónima to the rest of the local community. The steps they took came to include an Audiencia-wide manhunt for Gerónima, the public confiscation of Gerónima's home and material goods, which left her children homeless, and the interrogation of a total of forty-seven people, until the case ended with Gerónima's death while she was imprisoned in the city hospital and Cecilia's transportation to the Inquisition jail in Mexico City.

Targeting "bizarre" and "exotic" cases such as accusations of sorcery was one way that the colonial state, through institutions such as the Inquisition, attempted to reinscribe colonial authority and power in community life. However, competing cultures of sorcery, magical healing, and popular religious devotions, in which women played key roles, posed repeated challenges to Inquisitional authority in late-seventeenth-century Santiago de Guatemala. Witnesses from all social and ethnic groups recounted persistent rumors that Gerónima and a number of her female friends and clients cast spells on various political and religious officials in Santiago, including the president of the Audiencia, spells that allowed the women to continue their practices unmolested. The implications of these rumors were enormous—the perception that the Inquisition, despite all its inherent power, had fallen under the power of a female mixed-race sorcerer.

The actions of Gerónima de Barahona and her social ties to various inhabitants of the capital show how women's cultural challenges to the Inquisition's authority, viewed through the activities of so-called women who live evil lives, illuminate local relations of power under colonial rule. Gerónima first came to the attention of Inquisition authorities in the early 1680s.[71] By the 1690s Santiago's political and religious officials had attempted to put a halt to Gerónima's activities on numerous occasions. They arrested and imprisoned her in the city jail, and they also banished her from the capital. Yet, as one Inquisition official put it, Gerónima returned to her house in Santiago and continued her sorcery activities "with much brazenness." He added that Gerónima "had the devil in her body," and by providing her services for a fee to others in the capital, she "besmirched the reputations of elite and honorable women in Santiago de Guatemala."[72] Inquisition documents show that Gerónima was a well-known figure in Santiago in the 1690s. More than sixty persons referred to Gerónima by name and decribed her magical activities in the capital in detail.

It is not surprising, then, that in this context residents began gossiping and speculating publicly about how Gerónima, a mulata sorcerer, avoided the grasp of the Inquisition. The very publicness of her sorcery practices, which continued over a ten-year period, and the Inquisition's seeming inability to put a stop to them, challenged the Inquisition's authority and power at the local level.

By the early 1690s rumors of Gerónima's continued illegal activities seemed only to enhance her power as a sorcerer in the eyes of her clients, neighbors, and acquaintances. A number of men and women commented on Gerónima's supernatural power over colonial officials, including the Inquisition judge. Cecilia de Arriola stated that "many in the capital" knew that the Inquisition judge had banished Gerónima to the nearby town of Petapa as punishment. Cecilia added that only eight days after her banishment, Gerónima returned to her house in the capital "as if she had not committed a crime."

According to Cecilia, when the Inquisition authorities called Gerónima before them and placed her in shackles, she said that she had learned sorcery "from Indians who were already dead." Here she used the not uncommon strategy of blaming dead persons who could not be held accountable. Gerónima also claimed that "Indians" misled her, which is probably what the officials wanted, or expected, to hear: she was a weak woman misled by idolatrous Indians.

Though Gerónima used the strategy of blaming dead "Indians" when called before colonial authorities, she told Cecilia that what she did behind the scenes mattered more. Gerónima claimed that she used some herbs and a short incantation to "tame the Señor Comisario [the Inquisition judge] even though he acted very angrily toward her." She added that these same herbs also worked to bewitch *personas principales*, elite inhabitants of the capital. According to Cecilia, the incantation was as follows:

I enchant you and re-enchant you, and I subject you to me, so that you do me no harm, and do no harm to my belongings.

This simple incantation contains similar language used in sexual witchcraft to "tame" abusive and violent husbands. Perhaps Gerónima viewed the Inquisition judge and his power to imprison her as similar to how some husbands acted toward their wives. Gerónima also reportedly "tamed" the judge and her other enemies by making the sign of the cross on the ground with her left foot. In addition, the incantation supposedly not only protected Gerónima's person from harm and prosecution, it protected her material possessions as well, as a common punishment used against women for various transgressions was the confiscation of their homes and belongings.

Gerónima translated her reputation for having the power to use sorcery to avoid prosecution into a moneymaking opportunity. In September 1695 María de la Aruburu, an eighteen-year-old single mulata, regularly consulted Gerónima for various spells and curses. When Inquisition officials arrested María herself for "superstitious sorcery," Gerónima sold her spells "para librarse de la justicia," to free herself from colonial authorities. Apparently other female sorcerers offered similar services to their clients. A mestiza woman named Petrona, alias "La Pastora" (the Shepherd), who lived in the barrio of Santo Domingo, offered to sell María some powders "so that *la justicia* [justice officials] would not prosecute her."[73]

In addition to rumors that Gerónima avoided arrest and prosecution by bewitching Inquisition authorities, witnesses also reported that Gerónima used sorcery to murder her enemies. In 1694 Nicolasa González, a married thirty-year-old *mulata blanca cuaterona* (light-colored mulata) claimed that it was *pública voz y fama* (public knowledge) that eight or ten years earlier Gerónima used sorcery to murder a married woman named Felipa from the barrio of Santo Domingo.

Rumors also spread through the capital that doña Magdalena de Medrano (alias La Fiscala), wife of the Audiencia *fiscal* (Audiencia official) don Pedro de la Barrera, paid Gerónima for some potions designed to kill her husband while he lay sick in bed.[74] Many reported these rumors to the Inquisition as accepted fact in the local community, including Josefa de la Cruz, a single mulata born in Comayagua, Honduras, but then living in Santiago as the slave of a parish priest; María de la Candelaria, a thirty-two-year-old mestiza and legitimate wife of a postman; and two of doña Magdalena's servants, Josefa del Saz, an illegitimate, single, forty-year-old free mulata who lived in the barrio of San Francisco; and Elena de la Cruz, an illegitimate, single, twenty-eight-year-old mulata slave. All told basically the same story, that doña Magdalena de Medrano, the elite Spanish wife of an important colonial official, contracted the supernatural services of Gerónima de Barahona, a mulata woman with "evil fame as a witch and sorcerer," to kill her husband with bewitched powders.

Josefa de la Cruz told Inquisition authorities that doña Magdalena had consulted Gerónima for a potion to bewitch and kill her husband.[75] Josefa said she heard this from María de la Candelaria. María said that her sister Felipa, who was married to one of Gerónima's sons, told her that doña Magdalena paid Gerónima for the potion to kill her husband with clothing and money. Doña Magdalena then served the potion to her husband, don Pedro, and he died soon after.

The rumors did not stop there. Witnesses reported that after the death of her husband, doña Magdalena, newly widowed, continued to consult Gerónima for sexual witchcraft to attract two important Audiencia officials, the president, General Jacinto de Barrios Leal, himself a notorious figure in colonial politics, and the *oidor* (judge) José de Escals. All of the witnesses just mentioned, along with Juan de Fuentes, the mulato husband of Cecilia de Arriola, Antonia Martínez, a thirty-year-old single mulata, and Catalina Castillo, a thirty-year-old mulata slave of Captain don Gaspar de Viteri, recounted various ways that Gerónima aided doña Magdalena with supernatural rituals designed to bewitch and sexually attract the two colonial officials to her bed. Gerónima reportedly brought powders that doña Magdalena placed in some food and sent to the president. Gerónima and doña Magdalena together sprinkled powders on some bouquets of flowers "to bewitch the president and the judge."

Doña Magdalena's servant Josefa and her slave Elena both described how in the middle of the night they helped Gerónima and doña Magdalena carry water doctored with powders and urine and threw it on the windows and walls of the presidential palace "to incite" Barrios Leal. The women also threw the doctored waters on the windows of the judge's house. Josefa told Inquisition authorities that she thought the sorcery worked because President Barrios Leal "came many times . . . both early and late in the day" to visit her mistress. She added that doña Magdalena appeared to be *llevado de amores* (in love), implying that the two carried on an illicit affair. Josefa continued that doña Magdalena also appeared to be in love with the oidor Escals, who also visited her mistress, but only at night.

Although a number of sorcery accounts told by various community members directly linked doña Magdalena de Medrano to Gerónima de Barahona, Inquisition officials treated doña Magdalena, the elite Spanish wife of a colonial official, very differently from the accused mulata women. Despite the "secret" Inquisition proceedings, doña Magdalena also received word that her case was being pursued by the Inquisition. In what could be called a preemptive strike, doña Magdalena wrote a letter to the Inquisition giving her version of the events and sent it through a priest named don Francisco de Valenzuela, head of the Seminary College in Santiago. She wrote that she had sent don Francisco in her place "because she could not, herself, personally appear before the head of the Holy Tribunal of the Inquisition because of her elite status and [her] widowhood."

Inquisition officials began to focus on doña Magdalena's alleged sexual activities and her use of sexual witchcraft against various colonial officials that she purchased from Gerónima de Barahona. Doña Magdalena, however, never had to go before the Inquisition court. Instead, she continued to send letters through elite and respected intermediaries, including two priests, and through her mulato servant. Doña Magdalena confessed in writing that she had consulted a number of women for sorcery, including Gerónima, a mulata named Francisca Agreda, and an Indian woman named Petrona Mungía. She also confessed to having bewitched a Spanish woman named doña María Limon in a fit of jealousy, causing doña María to give birth to a stillborn baby and then "lose her mind."

In her letter-writing campaign, doña Magdalena played on seventeenth-century stereotypes of women and their potential for uncontrolled sexuality at the hands of the devil to explain her actions, while at the same time she used her status as an elite Spanish widow to ask for leniency:

> I, doña Magdalena, say that in the grip of the devil and pulled by animal [instincts], I consulted these persons to use love magic spells and avenge my jealousies, but by the mercy of God, I never denied any mystery of Our Lady of the Holy Roman Catholic Church . . . and I wish to reconcile myself with my Holy Mother Church.

Her words suggest that she consulted local female sorcerers for love magic and spells for revenge but still considered herself a good Catholic, or at least within the bounds of how a good Catholic woman should behave. Her strategy of relying on her reputation as an elite woman suggests that she expected to be treated leniently after she admitted purchasing the women's magical services.

In the Inquisition's uneven treatment of doña Magdalena and the castas Gerónima de Barahona and Cecilia de Arriola, we can see the tensions between how colonial institutions viewed all women—as weak and powerful at the same time, susceptible to corruption by the devil and the release of unbridled sexuality—and how they treated women differently according to ethnicity and emerging class status. Doña Magdalena, allowed to write letters instead of testifying and to send them to the court via priests as mediators, based her actions on her high social and ethnic status as a Spanish doña and the widowed wife of a political official. In a second letter to the Inquisition court, she pleaded for secrecy in the proceedings against her "for the benefit of my children who should not become infamous when they are not guilty."

Given the rumors and public knowledge of the intimate activities of Gerónima and her clients, it also apparently became widely known in the community that Juan de Fuentes had denounced Gerónima to the Inquisition. Gerónima decided to take immediate evasive action and fled to the countryside to escape arrest and prosecution. Hearing rumors of Gerónima's escape and concerned that she would again evade his grasp, Inquisition comisario Baños y Sotomayor retaliated. He notified all the priests and Indian justices in writing that they should be on the lookout for Gerónima on the roads to Santa María de Jesús and Alotenango, towns along the two routes to the Pacific coast, where she was rumored to have fled. He also notified customs officers who patrolled the *caminos reales* (royal roads) to watch for Gerónima.

Finally, Baños y Sotomayor read an edict during mass at the Cathedral in Santiago, calling for assistance in Gerónima's capture. He described Gerónima as in her fifties, of medium stature, and "somewhat corpulent," her skin color "more light than dark," with curly gray hair and small eyes. He added that Gerónima walked with a limp, was poorly clothed, and lived near the San Francisco arch on the last block on the right-hand side near the Pensativo River. The edict warned that anyone who aided Gerónima in her escape would be excommunicated and fined two hundred *ducados*, or, for persons of *inferior calidad* (inferior status), two hundred lashes and six years of labor without pay on a Manila galleon. Officials attached the edict to the doors of all the parish churches in the capital.

Gerónima's adopted son found her, with her legs gravely injured, at the shrine of Nuestra Señora de Masagua, a miraculous image of the Virgin of the Rosary in a town near Escuintla on the Pacific coastal plain.[76] At the shrine, her son, a member of the Franciscan lay group Third Order of San Francisco, either persuaded or forced Gerónima to

turn herself in. Or perhaps, severely injured and unable to flee, Gerónima decided to turn herself in and hope for leniency from the Inquisition court. Inquisition officials questioned Gerónima in very general
terms. In an effort to deflect the charges against her, she denounced
her comadre Cecilia de Arriola, a mulato named Antonio Larios, and a
Spanish woman named doña Juana Zuleta. In the end, Baños y Sotomayor decided she was too sick to be sent to the city jail and instead
placed her under guard at the Hospital San Juan de Dios, located two
blocks south of the central plaza. Cecilia de Arriola remained under
arrest at El Niñado.

At this point Baños y Sotomayor probably thought that the two
women were safely imprisoned. However, he learned that from her hospital bed Gerónima sent word to Cecilia in El Niñado that she was
plotting an escape. Gerónima used Catalina, her mulata slave relative, as the go-between. Madre doña Angela, head of El Niñado and
responsible for making sure that no "suspicious" persons talked with
Cecilia, eavesdropped on the conversation between the two women.
The nun foiled the escape plan by reporting the meeting to the Inquisition. Baños y Sotomayor then accused Cecilia of planning to murder
the nun during her escape from El Niñado and transferred her to the
city jail. Guatemalan authorities later sent Cecilia overland from Santiago to the Inquisition court in Mexico City, where she was convicted
and jailed. The last that is known about Cecilia is through a letter she
wrote to the Inquisition judge in Mexico City. Cecilia told him that she
was ill with pneumonia and near death and asked to be moved from her
cell on the bottom floor of the jail to an upper floor where the air was
less damp. Gerónima never recovered from her injuries and died in the
hospital in Santiago a few years later.

The events surrounding the activities of Gerónima de Barahona and
her accomplices illustrate how an intimate, personal event, in this case
a conflict between husband and wife, became, in effect, a public performance of the power of local female sorcerers, spread through the city
through rumor and gossip. Inhabitants of the capital described Gerónima's continued "illegal" activities and the perceived weakness of the
Inquisition in terms of Gerónima's reputed power to bewitch various
Inquisition officials, murder her enemies, and even bewitch the president of the Audiencia. The institution of the Inquisition, through Baños
y Sotomayor, the notary, parish priests, and others, was forced to take
decisive action in a local issue that needed immediate attention by conducting a public performance of its own: searching and confiscating

Gerónima's house and goods, leaving her children homeless, reading an arrest edict at Cathedral mass, and nailing "wanted posters" to parish church doors throughout the city. After Gerónima's arrest, Inquisition legal proceedings continued the public performance of Inquisition authority and power, as the Inquisition judge called dozens of witnesses to testify about Gerónima's and Cecilia's activities.

The struggle for authority and power at the local level was ultimately a struggle for control of rival public spaces and the activities that occurred there. Public perceptions within this struggle for authority and power in the late seventeenth century thus became critical to the maintenance of colonial rule in Santiago de Guatemala.

It was proven that [Manuel] Calderón
had expelled through his mouth and nose
various evil items associated with sorcery
when [Padre] Lima publicly performed
an exorcism in front of many witnesses in
the Church . . . of Nuestra Señora de los
Dolores. In particular, [Manuel] expelled
some ribbons that his mother had given
him four days earlier.

— LETTER FROM THE HEAD OF MEXICO'S
INQUISITION TO THE GUATEMALAN
INQUISITION, 25 JUNE 1733[1]

Magical Violence and the Body

The Politics of the Body under Spanish Colonial Rule

During Spanish conquest and settlement of the Americas, the human body became a central component of the symbolic and physical expression of power. Spanish authorities controlled the bodies of colonized peoples through slavery, religious conversion, forced labor, and the resettlement of subject populations into more easily policed, nucleated towns (*congregación*).[2] But the assertion of colonial power entailed more than outright violence. Poverty, racial and gender hierarchies of colonial rule, and epidemic diseases that repeatedly swept through the capital shaped social relations in daily life.

Recent work by historians and anthropologists has begun to broaden the concept of violence and what constitutes a violent act. By using multilayered analyses of violence, and placing representations of it in specific cultural and historical contexts, these scholars have begun to make cross-cultural comparisons.[3] Much of this work has been done in light of the rise of military governments across modern Latin America and the cultural responses to the use of state-directed repression against domestic populations.[4] There has been little work along these lines, however, for the colonial period in Guatemala.

Representations of violence were embedded in the complex webs of social relations in daily life in Santiago de Guatemala. Men and women often linked accounts of violent acts to beliefs about evil and the supernatural, experienced in intimate, physical terms. Bodies become a central site of women's use of supernatural violence, and the bodies of

male and female enemies, employers, colonial officials, and sexual partners constituted battlegrounds for local struggles for community authority and power.[5] In the process, men's and women's bodies became
at once personal and public, targets that experienced supernatural violence physically in graphic and often horrifying terms. The violent act
often became marked on the body through wounds, infections, expul-

FIGURE 1. Image of the Virgin Mary holding the Santísimo Rosario
(Holiest Rosary), published in Guatemala in the seventeenth century.
Courtesy of the John Carter Brown Library at Brown University.

sions, and even complete bodily transformations, expressions of ritual power designed to be seen and discussed by the wider community.[6] Furthermore, body images began to shape discourses of violence in colonial Guatemala, as men and women from all social groups in the capital connected community conflicts to monstrous, leaky, and malleable bodies, transformed by women's sorcery practices. In addition, some women used their own bodies and body parts as instruments and expressions of ritual power. Women's body parts and fluids associated with female sexuality became especially critical elements in practices of love magic and sexual witchcraft designed to control men's behavior.

In Guatemala, the focus of Spanish colonial authority and power on the control of bodies became intimately bound up with racial and gender hierarchies of power. The policy of the two republics and the initial structuring of the capital into a Spanish core ringed by Indian neighborhoods were expressions of these distinctions, as was the colonial legal system, which enacted different punishments for similar crimes according to race and social status. Gender hierarchies of power became intertwined with the racial politics of rule, as colonial civil and religious authorities and institutions sought to control women's bodies, in particular their sexuality, by establishing official norms of female and male behavior. Sexual violence and the threat of sexual violence formed a key aspect of the construction of patriarchy within the family and within the larger colonial society.[7]

The control of women's bodies and their sexuality, a primary focus of colonial authority and power, was in part achieved through the threat of sexual violence.[8] Women's historians have begun to historicize sexual violence and relate it to other forms of domination, including warfare, military rule, colonialism, and racial hierarchies of power.[9] Jacquelyn Dowd Hall has argued that in the American South, both rape and lynching were central to a society that upheld men's control over women as well as white men's control over European American and African American women and men. Hall has also described the desire to shield some women and not others from rape as the cornerstone of patriarchal control of women's sexuality and their bodies.

In Spanish colonial society, the desire to "protect" certain women from sexual violence became institutionalized in policies designed to control marriage practices and limit women's sexual activity to Christian marriage and family. The goal was to encourage stable colonial settlements and discourage informal sexual liaisons between Spanish and Indian populations. Authorities used the reforms of the Council of

Trent (1545–63) as well as the Holy Office of the Inquisition in their at- tempts to enforce Christian marriage. The tension between honor and sexuality affected women of all economic and racial groups in colonial Latin America through the designations *doncella,* signifying virgin or maiden, and *soltera,* signifying that the woman was not a virgin.[10]

Members of colonial society emphasized the importance of white European women's virginity and virtuous reputation. This ideal was expressed through the practice of the "enclosure" of women in a nun- nery or the home, under the vigilance of a male patriarch. The practice of enclosure played on fears of rape and its consequences for both male and female honor, as well as property rights, inheritance, and illegiti- mate births. At the same time, colonial society emphasized the control of Indian and African women's bodies for labor, which left them vul- nerable to forced and unforced sexual liaisons.[11] The use of both sexual and racial hierarchies of power played a key role in the construction of colonial rule in Spanish America.

The Body in Supernatural Violence

Through the threat and use of magical violence, sorcerers refashioned the body into a site of power in conflicts and confrontations in daily life in Santiago. Female sorcerers and their clients carried out violent acts in intimate physical terms, as in the magical attack on Padre José de Quevedo, an incident that one Inquisition official described as "so pub- lic in this city." In 1704 Padre Quevedo denounced Lorenza de Molina, a mestiza immigrant from Peru, and María de Santa Inéz, a *mulata prieta* (a black mulata) from the nearby pueblo of Amatitlán, for witchcraft.[12] The fifty-one-year-old Padre Quevedo went to sleep at nine o'clock one Saturday night after taking an indigenous-style sweat bath called a *temescal.* He awakened later that night to a series of loud noises outside his bedroom window. Because Padre Quevedo knew he was alone in the house with all the doors locked, he thought the noise was "robbers, of whom we have so many these days in this city, who especially prowl about at night."

As the noises became louder, Padre Quevedo claimed that the women somehow appeared in his room in the form of "two lights the size of, or bigger than, an orange" and that "soft hands that seemed as if they were made of cotton" held him by the wrists. Then he felt something yank the rosary from around his neck.[13] The women, apparently after chang- ing back into human form, pulled the priest out of bed and carried him

into another room. Padre Quevedo stated that he could not defend himself against the women because they rendered him "completely disabled
and totally passive."

The two women placed the priest on a "smooth and slippery material" on the floor. The fumes from the "vile material" caused his
"senses [to become] dazed." Next, the women pushed Padre Quevedo
onto a rough wooden beam, forced him into the shape of a cross (*puesto
en cruz*), and tied him down. The women beat him repeatedly on his but-
tocks, elbows, wrists, shoulders, and genitals. The women then turned
the cross upside down. The priest's blindfold briefly slipped from his
eyes, and he set a fantastic scene, describing himself as a martyr in the
face of the women's diabolical powers:

> From the glimmering light of the moon through the window, I saw
> that my entire body was not only naked, but covered in a muddy and
> foul-smelling material. I tried calling out to my neighbors, because the
> women were killing me with such a [relentless] vehemence from [the]
> martyrdom. Amid this I remembered some words the Virgin Mary
> [used] to repel the diabolical legions. Thus, in the name of the Holy
> Virgin and of my beloved patron, San Miguel, I said loudly: Who is
> there like God Our Father all-powerful, who from the heights watches
> over the humble in the heavens and the earth? Who besides Jesus
> Christ will redeem us from the tree of the cross and vanquish our
> enemies? Holy God, Holy Strength, Holy Immortal!

After Padre Quevedo cried out the prayers in an attempt to counteract the women's powers and to save his soul, he claimed that he felt
them "anoint" his nostrils with the fetid material. He again became
weak and "lost his senses" and felt something "soft like lips and a
tongue" suck the blood from his wounds. He woke up in his own bed at
about six o'clock the next morning dazed and weak, his body covered
with infected wounds.

Padre Quevedo's description of his confrontation with Lorenza de
Molina and María de Santa Inéz, who he later told colonial officials
he had repeatedly feuded with, contains telling descriptions of the possibilities and fears of women's power in colonial Guatemala. He cast
the beating in terms of the end of the world and himself as a Christ-
like figure, a "passive" man and a martyr, completely immobilized by
the women and unable to act. This theme of being unable to act in
the face of women's magical power runs through many men's testimonies against women accused of sorcery. In late-seventeenth- and

early-eighteenth-century Guatemala, both women and men feared falling under the influence of powerful women; in particular, Spanish men and women feared falling under the spell of casta, Indian, and Black women, who were seen as powerful sorcerers.[14]

The beating was the culmination of a series of tensions and conflicts between Lorenza de Molina and Padre Quevedo. Some time before, Padre Quevedo had befriended a poor, dying mestiza, became godfather to her children, and regularly helped her and her children with alms and gifts of food and firewood. One of his godsons, a young boy named Juan, stole some money from his aunt Lorenza de Molina, the sister of the poor woman, and then took refuge in Padre Quevedo's house to avoid punishment. Lorenza repeatedly went to the priest's house and asked for the return of the boy, but the priest refused. The escalating tensions between Lorenza and Padre Quevedo erupted into violence one weekend. Padre Quevedo emerged early in the morning on his way to say mass and found Lorenza waiting for him on his front doorstep. A shouting match ensued. Padre Quevedo described how Lorenza became angry and called him a pimp and a gossip. He charged that Lorenza yelled at him in the street in front of passersby, causing them to lose "all respect for [him] and [his] position." Padre Quevedo retrieved his pilgrim's staff from his doorstep and beat Lorenza about the head with it.

Padre Quevedo claimed that Lorenza then decided to take revenge on him and solicited the help of some women from the town of Amatitlán, including María de Santa Inéz, who had a citywide reputation for violence. According to the priest, other witnesses, and Inquisition officials, María "had an evil reputation for being a witch and a spellcaster." Many called her La Panesito (the Bread Roll) because she was rumored to have killed a woman using a bewitched chocolate roll. When colonial officials banished her from her home village of Santa Inéz, she moved to the nearby pueblo of Amatitlán, where she sold rosaries and grinding stones in the street.

When María de Santa Inéz showed up at Padre Quevedo's doorstep and introduced herself to him, he and his neighbors already knew of her reputation. She began a campaign of intimidation: she showed up at Padre Quevedo's house "at all hours" asking for alms and other items such as firewood, hot water, and a knife. Ritual objects associated with sorcery began to appear in the priest's home, including bones and *vuélvete loco* (crazy-making) leaves, and he repeatedly heard unexplained noises at night.

In addition to challenging the Spanish priest's authority and social position with the audacity and violence of their act, Lorenza and María marked his body with wounds and scars for all in Santiago to see, drawing attention to his weakness. Melchor de los Reyes, the neighborhood barber who examined the priest after the attack, carefully noted the number, size, shape, and placement of the wounds on his body and concluded that the women made some sort of alliance with demons. The barber asserted that "those witches [beat the priest] before the devil, torturing him."[15]

Padre Quevedo's claim that the women sucked the blood from his wounds during the attack, and the repeated references to a fetid material spread on his naked body, is reminiscent of descriptions of women's Sabbath rituals in medieval and early modern Europe, in which groups of women witches were said to gather to perform Satanic rituals and pacts with the devil.[16] European traditions characterized women as "ideal satanic accomplice[s]," susceptible to possession by the devil, a characterization that Padre Quevedo and Inquisition authorities drew on when they described Lorenza's and María's actions.[17]

The women's violence against the priest and the publicity and notoriety of the act were seen as dangerous and powerful in the context of local social relations. The attack also had larger implications, however; it suggested to Inquisition authorities the possibility that any woman, by making an unholy alliance with the devil, could empower herself. As the head of the Inquisition commented to Mexican Inquisition officials, the incident was "very public in this city [and] everyone is horrified."[18]

The control of the bodies of colonial peoples in Spanish America, specifically, the control of women's bodies and their sexuality, formed an integral part of the power relations of colonial rule and power relations between men and women in daily life. That Lorenza de Molina and María de Santa Inéz made Padre Quevedo's physical body the focus of their exercise of supernatural power, in addition to the sexual overtones of the assault, suggested a symbolic inversion of male sexual violence used against women. The body became the central site of conflict in women's magical attacks on men, used to intimidate and exact revenge in conflicts in daily life. These conflicts included personal arguments, public disrespect, and jealousies in sexual relations. The human body remained the site of ritual attack, and unexplained swellings of body parts, vomiting and expulsion of various substances from the body, and complete body transformations were seen as evidence of sorcery.

In 1696 a series of conflicts between two female neighbors left one of the women, an Indian servant named María de la Candelaria, near death.[19] José de Baños y Sotomayor, head of Guatemala's Inquisition, had heard numerous rumors that a mulata resident of the capital named Michaela de Molina had bewitched María de la Candelaria. Angry that no one had come to denounce the event to the Inquisition, Baños y Sotomayor decided to go to the house of doña Juana González, mistress of the Indian servant, to take the sick woman's testimony at her bedside.

Baños y Sotomayor described how for over a period of three years, María de la Candelaria had vomited and expelled a multitude of items from her body, including stones, locks of hair, crushed pieces of charcoal, corn husks, pieces of *huipil,* a traditional embroidered blouse worn by indigenous women, and balls of soap.[20] From Sunday through Thursday during the Feast of Corpus Christi that year, María repeatedly expelled blood and pieces of charcoal through her nose and mouth.[21] Several people witnessed María's expulsions, including her mistress, doña Juana González, a member of the Third Order of San Francisco; doña Juana's niece doña Rafaela; Padre Mathias Lobo de Utilla; Antonio García and Juan Moncada, both secular priests; Francisco de Pontaza, parish priest of the Church of Nuestra Señora de los Remedios; Capitán don Diego de Quiroga, a political official in Santiago; and don Diego de Arguello, a royal notary.[22]

Doña Rafaela described María's expulsions in graphic detail.

[Doña Rafaela] went to the house of her aunt doña Juana González to help, and she saw for the first time that María de la Candelaria was suffering from nausea. [María] then expelled from her mouth a bundle wrapped in a white rag, tied with string made from century plant fiber. Attached to the bundle was a small corn husk. Captain don Diego de Quiroga, mayor of this city, and don Diego de Arguello, royal notary, went to her aunt's house and were shown the two bundles that the servant expelled. The notary untied both of them, and inside of the [bundles], this witness saw that he found a bit of *cebo* [animal fat] that was in a rind similar to that of the seed of a *chicozapote,* a tangle of hairs around a tobacco cigar, a small piece of rose-colored cloth, a black ribbon, purple thread, a human tooth, half a clove of garlic, a piece of cacao tied with thread, and a small bit of charcoal.

To those involved, the objects that María vomited were consistent with local ideas about sorcery and women's powers. Men and women in Santiago de Guatemala portrayed female sorcerers as having the ability to curse others by attacking the body, revealed in this case by the expulsion from the body of various ritual objects. At one point María repeatedly vomited ground-up pieces of charcoal and "lost her senses." Thinking she was on the verge of death, María's employer, doña Juana, called a priest named Pontaza to administer *santo oleo,* holy oil used for anointing the sick, and give her last rites.[23] When Padre Pontaza witnessed María's expulsions, he refused to give her last rites, thinking that something "evil" possessed her.

In an effort to make sense of the expulsions, María, doña Juana, and doña Rafaela linked María's symptoms to a series of arguments and fights with María's "only enemy," Michaela de Molina, a mulata neighbor who sold sweets in the street. The conflict between the two women began during a holy day celebration in the countryside and ended in a physical altercation during which María dragged Michaela by the hair.[24] A few days after the incident María experienced fainting spells, nausea, and expulsions. A second argument between the two women concerned María's sexual relationship with an Indian man named Pablo Vallejo, the son-in-law of Michaela's close friend, who lived in the nearby town of Santa Isabel.

None of the women knew for certain if Michaela used spells or sorcery. All three, however, highlighted Michaela's intimate friendship with two Indian women, both of whom were reputed to be violent and to practice sorcery. One of the women, Gerónima García, lived with Michaela in her house in Santiago. The other woman, Teresa, lived in the nearby town of San Cristóbal el Bajo and often visited Michaela in the capital.[25] Teresa was rumored to have killed a mulata woman with a curse. Colonial authorities had previously imprisoned Teresa in the city jail for the murder, but she had reportedly escaped after feigning an illness.

The conflict between María, the Indian servant, and Michaela, the mulata street peddler, became the object of community gossip after María's illness. Doña Juana called both a doctor and a *partera* (midwife) to examine the woman, but neither could cure her. Doña Juana then brought a number of religious and political officials to her house to witness María's expulsions. In the process, the ongoing conflict between the Indian servant and her mulata neighbor became public knowledge throughout the neighborhood and city, as Baños y Sotomayor described in a letter to his superiors in Mexico City:

It is *pública voz y fama* [public knowledge] that a mulata resident of this city named Michaela de Molina, who sells candies, has put a spell on a female Indian servant of doña Juana González, a resident of this city, and this Indian woman is in danger of dying from the spell and no one has appeared to denounce this event.

No one came to denounce María's strange expulsions even though they had continued for three years. Baños y Sotomayor, acting on public rumors of the expulsions, used the rumors to act outside formal Inquisition procedure and intervene in the conflict.

In this case, a personal conflict that at first involved only two women and a fight at a fiesta, expanded to include María's employer, Michaela's friends, local religious and political officials, and the head of Guatemala's Inquisition. The Indian servant María de la Candelaria drew on informal networks of support from women and men of other social groups. Through ties of employment, María involved her Spanish mistress, doña Juana. Doña Juana, an elite Spanish woman and member of a lay religious order, called on the assistance of local political and religious officials. Michaela, the mulata candy seller, was not without her own social network. She called on her close friends, two Indian women in the community linked to witchcraft practices and violent acts. To doña Juana and her social network, however, María's close friendships with her two female Indian friends made Michaela seem all the more suspect.

Women's use of supernatural violence in community conflicts could also include body transformations of male and female targets. In 1695 Catarina de Rodríguez, a thirty-four-year-old mestiza healer (*curandera*), married to a mulato slave who lived on a nearby Jesuit sugar plantation, charged that Gerónima de Barahona, the mulata beef seller, "did evil" to a Spanish woman named María Antonia de Cabrera.[26] Catarina asserted that Gerónima transformed María Antonia's body (*la mudó*) so that she appeared to have "the sex of a man with a virile member," from which she suffered greatly. Catarina noted that in the course of ministering to the woman, she "repeatedly saw for herself that [María Antonia's] natural parts were like a man's."

Catarina attributed the transformation to a public confrontation between Gerónima and María Antonia. Gerónima had a citywide reputation as a witch and sorcerer. One day, María Antonia, for some unexplained reason, allowed Gerónima to enter her house. María Antonia's neighbors warned her of Gerónima's evil reputation, and so María Antonia decided to throw Gerónima out of her house in front of neighbors and passersby. A short time later, María Antonia's body was transformed. By casting Gerónima out of her house in such a fashion, María

Antonia publicly embarrassed Gerónima, and so, charged the healer Catarina, out of revenge Gerónima used supernatural powers to transform María Antonia's body.

To support her characterization of Gerónima as a dangerous woman, Catarina told how "Indians" who lived near Espíritu Santo burned down Gerónima's house "to drive her [from the neighborhood] so that they would not have such an evil neighbor." María Antonia's mother, doña Ursula, secretly went to call on Gerónima and asked her to cure her daughter. Gerónima denied causing María Antonia's body to change shape but said that she would send over some healing water for María Antonia to wash with. According to the curandera, María Antonia did not bathe in the healing water, and she died a few months later.

The transformation of María Antonia's body resonates with medieval and early modern women's experiences in Europe, especially the experiences of female religious. Caroline Walker Bynum has argued that the human body represented a sacred site for both male and female religious.[27] Activities such as fasting and self-flagellation provided access to the sacred through the physical manipulation of the body. This manipulation was manifested in trances and seizures, stigmata, body swelling and mystical pregnancy, ecstatic nosebleeds, and the miraculous elongation or enlargement of parts of the female body: "In short, women's bodies were more apt than men's to display unusual changes, closures, openings, or exudings."[28] When María Antonia publicly embarrassed Gerónima, Catarina and doña Ursula charged that Gerónima, in turn, used clandestine rituals to humiliate María Antonia by transforming her body, desexing her in a particularly striking act of supernatural violence.

Women's Bodies, Women's Power: Love Magic and Sexual Witchcraft

In practices of love magic, the human body, in particular, the female body and physical manifestations of female sexuality, became a ritual weapon in women's conflicts with men in daily life, for example, infidelity, physical abuse, and abandonment.[29] While there is some evidence that women used men's body parts such as hair and nail clippings against them in love magic, usually women employed their own body parts and fluids, for example, pubic and armpit hair, sweat, urine, feces, saliva, and water that had been used to rinse the breasts, armpits, and genitals.[30]

Women grounded their authority and power in their social roles as mothers and nurturers. They gained intimate knowledge of the human body through their roles in birth and death, washing the newborn and the dead, lactation, menstruation, and caring for the sick and elderly.[31] In Santiago de Guatemala, many inhabitants, both women and men, thought some women possessed the power to cause impotence, return unfaithful lovers and husbands, attract a lover along with small amounts of money or a house, and restrain abusive sexual partners. In love magic rituals, women regularly mixed body parts associated with female sexuality into food and drink.[32] These were then fed to the targeted man.[33] In this way, women took advantage of their social roles in food procurement and preparation and of men's dependence on them. The ritual food and drink symbolically penetrated men's bodies and influenced and controlled men's behavior.[34]

A mulata named María de la Aruburu wished to attract a priest with whom she had a sexual relationship. She made a soup, called *sopa dorada* (golden soup), that contained her urine and the water she had bathed in. By eating the soup, the priest would be "tied" to her and remain faithful.[35] Manuela Gutiérrez, a twenty-year-old single mulata servant, consulted the mulata sorcerer Gerónima de Barahona for sexual witchcraft to attract her lover. Gerónima sold her some powders and told Manuela to wash her *partes naturales* (natural parts, genitals) with water, then beat the powders and water into a hot chocolate drink and give it to the man she desired.[36] Nicolasa de Torres, a single, free, mulata servant, wanted to attract her employer. She consulted an Indian woman named Petrona Mungía, who told her to take her pubic hair and a small worm found under a certain type of stone and then mix everything together and put it in her employer's chocolate drink.[37]

Women's body hair, especially pubic and armpit hair, was an important component in women's sexual witchcraft practices. Generally, women mixed the hair with bath water, powders, ground-up human or animal bones, herbs, or worms. They then fed the mixture to their husbands or lovers in food or drink, spread it on his clothes or bed, or buried it under the front door of his house or bedroom window.

Mothers and daughters cooperated in their use of sexual witchcraft, passing ritual knowledge from one generation to the next. In 1705 a mulata slave accused her mistress, a wealthy mulata widow named Francisca de Agreda, and her daughter Juana, of practicing sexual witchcraft. The slave claimed that Francisca and her daughter concocted a bewitched chocolate drink to send to Francisca's lover, the parish priest of the primarily indigenous town of Santa María.[38] The slave asserted that the drink contained Francisca's pubic hair, gray hairs from her head, her fingernails and saliva, and Juana's hair.

The Catholic church and religious authorities in Europe and the New World encouraged and promoted this view of body parts as powerful ritual items but in the form of religious relics and the material remains of saints. A relic might consist of the entire body of a saint, or a body part such as the head, arm, hand, tongue, or that which had suffered during martyrdom. The faithful were attracted to relics in part because they hoped to receive a cure or some other miraculous occurrence.[39]

Religious officials in the churches and convents of Santiago de Guatemala also promoted the power of relics. In 1585 a box reportedly containing the relics of San Sebastián arrived from Spain and was deposited in the church in Santiago dedicated to that saint.[40] Santiago's churches continued to receive relics throughout the eighteenth century.[41] Relics of Santiago's own Pedro de San José de Betancurt, believed to have wrought miracles in the seventeenth century, were preserved in the Church of San Francisco.[42] Since official religious practices highlighted the power of religious relics, it is not surprising that women turned to the use of body parts in ritual claims of power over men.

It is significant that women used their own bodies, not those of the men they wished to control and not those of saints, in magical rituals. The use of body parts linked specifically to female sexuality spoke to many people's fears about women's ability to control men through witchcraft and magic. And, more important, all women's bodies held power; it did not matter if the practitioner or client was an elite Spanish woman, a poor Indian servant, or a Black slave. So, for example, María Luisa, a twenty-seven-year-old Black slave, described how she consulted a free mulata named Francisca de Avedaño for a spell to bring back her lover who had abandoned her and left her destitute. Francisca gave María Luisa some lotion and told her to wash her genitals with it. María Luisa explained to Inquisition authorities that her lotioned genitals had such a strong effect that her lover returned to her.[43]

Drinks made of chocolate proved among the most popular means for delivering spells in sexual witchcraft.[44] By the late seventeenth century, all social and ethnic groups in colonial Guatemala drank chocolate in large quantities in many contexts in daily life. Chocolate, especially in the form of an indigenous-style hot beverage, provided an ideal cover for items associated with sexual witchcraft because of its dark color and grainy texture.

Sexual witchcraft was not only practiced to attract men, it was also used to *desenojar al hombre* (to free the man of anger), indicating that husbands or sexual partners used physical violence. María de los Angeles, a thirty-year-old Spanish seamstress, mixed black powders and water she had used to wash her genitals into a *jícara* (gourd cup) filled with hot chocolate so that her lover "would lose his anger."[45] In 1682 a Spanish woman named doña Luisa de Gálvez, in search of relief from the physical abuse of her male partner, consulted an Indian woman named Anita to "to free him of his anger."[46] Anita gave doña Luisa some green- and cinnamon-colored powders. First doña Luisa washed her genitals with the water. She then mixed the water with the powders into a hot chocolate drink and fed it to the man.[47] Melchora de los Reyes, a single mulata blanca, began a sexual relationship with her lover before marriage, probably after he had promised to marry her.[48] The lover later abandoned Melchora, and because of the rumors surrounding the abandonment, she lost her reputation as a doncella. Melchora bought some powders from a sorcerer and mixed them into her lover's chocolate to make him "subject to her will," so that he would return, marry her, and restore her reputation.

Men sometimes took advantage of the association between hot chocolate drinks and sexual witchcraft in their sexual pursuit of women. Rosa de Arrevillaga was a twenty-eight-year-old mulata slave of a nun named Madre Manuela de San José, and the two women lived cloistered in the convent of Santa Catalina Martír in Santiago.[49] Inquisition authorities listed Rosa as "doncella," and despite her slave status, she had received an education in the convent, as evidenced by the letter she wrote to Inquisition authorities denouncing her confessor for solicitation in the confessional.

In the letter, Rosa described how she had gone to confess during the Easter holidays. As she waited, she served the priest, Padre Francisco de Castellanos, a cup of chocolate in front of the other priests "as it was the fashion and kindness that one does in the convent for the confessors." When she entered the confessional, Padre Francisco reportedly said many "amorous words" to her and called her "his soul, and his life, and his Rose of Jericho." As Rosa tried to fend off his unwanted sexual advances, Padre Francisco justified his actions by telling her that he knew she had put powders in the chocolate she served him "to gain his love."

Unstable Bodies: Shape-changing Sorcery and Representations of Women's Power

In colonial Guatemala, discourses of magical violence in community conflicts portrayed some women as having the power to transform the bodies of men and women or penetrate the body's boundaries with ritual objects. They also described how some women had the power to transform themselves into animals, insects, birds, and natural objects and thereby forcibly intervene in community conflicts. Goverment officials and inhabitants of the capital attributed this shape-changing ability to the most successful female sorcerers in the community. Shape-changing accounts represented women's bodies, in particular, casta, Black, and Indian women's bodies, as powerful and unstable, capable of wreaking supernatural revenge. Discourses of female sorcerers as shape-changers reflected both colonial and community perceptions of and preoccupations with the unfixed and changing nature of women's, especially nonwhite women's, roles in local social relations in late-seventeenth- and early-eighteenth-century Guatemala.

When Lorenza de Molina and her sister-in-law María de Santa Inéz assaulted Padre Quevedo, both the priest and his neighbors accused the two women of changing into various forms to attack him in an act of supernatural revenge.[50] According to Padre Quevedo, the women could shape-change into bright lights, an ability that appears to have been ascribed to those seen as the most powerful and dangerous sorcerers. The night following the attack, Padre Quevedo remained hidden in his house, afraid of another attack. He cleansed the rooms of his house with rosemary, an herb associated with protection from evil, and gathered together *reliquias* (holy items), a cross, and holy water. Despite the protection of the relics and ritual incense, Padre Quevedo claimed the supernatural intimidation continued that evening when "two lights the size of two bright nuts" entered his room and clods of earth began to fall from the ceiling.

As word of the attack spread through the community, Inquisition *comisario* Pedro López Ramalez noted in a letter to Mexican Inquisition authorities that at the same time strange birds began appearing around the city of Santiago. A nun, a woman "of much virtuousness" according to López Ramalez, came to him at nine o'clock one evening and reported that during the previous night's procession of the Holy Virgin, a "great multitude of large birds" took off and fluttered above them. The birds then perched on the walls of the Convent of Santa

Catarina Mártir. During another procession at Christmas, the nuns saw many *zopilotes* (turkey vultures) in the air. López Ramalez concluded his letter to the Mexican Inquisition:

> I have heard many times [the stories about the birds] in past years, and generally everyone says that they are *brujas* [female witches]. I repeated this news to your grace [so that you would] believe that they have infested this city.

Padre Quevedo's neighbors also noted strange animals, which they described in their testimonies as evidence that the two women shape-changed to carry out the violent attack. Juan de Velo, a twenty-one-year-old free mulato carpenter, spent the night after the attack with Padre Quevedo. Juan told of seeing "a white light, like the crown of a hat, moving under the bed." Juan de Aguilar, a thirty-six-year-old Spanish shoemaker, reported seeing birds associated with witches the night of the attack while he sat at the door of his shop. He also claimed to have seen a *gallo de la tierra* (turkey) "floating in the air." Another neighbor, Felipe de Mayen, a thirty-year-old mestizo shoemaker, reported that at about 11:00 P.M. on the day of the Assumption, as he sat at the doorstep of his shop, "[h]e heard animals, like cats, that fly about this time of year in the season of La Cruz [The Cross, meaning Easter] and San Juan [Saint John]." He also said that he had heard since he was a child that these are witches.

Also on the same night as the attack, the priest's neighbor, Domingo de Illescas, a manager at a nearby sugar plantation, heard the loud noise of what appeared to be a turkey flying over Padre Quevedo's roof. And Lorenza Cujante, a tall, barefoot, "freckle-faced" mulata, originally from the nearby town of Amatitlán and María de Santa Inéz's sister, heard an unexplained animal noise at about 9:00 P.M. According to her testimony, a turkey caused the sound, given its weight when it landed on the roof of the priest's bedroom, and because when she looked, the bird appeared "stocky and tall." Lorenza told colonial authorities that she made use of *remedios espirituales* (spiritual remedies), including holy water, to drive the evil turkey away.

In accusations of magical violence against female sorcerers, witnesses either connected the appearance of strange natural objects, animals, and birds to the female sorcerers' activities or considered them to be the sorcerers themselves in changed form. Men and women who gave testimony about Gerónima de Barahona, who reportedly transformed María Antonia's body, also claimed that she had the power to shape-change into a rattlesnake, a toad, a cat, various birds, a tiger, and "a large black animal that smelled of sulfur."[51] Witnesses described women, along with Indian and African men—social groups seen as particularly unstable and even dangerous in late-seventeenth- and early eighteenth-century—with the ability to shape-change into, or magically control, vultures, snakes, ants, bulls, and donkeys.

Both Mesoamerican and European beliefs about the supernatural included shape-changing. In preconquest Mesoamerican societies, the ability to shape-change expressed the authority and power of male and female witches, gods, and important charismatic individuals.[52] During Spanish colonial rule, various indigenous groups had their own words for shape-changers: *nahualli* in Nahuatl, *rajav a'a* in Kaqchikel, and *maestros nahualistas* and *brujo-nahual* in Spanish. In Nahua cultures, for example, a powerful female sorcerer named Quilaztli could appear in many shapes.[53]

The *Popul Vuh*, the K'iche' Maya book of creation, described how many gods and leaders possessed the ability to shape-change. This ability became an important expression of the connections between supernatural and political power in Maya culture:

> Their splendor and majesty grew among the K'iche'. . . . The lords were truly valued and had truly great respect. . . . And when war befell their canyons and citadels, it was by means of their genius that the Lord Plumed Serpent and the Lord Cotuha blazed with power. Plumed Serpent became a true Lord of Genius: On one occasion he would climb up into the sky; on another he would go down the road to Xibalbá [the Mayan underworld]. On another he would make himself aquiline, and on another feline; he would become an actual eagle or a jaguar in his appearance. On another occasion it would be a pool of blood; he would become nothing but a pool of blood. Truly his being was that of a Lord of Genius. All the other lords were fearful before him . . . when Lord Plumed Serpent made the signs of greatness.[54]

This excerpt from the *Popul Vuh* reveals the links made between political and religious power and community leadership, similar to those that can be seen in the context of women's shape-shifting witchcraft in postconquest Guatemalan society. "Lords of Genius" such as Plumed Serpent became powerful and respected political-religious leaders in Maya society. They were described as having the power to shape-change, especially in times of stress, such as war or other societal crises. Word of Lord Plumed Serpent's shape-changing abilities, his "signs of greatness," spread throughout the region, enhancing his authority and power—much as certain women's reputations for violence and success in sorcery enhanced their influence in their neighborhoods and even the city and also attracted paying clients.

Europeans, including Spaniards, possessed detailed and complicated ideas of how evil in general and the devil in particular functioned in the human world. In the Spanish colonial world, they used these ideas to interpret and take seriously indigenous religious practices, including descriptions of shape-changing.[55] In Spain, supposed witches were linked with owls, cats, snakes, and dogs, viewed as "demonic apparitions" and evidence of the witches' power.[56] In postconquest society, Mesoamerican ideas about shape-changers came to be associated with European ideas of witches and sorcerers who, according to Catholic ideology, gained access to evil sources of power through pacts with the devil. Shape-changers were criminalized as "evil sorcerers, capable of affecting transformations or at least the illusion of transformations."[57]

In cities such as Santiago de Guatemala with large populations of African descent, African beliefs about the connections among religion, power, and the supernatural entered into religious-cultural frameworks, integrating African practices such as the central role of revelation in religious life. In African-Christian practices in the New World, revelation and the exchange of information between the human world and supernatural beings could take place through a spirit medium, or a possessed object or animal.[58]

The reformulation and re-creation of postconquest ideas about shape-changers and their powers can be seen in both indigenous and Spanish accounts of conquest. A postconquest K'iche' Maya account of the wars of conquest in Guatemala described how the provincial leader Izquín Najaib transformed into lightning and attemped to kill Pedro de Alvarado, head of the Spanish forces, during the decisive battle on the plains outside present-day Quetzaltenango:

In the year 1524 . . . these Indians, unable to kill Tonatiú [Alvarado], this time sent another Indian captain, turned into a lightning bolt, called Izquín Najaib . . . and this Najaib went to where the Spaniards were and in the form of a lightning bolt tried to kill the Adelantado [Alvarado]. When he got there, he found that a white dove was perched above the Spaniards, defending them. The second time he attacked, he fell to the earth blinded and could not get up. Three more times this captain tried to attack the Spaniards as a lightning bolt, but each time he fell to the ground.[59]

In this case, the local K'iche' leader Najaib drew on his ability to shape-shift into a natural form in a last-ditch attempt to defeat the Spanish enemy in the midst of a decisive battle.

In preconquest Mesoamerican societies, shape-changers could perform both good and evil acts. With the imposition of Spanish colonial rule, the role of shape-changers came to be influenced by European ideas about black magic, creating new discourses in postconquest society that characterized shape-changers as witches. The following eighteenth-century Spanish account of the K'iche' leader Tecum Uman reflected the competing postconquest accounts of shape-changers as witches:

> They say that the King of the K'iche' Tecum Uman is a *gran brujo* [great witch], and that he flew over all his armies in the form of a bird called a Quetzal, with very long feathers, green and showy. With a scepter of emeralds in his hand, he went about giving orders to his captains and urging on his soldiers. They also say that he had the same ability as the brujos and many lords that go about in the form of lions and eagles and other animals. . . . [I]t is certain that . . . the K'iche' kings are grandes brujos and can transform themselves into various animals, and one knows that this wicked pact with the devil exists to this day between some Indians, and so it is not unbelievable that this King Tecum Uman was a brujo and could transform himself into a Quetzal bird.[60]

In this account of the wars of conquest Tecum Uman's leadership is associated with shape-shifting abilities, but he is reconstructed as a witch who made a pact with the devil.[61]

Beliefs that certain subjects had the power to shape-change carried through into the colonial period and continue in Mesoamerica and the Andes to the present day.[62] There appears to be a hierarchy based on which animal or natural form the shape-changer adopted.[63] The most powerful and important sorcerers transformed into jaguars, eagles, quetzal birds, or natural forms associated with Maya ideas of kingship and high status, such as pools of blood and lightning. Less powerful sorcerers transformed into lower-status animal and bird forms, such as turkeys and vultures.

Shape-changing accounts from seventeenth- and eighteenth-century Guatemala contain descriptions of individuals, especially women, Indians, and castas, who had the ability to transform themselves. In 1706 an eighteen-year-old Indian servant named Simona de los Santos accused her Spanish mistress, Antonia Santiago, and her mistress's sister, Sebastiana, of shape-changing into turkeys to gain wealth.[64] Simona, an orphan left on the doorstep of the Estancia de Tuluché del Pasón, was raised in the Santiago household, where she remained as a servant in her adulthood. Simona recounted that a year before, while she slept in the same room with Antonia, a noise awoke her, and so she lit a candle. She looked over at Antonia and saw her sleeping face up. Next to Antonia, she saw a large bird with yellow feet that resembled a turkey. Simona became frightened and tried to wake Antonia, but Antonia "appeared dead." Simona then saw the turkey enter Antonia's body through her mouth, and she said that "[the turkey] did not leave again." At that instant, Antonia awoke and asked why Simona lit the candle, but Simona said nothing.

A few days later, Sebastiana came to visit. Simona noticed that the two women gathered eggshells and then entered a room. Simona followed and found the two women sleeping face-up. She then saw two turkeys enter the room, one the same as before, the other roughly similar but with a golden beak. The turkeys then entered the women's bodies through their mouths. The two sisters woke up and told Simona not to tell anyone what happened.

Simona denounced the women as *mujeres de mal vivir* and claimed that they shape-changed into turkeys to bring back riches, including five chests and four cases of satin and silk clothing, silver spoons, and other items, adding that the women dressed themselves in this finery to attend church. Though both sisters were married, Antonia to an Indian man from Quetzaltenango and Sebastiana to a Spanish silversmith from Santiago de Guatemala, neither lived with her husband. In his letter to the Mexican Holy Office, the Guatemalan Inquisition judge concurred that the sisters were *mal opinionados* (not well thought of) because they did not live with their husbands.

Simona's account of the shape-changing sisters reveals intersecting themes of gender, ethnicity, and society in colonial Guatemala. First, an Indian servant denounced her Spanish mistresses for acting as mujeres de mal vivir, perhaps out of revenge or jealousy. Sebastiana and Antonia apparently flouted the traditional marriage prescriptions for elite Spanish women; they did not live with their husbands and so remained outside of men's control. In addition, the sisters possessed a fair amount of material wealth, which probably translated into high social status for the two women in community life, enhanced through the display of rich clothing at church. Simona represented her employer's unorthodox behavior and unexplained wealth in terms of using the ability to shape-change to steal from others.

Supernatural Violence and Magical Bodies

The central theme of the physical body in community conflicts, both as a battleground in interpersonal conflicts and as a metaphor of violence in daily life, came together in graphic form in the following sorcery, shape-changing, and exorcism account. In 1730 Manuel Antonio Calderón, a twenty-one-year-old free mulato who worked as a weaver, wrote a letter to Inquisition authorities accusing his seventeen-year-old wife, María Magdalena, also a weaver, of sorcery.[65] He later explained that he denounced his wife in writing because he suffered from an "affliction of reason" caused by demons that had entered his body when his wife bewitched him.

Manuel described his marriage to María Magdalena as filled with discord, declaring that "there has not been one day that they have not fought, because she mistreated him in word and deed." A few weeks earlier, in late December, Manuel's mother had given him a gift of some stockings decorated with silk ribbons, which he brought home for his wife, who placed them on top of the loom. The two then began to argue, and Manuel briefly left the house.

When he returned, Manuel found a vulture in the middle of the front room, with the ribbons tied around its claws, suggesting that his wife had shape-changed in his absence. He wrote: "I became filled with terror at the sight of the vulture with the ribbons." The vulture then flew through the door into the kitchen. Immediately after that, María Magdalena came back through the kitchen door with the ribbons in her hands, supposedly having shape-changed back into human form. The two again fought, and María Magdalena, still with the ribbons in her hands, said to Manuel: "This insanity has returned to you." She then placed her hands, which were covered in fat, on his head to heal him. Manuel had recognized María Magdalena in her transformed state because the vulture had the ribbons he had just given her tied around its feet. Manuel claimed that about an hour after the experience, "I took the stockings and I found that they no longer had the ribbons attached." Manuel explained the ongoing conflicts with his wife and his repeated bouts of insanity and confusion in terms of having demons in his body, placed there by his wife. Furthermore, he described how María Magdalena could control the demons in his body; she could use her powers of sorcery to cause his insanity to come and go, sometimes bringing it on with a bewitched cigar that caused him "to feel as if his head were suffocating." Sometimes, he said, she touched his head, and he returned to normal. He also spoke of his wife's power over him in terms of her ability to penetrate his body with ritual items hidden in smoke and food.

According to Padre Lima, the thirty-three-year-old Spanish priest of the Church of Our Lady of Dolores de Abajo, María Magdalena had shape-changed into a vulture previously, during one of the couple's arguments. Padre Lima claimed that Manuel told him he found a vulture in his bedroom one night. Feeling desperate, Manuel decided to attack the vulture. He grabbed the bird by its feet, but it seemed very heavy. The vulture clawed Manuel's hands, and so he "whacked" the vulture on the head. After the incident, Manuel told Padre Lima that he found his wife with a wounded head, and he showed the priest his scratched hands. The priest reported to Inquisition authorities that when Manuel Antonio slept, a siren (*sirena*) who had the body of a fish and the face of his wife laid down in bed with him.

Manuel had apparently battled the demons in his body for at least a few months before he wrote the letter denouncing his wife. He alternately explained the symptoms as *perturbación* (confusion, disquiet of mind), *locura* (insanity), and losing his *juicio* (judgment). He pointed to a series of incidents that led him to believe his wife had bewitched him. One night six months earlier, María Magdalena, along with Manuel's mother-in-law and sister-in-law, offered him a cup of hot chocolate. When Manuel took the cup of chocolate, he noticed it was heavier than usual and became suspicious. He took the chocolate over to the light and found in the foam some "suspicious items placed there for evil ends."

Manuel decided not to drink the cup of chocolate and placed it in the corner of the room. He set some rosemary next to the cup, an herb associated with ritual cleansing and protection from evil in Spanish culture. When he returned to his wife, her mother, and sister, he saw that they watched him and then "laugh[ed] at me, taking me for an idiot." Manuel, however, felt he had been right in thinking his wife had tried to bewitch him. "I found the cup of chocolate filled with such a large quantity of white worms," he wrote, "that the cup of chocolate appeared to move on its own, which horrified me."

According to the neighbors, María Magdalena had a history of using supernatural violence. She would introduce ritual items into the target's body through food and drink. The effects of the spell were then expressed physically, through the bodily expulsions of a wide array of ritual items. Petrona Mártir, Manuel's mother, related that María Magdalena had bewitched an Indian shepherd named Cipriano with *atole*, an indigenous corn drink. Manuel's mother asserted that the bewitched atole was meant for her husband, who drank some of it and then "vomited for two days." Her husband gave the rest to Cipriano, who drank the atole, "became dried out" (*se fue secado*), and died four months later. Teresa de Jesús, a sixty-year-old Indian laundress and Cipriano's mother-in-law, added more detail. María Magdalena sent bewitched atole to Manuel's father, who took a few sips and vomited. Manuel's father then gave the atole to Cipriano, who drank it and immediately became gravely ill. "[Cipriano] began to dry out," claimed Teresa, "[and] he felt great heat waves in his bowels, until he lost his life."

Others reported that María Magdalena also bewitched a woman named Rosa, who was married to a musician, after the two women fought in a store that Rosa operated from the front of her home.[66] María Magdalena bewitched her in revenge according to Manuel, causing Rosa to become ill and "expel evil things that suggested a curse." Acting on Manuel's information, Inquisition officials hurried to question Rosa. They found her on her deathbed, *in articulo mortis*. Officials questioned her anyway, asking if someone had "cast a spell on her."

Rosa replied that she had been ill for four years but that it "appeared to be natural." For part of that time, however, she was in the Hospital San Juan de Dios. During her stay, she "expelled from below" various types of seeds (*pepitas*). The priest-administrators examined the seeds that Rosa expelled and told her that she suffered from sorcery. Rosa said she ignored their diagnosis. The questioning ended soon after, when Rosa began to suffer *grandes fatigas* (great waves of nausea).

Manuel, afraid after his wife shape-changed into a vulture and worried that his confusion would return, went to the house of a male friend, and then the two of them went to see Padre Lima. Manuel described what happened next:

> [The priest] placed his hands on my head and said an *evangelio* over me, and I immediately regained my memory, and I expelled one of the silk ribbons from my mouth, along with other evil things.[67]

The priest, intrigued by Manuel's accounts of his wife's sorcery and eager to intercede, persuaded Manuel to take him to his house to recover the sorcery items.

The following day, Padre Lima brought Manuel to his small church and began an exorcism ritual that lasted seven days. The exorcism, conducted in public, acted as a counterdisplay of the corporeal power of Catholicism and his ritual role as priest. When Padre Lima drove the demons out of Manuel's body, the witnesses saw for themselves the church's power over women's witchcraft and later described Manuel's dramatic expulsions to the Inquisition. Having others bear witness was an important aspect of demonstrating power, whether over "evil" or within local social relations. During the exorcism, the priest fought for control of Manuel's body, which became a battleground between the forces of righteousness, of the priest and the Catholic church in alliance with the Virgin of Dolores, and the forces of evil, a woman and her sorcery powers in alliance with demons.

Priests who conducted exorcisms from demonic possession followed formal guidelines and procedures, such as those found in a seventeenth-century Guatemalan religious manual. Exorcism manuals described in detail how to recognize demonic possession and how to heal it, listing the prayers to be read, the ritual steps to follow, and how to avoid being tricked by the demons:

> The cunning and deceit of the demon used to trick man are many, and so to avoid being tricked, the Exorcist must act cautiously. . . . There are many types of demons, according to Our Lord, that will leave only through prayer and fasting. [The exorcist must use] these two remedies to ask for divine intercession and expel the demons using the model of the Holy Fathers.[68]

Catholic beliefs regarding the possibilities of demonic possession characterized the body's boundary as unstable and open to intrusion by demons and the devil, who revealed their presence inside the body physically: "Every time you see the possessed [person] in pain in some part of the body, or that some part swells up, make the sign of the cross and rub him [there] with holy water."[69]

Inside the church, Manuel knelt, and the priest said a prayer to the Holy Virgin and said another evangelio. Soon Manuel began to feel "a great [amount] of nausea" and vomited a corn husk, which the priest carried to the altar of the Virgin of Dolores.

The priest repeated the evangelio and Manuel "vomited and expelled" a corn husk leaf, copper nails, some tobacco, and the other ribbon from María's stockings, all of which the priest saved to present to Inquisition authorities. According to the handbook, expulsions played a central role in exorcisms of the possessed, who became ritually cleansed after they rid their bodies of demons and other evil items:

> While you conduct the exorcism, use more words from the sacred scripture than your own [to] ask [the demon] if he is in the body from magical works, or [by] evil signs or instruments, and take the possessed by the mouth, and help him expel them.[70]

The priest commented to the Inquisition that he "publicly conducted" the exorcisms in the church before numerous witnesses, who watched Manuel expel the sorcery items through his mouth and nose. One aspect of demonstrating power, whether over "evil" or within local social relations, was through having others bear witness. In this case the priest conducted the exorcism publicly in front of witnesses, many of whom recalled in a detailed fashion exactly what, when, and how much Manuel vomited and expelled from his body.

Sebastián de Morzano, a thirty-three-year-old farmer, watched Padre Lima perform the exorcism on Manuel four times in the church and another three times in the priest's house. He recalled that Manuel expelled "various evil things through his mouth": a cigar butt, pieces of ribbon, blue thread, silk, pieces of paper, three pieces of bone, a piece of ribbon made with white thread, copper nails, tobacco leaves, and many other things that he said he could not remember.

Francisco de los Santos, a fifty-year-old tailor, had accompanied Padre Lima and Manuel when they returned to Manuel's house to recover the items his wife had used in her sorcery. In the house, Manuel expelled a small ball of hair, "which [Padre Lima] pulled from [Manuel's] nose in his presence, with great performance." Later Francisco witnessed the exorcism and saw Manuel expel a piece of charcoal and a nail from his mouth. He also said he "heard" that Manuel had also expelled two pieces of red-colored ribbon and many other things, all of which appeared to him to be *diabólica* (diabolical). Pedro Flores, a married, thirty-eight-year-old mestizo tailor, saw Manuel expel from his mouth some thorns, charcoal, fibers tied with blue thread, and wax mixed with bits of glass, and he heard that Manuel also expelled ribbons, corn husks, and other "evil" items.

María Manuela, with the help of the demons she supposedly either controlled or allied herself with, counteracted the priest's exorcism. Padre Lima waited seven days to see if the exorcism succeeded, keeping Manuel in his house for observation. Since Manuel had not expelled anything further, the priest decided to send him back to his job as a weaver. Manuel left the priest's house, but after walking only a block, he claimed he met the four demons who had left his body, one standing on each of the four corners of the street.

Manuel described one of the demons as a siren that had the head of his wife but the body of a fish. The demons attacked him and tried to force him to return to his wife's house. The account becomes convoluted here, but Manuel later found himself in a nearby rural town, taken there by a figure who at times appeared to be his wife, María Magdalena, and at other times appeared to be his wife in the form of the siren.

Padre Lima claimed that María Magdalena again bewitched Manuel during the trip, magically seizing him so he could not move his hands. María Magdalena then apparently taunted Manuel, telling him that "not every day [did] the Virgin of Dolores perform a miracle," and then caused Manuel to expel a leaf from a corn plant from his body, which then shape-changed into a large toad, along with "other poisonous animals."

In both institutional and informal exercises of power, the body formed a central physical and symbolic battleground in the struggle for power in daily life in colonial Guatemala. Inhabitants from all social and ethnic groups in the capital and surrounding towns attributed to certain women the power to use supernatural means to shape-change to intervene in conflicts and feuds, exact revenge, or gain wealth. Accounts of female shape-changers and their use of magical violence reveal discourses on women's power in community life and represented women's bodies as unstable and capable of transformation in strategies of witchcraft and sorcery.

Colonial authorities actively sought out accounts of female shape-changers. By pursuing and prosecuting the individuals involved, they attempted to transform discourses of women's magical power into discourses of colonial control, marking them as deviant and criminal practitioners of illegal religion. In the process, Inquisition authorities capitalized on accounts of women's use of magical violence in local conflicts and used them to reinforce and extend colonial authority into community life.

4

Illness, Healing, and the Supernatural World

For the love of God take this evil that is in my body, because it is not the word of God, this evil that you are killing me with.

—TESTIMONY OF ANDRÉS YOS
RECOUNTING HIS WIFE'S ACCUSATION
AGAINST A MIDWIFE FOR USING SORCERY
TO INTERFERE WITH HER PREGNANCY,
PINULA, 1660[1]

In colonial Guatemala, female curanderas and parteras played important curing roles in community life, attracting both male and female patients from all ethnic and social groups in Santiago and surrounding towns.[2] Women based their healing practices on their gendered social roles, re-created and extended by drawing on knowledge of the natural world, including herbs, plants, and food procurement and preparation, along with Spanish, African, and Maya ideas about religion and the supernatural.[3] The use of this knowledge formed a central part of women's cultural authority and power in colonial Santiago de Guatemala.[4]

Descriptions of experiences of illness and healing practices not only offer evidence of how women claimed authority and power in daily life, they provide information about social relations within multiethnic urban communities and about how communities perceived themselves in relation to the Spanish colonial state.[5] A major social change in seventeenth-century Santiago de Guatemala was the emergence of a multiracial population by the 1650s. This large population of castas, free and slave Blacks, hispanicized Indians, and urban poor occupied a fluid cultural and economic border linking elite Spanish populations and the mainly indigenous hinterland. The operation of this border can be viewed, in part, through accusations of supernatural illness prosecuted by Inquisition and civil authorities in Santiago. The sick, their family members, and their neighbors accused certain female healers and midwives of using sorcery to cause illnesses that could result in blindness, strange bodily expulsions, and deformed babies. Community

FIGURE 2. Image of Santa Catarina (Saint Catherine) in a prayer book dedicated to her, published in Guatemala in 1716. The caption reads "Pray for us." Courtesy of the John Carter Brown Library at Brown University.

members distinguished what they perceived as supernatural illnesses from other illnesses with the phrase *no era palabra de Dios* (it was not the word of God).

Ethnicity, class, and gender played an important role in who was considered most suspect—usually women, castas, Mayas, Afro-Guatemalans, and the poor, who were publicly known as magical healers and sorcerers or were thought to have associated with or consulted one. Illness accusations, and how the afflicted physically experienced sickness, illuminate the central role of local cultural practices in reflecting and reshaping lived experiences in the capital.[6] Whether made by local ecclesiastical and civil officials, Indian justices, or community members themselves, the accusations also provided the opportunity for the Spanish state to capitalize on the suffering of local populations and use it to reinscribe colonial power.

Despite the dangers of denunciation and prosecution, female healers and midwives practiced curing and used, or threatened to use, their powers to cause illness. The perceived ability to both cure and cause illnesses contributed to their power in local community relations and aided in the intimidation and coercion of others in personal conflicts. In addition, for those seen as skillful and successful curers and midwives, healing offered a viable economic option and provided access to cash and social status. Illness accusations against female healers and midwives reflected and critiqued the often conflictive social relations and the difficulties women faced in Santiago de Guatemala under Spanish colonial rule. Illness accounts also illustrate women's creative use of European, Maya, and African religious beliefs and practices in local healing cultures.[7]

Conceptions of Illness and Healing Practices in Colonial Guatemala

The regulation of official medical practice in New Spain and the Audiencia of Guatemala closely followed the Spanish model. In 1477 the Spanish crown established the Protomedicato, an institution designed to regulate medicine through examinations, licensing, and the court system. The Spanish crown continued the institution in New Spain, and in 1525 the municipal council of Mexico City named its first director, or *protomédico*, to regulate medical practices there. The Protomedicato did not license Muslim or Jewish doctors, nor did it license native healers.

For much of the colonial period, especially outside of urban centers, there was a chronic shortage of licensed physicians in New Spain.[8] After 1646 only those doctors with university degrees could legally practice medicine. Inhabitants devised multiple healing strategies, however, that included consulting doctors, surgeons, and barbers, native healers, midwives, and pilgrimages to healing shrines, strategies often used in conjunction with one another.[9]

In the wake of the epidemics that accompanied the Spanish conquest of the Americas, colonial authorities began to establish institutions to address the problem. As early as 1502, the Spanish crown instructed settlers to build hospitals in the New World to house both Spaniards and Indians.[10] Church officials, based on their experiences during the Reconquest, saw hospitals as a way to aid in the conversion of native peoples to Catholicism and began to be active in healing activities. The regular orders, responsible for the conversion of indigenous groups, also administered colonial hospitals, and this was true in Guatemala as well, which did not have any European-trained doctors until the late sixteenth century.[11]

In Guatemala and elsewhere in Spanish America, hospitals cared for specific social and racial groups. In 1541 Bishop Marroquín founded the first hospital in Santiago de Guatemala, the Hospital Real de Santiago (Royal Hospital of Santiago) and designated it specifically for Spaniards.[12] Construction was completed in 1553.[13] The Hospital San Alejo cared for Indians. In 1630 the religious order of San Juan de Dios took over the administration of both hospitals and continued to segregate the sick by ethnicity: San Alejo administered specifically to Indians, and San Juan de Dios cared for Spaniards and gente ladina (castas, blacks, and nontributary Indians).[14] The Hospital de San Pedro admitted only priests.

In 1630 Alvaro Quiñónez de Osorio, president of the Audiencia of Guatemala, donated money to establish the Hospital de San Lázaro, also known as the Hospital de los Incurables, to house the large numbers of lepers he saw in the streets of the capital. It effectively functioned as a place to quarantine and imprison lepers, as officials believed that the disease would easily spread to the rest of the population.[15] By the late seventeenth century, friars of the order of San Juan de Dios administered all of Santiago de Guatemala's hospitals, which reinforced the connections between religion and healing in the capital.[16]

Shortages of beds and medicines continually plagued the capital.[17] By the early 1680s, for example, the Hospital Real had only twenty-four beds for Indians and another twenty-four beds for Spaniards and gente ladino, fourteen of those for men and ten for women. Authorities in the capital repeatedly requested funds to improve hospital buildings and increase the number of beds.

Many such requests came in the aftermath of the epidemics that continued to sweep through Santiago and the Audiencia of Guatemala throughout the colonial period, affecting rich and poor alike. An epidemic of typhus or pneumonic plague lasted from 1686 into 1687 and hit Santiago and the surrounding area hard. Colonial officials estimated that the epidemic killed one-tenth of the population, mostly Indians and the poor.[18] Priests of the order of San Juan de Dios, who administered the Hospital Real, had to turn away most of the afflicted because of a severe shortage of beds. One priest estimated that they would need at least another two hundred beds to adequately minister to the sick.[19]

Political officials, church leaders, and inhabitants of Santiago struggled to make sense of the widespread and devastating epidemics. So many people died that there were no spaces left in church cemeteries to bury them. Instead, the dead were buried in communal graves without the usual funeral rites.[20] Santiago's cabildo agreed to contribute part of the money needed to increase the number of beds for poor patients and also called on the regidores to ensure the cleanliness of their barrios.[21]

Authorities supplemented these political measures with religious strategies. Church officials organized a *procesión de sangre* (procession of blood), during which the bishop of Guatemala walked barefoot and participants carried the image of Christ from the Cathedral through the streets of the capital. The convent of Santo Domingo held a *novenario,* a religious celebration that took place over nine days, calling for the intercession of Madre de Dios del Rosario. Priests also carried the Virgen de Plata in a public procession.[22]

Periodic epidemics not only disrupted the lives of the urban poor but also affected the functioning of Santiago's local government. During a smallpox outbreak that began in 1693 and continued into 1694, a number of cabildo members had to be excused from a 20 April 1694 meeting for reasons related to the epidemic: Captain don José Fernandez de Cordovaso's entire family fell ill; Ayudante General Jacobo de Alcayaga's son fell ill and remained confined to his sickbed; and the chronicler Francisco Antonio Fuentes y Guzmán was unable to attend because he lay sick.[23] The Cathedral held a novenario to battle the epidemic, and nuns from the orders of Santa Catarina and Santa Teresa carried the image of Nuestra Santíssima Señora de María de Socorro through the streets of the capital.[24]

Natural and Supernatural Illness and Female Healers

Much of the population in Spanish America did not have access to hospitals and licensed medical doctors and relied instead on local ideas about what caused illness and about healing strategies. In colonial Guatemalan society, popular beliefs about sickness and healing separated sicknesses into two categories, "natural," or *de Dios* (from God), and "supernatural," caused by the intervention of evil beings or humans acting as witches or sorcerers.[25] This binary model of illness causation can be found in Catholic, Maya, and African popular healing traditions. In Mesoamerica the division of illness into natural and supernatural origins goes back to precolonial times. The precontact Maya conceived of the underworld, Xibalbá, as stinking and disease-ridden.[26] In the *Popul Vuh*, the K'iche' Maya authors attribute the power to cause illness and death to the Lords of Xibalbá.[27] Ahal Puh, or Pus Maker, had the power to cause infection. Chamiya Holom, or Skull Staff, turned people into skulls and bones, images associated with *hidropesia* (dropsy). Ahal Q'ana, or Bile-maker, caused people to become ill and swell up.[28] The Lords of Xibalabá were distinguished from humans by their diseases and horrible smells, and glyphs representing these lords on pottery and stone contain foliated scrolls indicating the foul odors they expelled.[29]

In the Spanish colonial period, Maya cultures continued to hold that evil caused serious illness, that "to be ill is to be the object of malevolence, the curses of others."[30] Indigenous peoples of Guatemala and Mexico associated witchcraft with illness and the activities of supernatural beings, as well as brujos, hechiceros, and other ritual specialists.[31] It was thought that certain community members had the power to inflict illnesses through the penetration of the body's boundary with ritual objects such as doctored food and drink, herbs, leaves, and powders and via various insects, animals, and birds. Mayas practiced bloodletting, sometimes called "cupping," to extract the offending material from the afflicted's body. The healer made small cuts on the body with lances and then placed a gourd over the opening to extract live or dead animals and insects, corn and corn husks, hay, and other items. Cupping appears to have been practiced widely among healers of all ethnic and social groups in colonial Guatemala, including elite Spaniards.[32]

African cultures also have seen a connection between curing and sorcery. For example, the Ibo of southern Nigeria "believe that witches can infect innocent people by putting a spiritual substance into their food."[33] In many African societies, in particular, those in Central Africa, healers acted as liaisons between the natural and supernatural worlds through spirit mediumship, in which a saint or a deceased ancestor possessed the medium and told where a sickness came from and how to heal it.[34]

Afro–Latin American populations drew on African ideas about illness and healing, combined them with indigenous and European ideas, and created new practices in colonial Spanish America. Solange Alberro documented this process in her study of the Mexican Inquisition, noting the role of free and freed Blacks in healing and sorcery.[35] The fear that Afro-Latin American religious leaders and healers possessed knowledge of sorcery and had the ability to cause supernatural illness can also be found in colonial Brazil, where planters and colonial officials considered "old black women" particularly dangerous, because of their reputed familiarity with poisons and their uses. Many feared that these women would teach slaves how to use the poisons to tame, bewitch, or kill their masters.[36]

The European view of sickness and healing, formalized and supported by the Catholic church, held that sin could cause illness and that grace could bring a miraculous cure. Also, according to this view, certain illnesses were the physical expression of divine punishment.[37] Many regarded a 1568 syphilis epidemic in Seville, which led to the regulation of prostitution there, as not simply a disease but a "'divine illness' imposed by God as punishment for excess lust."[38]

Concerns that sickness represented punishment from God infused descriptions of illness experiences in colonial Santiago as well. During a 1651 epidemic of pestilence and bubonic plague, the priest Pedro de San José de Betancurt became disturbed by the large numbers of sick people in the city.[39] At the moment he entered the city over the San Juan Gascón Bridge, Betancurt felt the ground tremble and attributed both the epidemic and the earthquake tremor to punishment sent by God to the city of Santiago for his personal sins. Betancurt reportedly then walked into the city, and as he reached the Arco de las Monjas near the convent of the Conceptionist nuns, he knelt on the ground in public and asked God to pardon him and the city, reportedly saying: "Oh Lord, Lord, I have seen that because such a great sinner as myself entered [Santiago de Guatemala], you send this punishment to the city."[40]

Another seventeenth-century account also captures a worldview wherein illness was the result of divine punishment, meted out not only to communities but also to specific individuals. Fray Antonio de Molina, a Dominican priest living in Santiago de Guatemala, related the story of a double murder that occurred there in 1657 to illustrate how the wrath of God manifested itself through bizarre and often incurable illnesses. As Molina told it, one day don Claudio de Quiñónez, accompanied by his unnamed Black servant, came home to find his wife in the company of a priest. In a fit of jealousy, don Claudio stabbed both of them to death.

As don Claudio stabbed the priest, his wife attempted to escape out the window, but the servant prevented her from leaving and don Claudio stabbed her to death as well. Because public opinion held that the wife and the priest were *compadres* (perhaps the priest acted as god-father to her children), and thus their meeting alone was legitimate, Molina declared that the husband and his servant were at fault for the murders, and so "God punished them both for what they did." Don Claudio ended his days in exile in "the mountains" and died without re-ceiving the sacraments. The servant, who Molina deemed particularly guilty for preventing the wife's escape, became a leper, and his body filled with worms "so that when he sat down, the worms would [crawl] in and out of his sores."[41]

Even as inhabitants of colonial Santiago described disease and ill-ness as the result of divine punishment, so too could miraculous cures be attributed to divine intervention, the result of pious works, or a particular public act of grace. To illustrate this, Fray Molina related another story of the miraculous healing of Fray Damián Delgado in 1666. Fray Delgado, known as the "Great Minister to the Indians," dedicated his life to serving his Maya parishioners. He spoke both K'iche' and Kaqchikel Maya and wrote a number of works in these languages including an *arte* of the K'iche' language.[42] Fray Delgado re-portedly told Molina that he regularly "suffered from vehement pains all over his body, but when he said mass, preached, or ministered to Indians, he found himself healed and completely without pain."[43]

In Europe and the Americas, healing shrines became public forums where divine grace could be dispensed. The sick, especially those suf-fering from long-term and seemingly incurable illnesses, sought out the shrines and the miraculous powers of images, statues, ex-votos, and relics.[44] In sixteenth-century Spain, more than two-thirds of the shrines known for healing miracles were associated with the Virgin Mary.[45]

In 1601 a plague swept through Santiago and the surrounding area, killing many people. Local priests asserted that the oil in the lamp placed before the image of Nuestra Señora de Alcántara (an image of the Virgin Mary), could be used to ward off contagion and protect the healthy.[46] The image of the Black Christ of Esquipulas also became known in the early seventeenth century for bringing about miraculous cures. The sick from all ethnic and social groups in Guatemala visited the Black Christ, which reportedly had the power to cure a wide variety of illnesses, including blindness, paralysis, rabies, and open sores. The cure was said to come after a sick person ate the earth at the shrine. In 1737 Church officials formally recognized the shrine after the archbishop of Guatemala, seeking relief from an unexplained illness, visited the image and received a miraculous cure.[47]

Santiago's multiethnic population shared the binary explanation of illness causation and healing practices in colonial society. But while official explanations for the causes of illness combined concerns about lax public health measures and the breakdown of an individual's or community's relationship with God, many attributed certain illnesses to the activities of female sorcerers and magical healers, working alone or with the aid of supernatural beings at the behest of the sick person's enemies. The sick, their family members, and colonial officials often connected strange and incurable illnesses to intracommunity conflicts and violence associated with theft, sexual and physical abuse, public disrespect, a sexual partner's unfaithfulness or abandonment, the inability to repay small loans, or the desire to drive a competitor out of business.

As many believed that healers also had the power to cause illness, suspicions of supernatural illness could lead to accusations against those who were seen as especially successful and powerful curers.[48] Colonial officials did not hesitate to refer rumors as well as official accusations of supernatural illness to Inquisition and criminal courts. Angry or disgruntled servants, slaves, neighbors, employers, and family members might accuse women seen as sorcerers of having the power to cause supernatural sickness and even death. The accusations against healers and midwives also revealed larger community preoccupations with and fear of "women who live evil lives," especially casta, Black, and Indian women, in late-seventeenth- and eighteenth-century Santiago and the Audiencia of Guatemala.

Accusations of Supernatural Illness and the Search for a Cure

In 1706 Felipa de Xérez, a thirty-year-old widowed mestiza servant, described how, on the night of 25 August of the previous year, a female street peddler blinded her with hechizos.[49] Felipa worked as a servant for doña Juana de Aragón, in a house located just off the plaza mayor. Felipa told authorities that one night around eight o'clock, as she mixed chocolate in the kitchen, she heard a knock.[50] When she answered the door, she saw a stranger, a tall woman whose head was covered with a black mantilla.[51] The woman tried to sell Felipa a scarf and some thread, but Felipa said she did not want to buy anything. The woman insisted. Felipa took the items in her hands but again declined. She returned the items to the woman and shut the door. As she moved back toward the kitchen, she claimed she immediately felt severe pain in her head and eyes, so severe she could not finish making the chocolate, and she went straight to bed.

When her employer, doña Juana, returned home that night from tending her dying aunt, she found Felipa "screaming desperately" from severe pain in her eyes and head. Doña Juana, a native of Santiago de Guatemala, was the thirty-seven-year-old legitimate daughter of Second Lieutenant Pedro de Aragón and doña Luisa Marquez. She was the widow of Second Lieutenant don Luis Fernando Galindo. Doña Juana applied various *remedios* (cures) with no success, and when she placed a candle in front of Felipa, Felipa could not see it.

The next day, doña Juana called a physician, Licenciado don Vicente González, to come to cure Felipa. After he examined Felipa, he said he doubted she would recover her sight, and if she did, it would not be permanent. Despite his dire predictions, the doctor prescribed various cures, which Felipa and her mistress earnestly followed. Felipa did not recover her sight, however, and doña Juana declared that "it is public in this city that [Felipa] is blind despite having clear eyes," hinting that the blindness might have been caused by sorcery.

In seventeenth- and eighteenth-century illness accusations, the sick often attributed their symptoms to a previous conflict or act of violence with a personal enemy. Supernatural illnesses were transmitted differently than other illnesses, through touch, evil air (*mal aire*), ritual objects hidden in food and beverages, and the intervention of evil beings. Supernatural illnesses were often accompanied by signs, including the appearance of strange animals, birds, or insects and ritual objects buried under the door to the street. Community members often discussed and analyzed the often gruesome symptoms and speculated about causes, so that details about supernatural illnesses became widely known and discussed thoughout the capital.

Supernatural illness could be attributed to conflicts over a wide range of issues. In Felipa's case, her sisters, Cecilia and Luciana, and a neighbor, doña Isabel Sánchez de León, a married Spanish woman and cousin of doña Juana, all testified that Felipa's blindness occurred after she held and then refused to buy the items offered for sale by the mysterious woman street peddler. Residents of the capital also described how certain women known in the community as sorcerers and spell-casters transmitted supernatural illness through doctored food and drink, bewitched clothing, the burial of ritual items under the door to the street or in the interior courtyard, rubbing foul-smelling substances such as animal or snake fat around door frames, and throwing or sprinkling bewitched urine or water against the house, door, or bedroom windows of the target.

Nicolasa de Torres, a thirty-six-year-old single free mulata, traced her illness, which she believed to be rabies (*rabia*), to Petrona Mungía, the Indian servant of her neighbor.[52] One day Petrona went to Nicolasa's house and asked to borrow some clothing for her mistress. For some unexplained reason, when Petrona returned the clothing to Nicolasa, she threw the items on the floor, which led to a heated argument between the two women. Nicolasa claimed that right after the incident "disgusting things" appeared in her home, and she herself became ill with rabies the next year. When Nicolasa's neighbor, a mestiza married to a slave, heard of Nicolasa's illness, she told Nicolasa that Petrona had caused it—Petrona had done the same thing to her after borrowing some clothing. When Nicolasa confronted Petrona, Petrona denied causing the rabies. She did, however, say that someone else placed a *daño* (curse) on Nicolasa, and they needed to dig up the items buried under the doorway and burn them to rid her of the illness. Petrona also gave Nicolasa a curative drink containing tobacco. Nicolasa drank the beverage and with Petrona's help vomited the offending materials. Nicolasa reported that the drink healed her of the rabies.[53]

In addition to the signs associated with supernatural illness—for example, noises at night and sightings of certain animals—many in seventeenth-century Santiago also described how certain incurable and painful physical symptoms, including sores or pimples, particularly on the genitals, unexplainable swelling of the abdomen and other body parts, and even complete bodily transformations, indicated supernatural illness. In Felipa's case, a stranger wearing a black mourning veil appeared at night when she was alone in the house. And even though Felipa's eyes were clear, she remained blind despite the use of many "strong" remedios.

Even the elite described experiencing supernatural illnesses that they attributed to personal conflicts. Doña Catarina Delgado, a twenty-eight-year-old Spanish woman, accused a woman named Agustina of using sorcery.[54] Doña Catarina's husband, Sergeant Nicolás Callejos, also a Spaniard, had been conducting an illicit affair with Agustina, a mulata servant who lived in her employer's house near the University of San Carlos.[55] According to doña Catarina, one day Agustina "with much *osadía* [brazenness]" came to their home and fought in public with her husband.

After a few days, Agustina and a woman named "Chana de don Jorge" brought them some chocolate as a peace offering.[56] Doña Catarina, her husband, and their female Indian servant drank the chocolate. Doña Catarina fell ill. She described her sickness as "echando el curso negro o amarillo" (expelling the black or yellow flow), where she alternately expelled yellow, green, and blood-colored watery substances through her mouth. The Indian servant fell ill with the same sickness and died, while the husband apparently remained healthy. Doña Catarina said Chana's daughter told her that her mother and Agustina had ground up chocolate to make the maleficio, adding that Agustina and Chana had "a great friendship" to support her contention that the two women cooperated to cast the spell.

Juana Manuela de Heredia, alias "Chana Lucrecia," a thirty-year-old single mestiza, claimed that Gerónima de Barahona, the mulata meat seller, had bewitched her by throwing a number of ritual items at her door, including a *floripundo* (a type of plant called angel's trumpet), white powders "like flour," and some green water.[57] Immediately afterward, Juana Manuela found a "large toad with black and yellow stripes" in her parlor, and when she picked up a stone to kill it, the toad disappeared. Juana Manuela then became ill and suffered for two years, during which "she found herself acting like a dazed person."[58] A mulata woman named Antonia de las Mineras confessed on her deathbed that she paid Gerónima to cause the illness. Gerónima herself had also confirmed this to the sick woman.

Such gruesome and often incurable afflictions became public events, in that the events and symptoms occurred in front of witnesses and were discussed and gossiped about by friends and neighbors. The public nature of supernatural illnesses demonstrated the power of the person thought to have inflicted the illness and also legitimized the actions taken by the afflicted and their family, either calling for the intervention of a local healer-sorcerer or involving colonial authorities.

Because such illnesses were often dramatic and involved conflicts between individuals in the community known to everyone, inhabitants gossiped about the details and speculated about the causes and possible cures. Doña Juana commented that her servant Felipa's illness was public knowledge, indicating that her blindness became a popular topic of gossip in her neighborhood and other parts of the city. Through gossiping, spying, or witnessing fights, cures, and symptoms, community members discussed, criticized, and accused certain women of having the power and the motive to cause illness. Those involved in helping Felipa—doña Juana, Juana's neighbor and cousin doña Isabel, Felipa's sisters, Cecilia, an unmarried mestiza kitchen servant in another household in the city, and Luciana, a widowed mestiza weaver from nearby Santa Lucia—and blind Felipa herself all agreed on the same sequence of events and many of the details.

Colonial authorities appropriated gossip and "public knowledge" about the powers and practices of certain women in the community and used it to intervene in community conflicts, even when news of such occurrences reached them through unofficial channels. An example of this is don José de Baños y Sotomayor's decision to involve himself in the case of María de la Candelaria's strange illness, which was widely known in the city but had not been formally brought to the attention of the Holy Office.

Blind Felipa was no longer able to perform her duties as a kitchen servant and instead worked as a laundress. She relied on her young daughter to serve as her *gomecilla* (blind person's guide). Together, they made the trip from the capital to the nearby pueblo of Ciudad Vieja to wash clothes in the river there.[59] During her blindness, Felipa continued to search for cures, none of which succeeded, and her employer complained that Felipa sold all of her material possessions to pay for them. One day while she was washing clothes, a mestiza widow named María García, who had a reputation in the capital and surrounding towns as a successful curer, approached Felipa.[60] María offered to cure Felipa for a price if she came to her house. Felipa said no, perhaps because she no longer had any money or because she did not trust María.

About a month later, a woman approached Felipa, this time at her home, and offered a cure. Felipa said that it seemed like the woman was María offering her services again, but she could not tell for sure because she could not see.[61] The curandera offered to cure Felipa for twenty pesos, but Felipa again said no, because she "had already sold everything that she could" and had no more money. The women bargained, and the price dropped to ten pesos. Finally, Felipa told the curandera she had scraped together the money to pay for the cure.

At this point in the accounts, the participants' descriptions become ambiguous and surreal. The mysterious curandera came to the house the next night, *el día de San Francisco Xavier*, to heal Felipa. Felipa's mistress, doña Juana, did not want her to go and so with the help of Felipa's sister Cecilia tried to set a trap to prevent the curandera from taking Felipa. Felipa told Inquisition authorities that she waited *cargada de reliquías* (laden with relics) of the Holy Trinity, to protect her from evil. The mysterious cuandera, who Felipa later described as María García, managed to take Felipa from the house without being seen by doña Juana or Cecilia. Felipa and others involved commented that María García had a reputation in both the city and countryside as a successful healer, even as they denounced her.

Women's power within local cultures of healing depended on a reputation for being successful, spread through gossip, word of mouth, and practicing cures in front of family members and neighbors. Men and women, who often paid for the healing services with goods or cash, sought out and consulted those considered by local community members as the most successful healers for their specific needs.[62] Felipa commented that María García specialized in healing illnesses caused by spell-casting: "They say that María García who cures hechizos has a hospital in her house because many people go there to be cured."

Accusations of Supernatural Illness and the Intervention of Colonial Authorities

Women's activities as healers and midwives left them open to denunciations by other community members, including their patients, for using sorcery and witchcraft. Even though Felipa credited María with restoring her sight, she cooperated in the Inquisition's investigation of María for using spells in her curing rituals. Felipa described how after they arrived at María's house in Ciudad Vieja, María placed her in a chair and began to cure her. She put "strong powders" in Felipa's eyes, gave her a healing bath, and then covered her eyes with a cloth. Felipa stated that she felt *atarantada* (dazed) from the effects of the cure and did not know what she was doing or saying.

In this state, Felipa attempted to make her way back to Santiago de Guatemala and somehow ended up at her sister Luciana's house in Santa Lucia at one o'clock in the morning.[63] During her walk, Felipa apparently tripped over bricks from the church that had fallen to the ground during a recent earthquake. Luciana described how Felipa arrived at the house in the middle of the night "dazed and stunned" from the cure and said that she had *hierbas y tierra* (herbs and earth) clutched in her hands. Luciana took the items from Felipa's hands and burned them. The next day Felipa found herself miraculously cured and went to give thanks in the Church of Santa Lucia for recovering her sight. Santa Lucia, the patron saint of eye troubles who is invoked against blindness, is portrayed in religious iconography holding a palm leaf and two eyes on a plate.[64]

Curing rituals for supernatural illnesses varied widely but most involved the use of herbs or roots, often mixed into a healing drink, the extraction of items associated with sorcery from the patient's body through vomiting, lancing the skin or using a cupping gourd, and a ritual bath, or temescal.[65] Healers and their patients often combined these procedures with some type of explicitly religious action, such as visiting a healing shrine or parish church, lighting candles to a particular saint, and carrying a religious object or a purifying *sahumario* (ritual incensing) of rosemary or copal as protection against evil and further supernatural illness.

Accusations that María used supernatural means to cure Felipa's illness show the precarious nature of women's roles as healers in colonial Guatemala, when their patients or their employers brought Inquisition authorities into the process. In her testimony, Felipa described how the mysterious female healer took her on a fantastical and roundabout trip from her house in the capital to Ciudad Vieja. Felipa claimed that she "felt as though she flew through the air" past religious sites about the city and countryside — the Alameda, the Campo de Calvario, the Convent of La Concepción, and the Church of Santa Lucia.

Felipa's sisters, Cecilia and Luciana, also claimed that the curandera María "la llevaba [Felipa] por el aire" (carried Felipa though the air). Felipa's employer, doña Juana, added that a *cabrito*, a small male goat, followed Felipa back to her sister's house after María cured her and that Felipa "saw bulls dance." Felipa and Cecilia also reported seeing an apparition of a woman in white, an unmistakable sign to both that there was supernatural involvement in Felipa's illness.[66] The women's accounts portrayed life in colonial society, and in an urban and rural landscape, as rife with religious and mystical references.

When questioned by the Inquisition, María said she practiced healing, especially of stomach illnesses, and that she had practiced this *ministro* (calling) for many years, but she denied using spells or sorcery. María told how she healed people "of all status groups and ethnicities in the city of Guatemala" (de todos estados y calidades de la ciudad de Guatemala), including a Franciscan priest named José Velez, whom she cured of hechizos, and an unnamed Black woman, whom she cured of *hidropesia* (dropsy). María used the herb *tesumpate*, mixed with other items, to make a drink that she administered to her patients.[67] She then kept the patients in her home for "eight or more days" until they recovered.

Inquisition authorities became particularly alarmed at the rumors that the curative drink María administered to the sick Black woman was actually designed to cause the woman to abort her unborn child.[68] Rumors that María could cause women to abort made her even more suspect, and her home was searched for further evidence. Inside the house, officials found many of the materials necessary to practice healing: roots and herbs, reliquías, cotton, and various types of seeds. When confronted with the items, María asserted that she used them to heal different kinds of sicknesses and pains of the teeth, side, and stomach. The authorities ordered her never to practice healing again and placed her under the supervision of a local parish priest. It is unclear whether María García complied with the restrictions.

Gender, Ethnicity, and Cultures of Healing

Both men and women in Santiago and the surrounding rural towns participated in popular healing, including magical healing. For the most part, however, colonial authorities did not pursue and prosecute male healers: for the period 1680–99, I have uncovered only two Inquisition legajos targeting male magical healers. Men's magical healing activities are mentioned in a number of Inquisition testimonies, but apparently authorities chose not to pursue them further. During the same period, the Inquisition targeted fourteen women for magical healing.

The relative absence of Inquisition cases against male healers in Santiago, despite evidence that they were also very active, reveals the gender and ethnicity components of church and colonial policies. Among the women targeted by the Inquisition, the majority were listed as mulata, women of mixed African and Spanish or Indian descent. Colonial authorities perceived women's power as located within the cultural realm of curing, which combined religious activities, magical somatic knowledge, and personal, face-to-face interactions across racial and class lines. The Inquisition's pursuit of female healers accused of sorcery shows colonial concern that their activities had the potential to corrupt those who sought their help.

Although political and religious authorities did not prosecute many formal cases against male healer-sorcerers, they are mentioned in accounts of other illicit activities or in denunciations that were not pursued. Cecilia de Arriola, a married mulata blanca, and her husband, Juan de Fuentes, consulted Matheo de Maedes, a mulato prieto, for protection from supernatural illnesses and other types of "evil."[69] Matheo was from "the coast" and had traveled through the Audiencia of Guatemala but currently lived on a ranch near Santiago. Although he lived on a ranch in the countryside, he plied his trade in the capital as well. Matheo made two bags of ritual items for Juan to carry with him so that no one would "do evil to him." Cecilia and Juan also asked Matheo to protect their home. With Juan's help, Matheo buried a *tinajuela* (an earthen container or jug, often with a handle) under the door to their house.

Matheo placed a number of items inside the tinajuela to ward off evil: garlic, rosemary, chile de chocolate,[70] the plant *contrayerva*, and two needles in the shape of a cross. The area under the door to the street was an important gateway linking the public world to the internal, domestic world, and so it was a logical place to establish a ritual barrier to protect the home and those inside from evil. A house's doorway to the street seems to have been a dangerous place as well, where items and curses to cause illness were placed, where sexual witchcraft was practiced, and where evil in general was promoted. Matheo explained to the couple that if someone tried to cast a spell, the buried tinajuela would trap the evil before it reached them. After some time passed and Cecilia and Juan decided to move to a new house, Juan dug up the tinajuela to take it with them, presumably to rebury it under their new front door. Juan apparently could not resist opening the box to see what it had trapped. Inside the container Juan found a toad, an animal closely associated with sorcery, especially the transmission of supernatural illness.

The Inquisition's mandate to enforce religious orthodoxy included all peoples in New Spain, with the important exception of the colony's majority—the indigenous population, which had been formally removed from its jurisdiction by order of King Philip II in 1571. Accounts of the activities of Indian healers, however, can still be found in colonial records. The Inquisition often conducted a preliminary round of questioning before referring the case to the civil courts. During the testimony, a witness often mentioned people who were not directly involved in the case, including Indian men and women. Nicolasa de Torres, the mulata who told Inquisition authorities that the Indian woman Petrona bewitched her with rabies, consulted another healer, a man named

Mapola, a tributary Indian from the barrio of San Antonio, when her rabies returned a year later.[71]

As the above case illustrates, the sick and their caretakers often consulted more than one healer when an illness lingered or intensified or when alarming symptoms such as expulsions or body transformations were exhibited. Mapola specialized in healing supernatural illnesses and in the ritual cleansing of the home. Nicolasa told Mapola that she suspected sorcery caused her illness because at night she heard noisy cats on her roof. She noted that the cats never bothered her pigeons, however, suggesting that since the cats did not behave like regular cats (they did not pursue her pigeons), they were sorcerers in disguise. Nicolasa then consulted sorcerer-healer Mapola to counteract the sorcerer-healer Petrona Mungía.

Mapola told Nicolasa that Petrona had indeed cursed her with an illness that would cause her to "waste away until she lost her life" and that the cat noises on the roof also came from Petrona's witchcraft activities. Nicolasa's house contained her living quarters at the back and a small shop in the front. From underneath the shop doorway to the street, Mapola dug up a shoe, a large key buried with the sharp end up, a bundle of straw, feathers, and other items tied with rags. At dawn the next day, Mapola also dug up a *muñeco* (doll), a toad, and numerous rags and small feathers, "all of which smelled very bad." To counteract the sorcery, Mapola burned everything with rosemary. Mapola gave Nicolasa a ritual bath to heal her of the illness, as well as a *figurita*, perhaps a small religious figure that worked as a type of amulet, for protection. Nicolasa told Inquisition authorities that she kept the figurita in a box, where "it moved on its own."[72]

In the 1690s the Holy Office began proceedings against two male healer-sorcerers in the capital, Antonio Álvarez, a black slave owned by the Cathedral, and Antonio de Larios, a free mulato.[73] Though both men died before they could be questioned, descriptions of their activities remain in various testimonies. Antonio Álvarez acted as a healer-sorcerer despite his status as a slave. According to witnesses, he had the ability to heal both natural and supernatural illnesses. A number of inhabitants in the capital consulted Antonio for magical healing, including Spaniards. Doña Juana Zuleta, a widowed Spanish woman who had been married to a colonial official, consulted Antonio to cure a maleficio supposedly cast by Sebastiana de Aguilar, a thirty-year-old Spanish widow. To cure the maleficio, Antonio gave doña Juana two small bewitched sticks that she attached to her leg. Cecilia de Arriola consulted Antonio for some *pelotillas* (small balls) of an unknown material to aid her sorcery activities. Antonio claimed that with the pelotillas "female witches can do whatever they want" (las brujas hacian lo que querian).

Antonio de Larios, a single free mulato, also practiced magical healing and other sorcery activities.[74] Antonio was tall, with grayish-white hair, and between forty and fifty years old. Originally from San Salvador, Antonio earned his living as a trader, traveling throughout the Audiencia of Guatemala and occasionally stopping in the capital. A forty-year-old married mulata claimed that Antonio "was publicly held to be a sorcerer." Others concurred, including María de la Natividad, a thirty-two-year-old mestiza who had an on-again, off-again sexual relationship with Antonio. María claimed that Antonio had placed a curse on her, causing her to suffer a gruesome and painful illness. One night the couple fought because she suspected that Antonio had used sexual witchcraft designed to "tame her" (*amansandola*). Antonio returned to her house to make up with her and reestablish their relationship. After she agreed, he gave her some *barbas de chuntal* (turkey wattles) and five black kernels of corn.[75] He told her to bury the items under the door of the house and she did, even though she was afraid. When Antonio returned about two weeks later, he asked for the items back, and María returned them.

Approximately four weeks after María returned the ritual items to Antonio, she fell gravely ill. The bottom half of María's body became crippled and her airways closed, making it difficult and painful to breath. Five *llagas* (open sores) appeared on her genitals, and pimples covered her body. The pimples itched and made her uncomfortable until they finally burst two months later. Dominga, María's ten-year-old servant, told her that someone "must have done evil to her to cause her to be so afflicted." María agreed and eventually denounced Antonio to the Inquisition. She attributed the five sores on her genitals to the five black kernels of corn that she had buried for Antonio. María searched the *corral*, the interior patio of her house, where she believed her illness began. Dominga pointed to a spot where she thought she had seen Antonio bury something, and María dug up some bones, but she was not sure if they were human.

While María de la Natividad seemed reluctant to overstate the supernatural aspects of her illness, Francisca González, a single thirty-seven-year-old mulata blanca cuaterona, filled in more of the lurid details about María's illness, which she learned from a mulata healer who

María consulted for a cure.[76] According to Francisca, Antonio de Larios gave María the five kernels of corn and the turkey wattles and told her to bathe *sus carnes* (her genitals) with water in which the items had been soaked. María reportedly told Antonio "anda puerco que me avias de hacer" (roughly, "behave yourself toward me"). Antonio then went into the courtyard and buried some ritual items. When María uncovered the hole in the courtyard, she found "some skeleton bones," and she unearthed the corn and turkey wattles from under the door. Francisca noted that a short time after this María became ill and that her *partes bajas* (lit. "lower parts"; genitals) swelled up and her thighs "turned black and mangy like the skin of a toad."

Descriptions of María de la Natividad's illness, attributed to Antonio de Larios who was known as a sorcerer, showed to those involved the unmistakable signs of supernatural intervention. Both María and Francisca attributed the onset of the illness to a fight between María and Antonio, unleashed by the burial of items associated with sorcery. In addition, the incurable nature of Maria's illness and its peculiar symptoms led María and others to suspect supernatural intervention, and so she denounced Antonio to the Inquisition.

In general, descriptions of the activities of healers in the city of Santiago show no discernible difference in the healing powers of men and women, nor is there any evidence that residents believed either men or women healed more successfully. Community-generated consensus on successful healers of natural and supernatural illnesses seemed to depend more on individual reputation and specialization, such as blindness, illnesses of the stomach, and broken bones.

Male and female healers were also active in the mainly indigenous rural towns that surrounded Santiago. Accounts of illness and healing indicate that in general men and women had similar healing powers. The gender of the practitioner did not seem to alter local and regional respect for and fear of sorcery. Aside from midwifery as a primarily female specialty, one major difference was that descriptions of the powers of rural Indian male healers often contained specific references to their role as blood specialists, or *curandero sangradores* (healer-bleeders). This is not to say that women did not practice bloodletting. Both men and women cured both natural and supernatural illnesses by extracting ritual items, such as toads, snakes, stones, and sawdust, from openings made in the body through the area in pain, or in key areas associated with health, such as joints and the crown of the head.[77] When healers needed to cut the patient's body to extract the offending items, they pierced the skin with *lancetas* (lances) or used a *ventosa* or *ventosa seca,* whereby a cut was made and a gourd placed over the wound. While the gourd filled with blood, the healer extracted the items from the patient's body.[78] And, of course, midwives dealt with the bleeding associated with menstruation and childbirth. The term *sangrador* (bleeder), however, did not seem to be included in the formal titles of female healers, and accounts of women's healing and sorcery practices did not highlight the role of bloodletting as they did for Indian men.[79]

A number of male Indian healers, active in and around the rural town of Santa Cruz Chinautla, came to the attention of Captain Sebastian Loayso y Ledesema, an *alcalde ordinario* (member of Santiago's city council).[80] On 1 January 1705 a local priest named Tomás de Arrevillaga sent a letter to authorities in the capital denouncing a number of well-known healers in the area as brujo-hechiceros.[81] Padre Tomás charged that the mainly Pokomán pueblo of Chinautla contained many *grandes adivinos y médicos* (great soothsayers and doctors) whose activities were "very pernicious." Although these men appeared to be successful curers, Padre Tomás claimed that they were "fooling" the local Indian population and demanded that authorities take action to "untrain" the healers "to save the poor Indians." Overall, his letter reveals the tenuousness of colonial control over religious cultures in rural areas. Perhaps adding to the priest's alarm was the *peste* (plague) that had recently swept through the town that some suspected had been caused by sorcery.

Padre Tomás characterized a number of local Maya men as "Indian sorcerers." He denounced Gerónimo Hernández as a "hechicero muy afamado," a famed and well-known sorcerer. Originally from the pueblo of San Juan Amatitlán, Gerónimo not only worked in his own community but ranged widely to practice healing. Gerónimo had traveled the year before to Escuintla to cure and divine, and the priest noted that there was a great deal of gossip in Chinautla about his activities there.[82] When questioned by Indian justices from Amatitlán, Gerónimo acknowledged his specialty was curing spells. On his own, Padre Tomás questioned an Indian woman, also from Amatitlán, who told him that Gerónimo had cured her of a spell. When the priest asked how he cured her, the woman said that Gerónimo "touched her all over her body."[83] The woman added that Gerónimo had a wide reputation in all the pueblos for his ability to cure people of spells.

After receiving Padre Tomás's letter, alcalde ordinario Loaysa transferred Gerónimo and the other accused curanderos who had been imprisoned in Chinautla to Santiago's city jail and began hearings on the matter. Searching for more details, Loaysa questioned a number of Indian justices who had already begun an investigation. The alcalde ordinario did not question Padre Tomás, nor did he question any of the curanderos' clients.

Indian authorities from Chinautla, however, identified more specifically the men's magical healing specialties and activities. Domingo Martín, the *alguacil mayor* (chief constable) of Chinautla, testified that Gerónimo Hernández practiced healing using lances and cupping gourds to cure patients of both natural sicknesses and spells. Gerónimo was well known for his ability to cure spells, and many people consulted him, not just the "poor Indians" of whom Padre Tomás wrote, but also the gente ladina. Gerónimo cured with *sacates*, probably a type of healing poultice, that contained grass and dried wheat or cornstalks designed to draw out material from the body. Domingo commented on Gerónimo's reputation by saying that he "cures some but not others." José López, the *alcalde actual* (current mayor) of Chinautla, called Gerónimo a healer-bleeder who used cupping gourds to heal people of spells. The town's regidor described Gerónimo's use of "ventosas lancetas," probably a combination of the two procedures whereby he used the lancetas to make openings in the skin and then applied a cupping gourd to extract blood and objects associated with sorcery from the sick person's body.

Pablo López was also a curandero sangrador, and he attracted patients claiming to be bewitched from a wide area, including Santiago and the pueblos in the Valley of Guatemala. Pablo specialized in various bleeding strategies, including the use of lancetas and cupping gourds, bleeding, and the extraction of supernatural objects. Pablo also cured with a poultice made from *chichicaste molido* (ground nettles) and *hojas de chiguera* (leaves from the chiguera plant) that he placed on the sick person's head and body. Padre Tomás wrote that a Spanish man came to him and told him that he had been ill and that "the doctors in [Santiago de] Guatemala could not cure him." When the Spaniard heard of Pablo López's reputation as a healer, he consulted him for a cure. Pablo brought the Spaniard some copal and green ears of wheat and burned them to purify the room and his patient.

Officials arrested and jailed Francisco Cajero, an Indian from Chinautla, for his activities as a healer and diviner. Domingo Martín, the alguacil mayor, described Francisco as a curandero sangrador as well, because Francisco cured "those who are bewitched and those who have whatever type of sickness" using various bloodletting strategies. Francisco's divination involved finding lost items and giving advice on auspicious days to his clients. Witnesses claimed that many in the surrounding area consulted Francisco for his skills as a healer and diviner.

Although male healers appear to have specialized in bloodletting, some women did so as well. In late-seventeenth-century Santiago, Pasquala, a married Spanish or mestiza woman (witnesses could not agree), became known as "la curandera de los indios" (the healer of Indians), and she was widely known in both the city and the countryside as a successful healer who cured Indian patients of spells and curses.[84] As a Guatemalan Inquisition official wrote:

> It is public and notorious that Pasquala uses divination to find lost objects and hechizos to cure Indians, who come to her house in large numbers from all around the circumference of the capital.

Victorina de San Joseph, a married forty-eight-year-old Spanish woman and a beata, denounced Pasquala to the Inquisition when she became alarmed at the "large numbers" of Indians who repeatedly showed up at Pasquala's door.[85] Victorina stated that Indians from the outlying pueblos traveled to the capital to consult Pasquala because of her reputation as a successful healer. Pasquala lived with her husband in the barrio of Candelaria, on Matheo de Morga Street. Francisco de la Cruz, an *indio natural* (tributary Indian) from the outlying pueblo of Santa Isabel, went to the capital to consult Pasquala for a cure for his illness.[86] Pasquala reportedly told Francisco that an *hechizo antiguo*, an old spell, was causing his pain. To heal him, Pasquala applied a cupping gourd and squeezed Francisco's shoulders to extract live ants from his body.

Sebastiana de Céspedes, a sixty-year-old widowed mestiza from the nearby town of Santa Ana, also described how Pasquala cured bewitched Indians. According to Sebastiana, Pasquala used a cupping gourd to extract items and also caused her patients to vomit and thus rid their bodies of "worms, corn husks, and ants." Pasquala also healed a sick Indian named Tomás, also from Santa Ana. Again using a cupping gourd, Pasquala extracted corn husks from the sick man's shoulders. She then put her hand in Tomás's mouth, helping him to vomit gravel and "many fat worms with black heads."

A criminal case carried out in 1688–89 against two curanderos, Magdalena Méndez and Joaquín Sánchez, further outlines official and pop-

ular attitudes about men's and women's practices of healing supernatural illness.[87] Antonio Hernández of San Miguel Milpas Dueñas,[88]
afflicted with what he believed to be a supernatural illness, accused
Magdalena and Joaquín of being sorcerer-witches. Magdalena and
Joaquín were both well known locally and specialized in healing stomach ailments by administering pig hairs mixed with animal fat to the
patient through the mouth. Pablo Hernández, the Indian alcalde of
Dueñas, brought the case to the attention of don Antonio Felipe, gover-
nor of the jurisdiction of Almolonga (also known as Ciudad Vieja), who
immediately began to pursue the case. Don Antonio and other Indian
officials arrested and interrogated Magdalena.

As the men whipped Magdalena, she confessed that she had cast a
spell on the sick man, and she also implicated Joaquín in the deed. Don
Antonio arrested Joaquín, who also confessed while being whipped.
The Indian justices of the towns, under don Antonio's leadership,
then brought the case before the judge in Santiago, José de Baños
y Sotomayor, head of Guatemala's Inquisition.[89] Baños y Sotomayor
immediately opened a case against the two, accusing both of being
hechiceros-brujos, and transferred them to the public jail in Santiago
de Guatemala.

Initially, Baños y Sotomayor questioned six witnesses, all Indian
men from towns near Almolonga. Most of the men played significant
political roles as justice officials in their respective towns, including the
gobernador, a regidor, and an alcalde. Others described themselves as
principales, recognized in their communities and by colonial officials as
members of the local Indian elite.[90] Only two of the Indian witnesses
spoke Spanish; the others spoke Kaqchikel and testified through an interpreter. The sick man died before he could be questioned by Baños y
Sotomayor, who called no other witnesses to testify about Magdalena
and Joaquín's healing-sorcery activities.

Antonio's supernatural illness began after the wedding and fiesta of
one of his children, to which Magdalena and Joaquín had not been
invited. The Indian officials portrayed both Magdalena and Joaquín
as having similar powers, including the ability to cause supernatural illness, to shape-shift into tigers and lions to gain revenge against
their enemies, and to cure spells and curses by extracting supernatural
items from the patient's body. There are important differences, however, in the characterization of each healer's powers: witnesses noted
that Magdalena had inflicted supernatural illnesses on community
members in the past, bewitching an Indian town official and the wife of

another Indian official by feeding her chile pepper seeds until she died. In addition, two witnesses denounced Magdalena for killing the infants and children of Dueñas by casting spells on them. The afflicted community members and local officials included elements in their illness accounts that signaled Antonio Hernández had a supernatural illness: he became ill with a seemingly incurable sickness, and the illness began after a public slight against Magdalena and Joaquín when he did not invite them to the wedding and fiesta. One Indian official produced what he claimed was the *jícara peste*, or infected gourd, that had contained the ritual items used to bewitch Antonio.

In addition, Magdalena and Joaquín behaved suspiciously, and Indian officials suggested they shape-changed into various animals to exact revenge from their enemies and steal chickens from nearby farms. Tomás Hernández even claimed that he saw Magdalena in the shape of a cat near the sick man's bedside and that animals followed and harassed him when he walked in the countryside. Finally, when the gobernador ordered Magdalena and Joaquín to heal the bewitched man, the two complied and massaged his belly and caused him to expel lardlike material mixed with pig hairs from his mouth and lungs. The sick man's condition worsened, however, and he died a short time later.

By 27 May 1688, after hearing the Indian officials' testimonies, Baños y Sotomayor interrogated both Joaquín and Magdalena in the city jail. Also present were the counsel for the defense, the public notary, and an interpreter, as neither Magadalena nor Joaquín spoke Spanish. Magdalena, the legitimate daughter of Indian parents and married to an Indian, was originally from the town of Santiago de Zamora but currently lived in San Miguel Milpas Dueñas.[91] Baños y Sotomayor asked her if she cast a spell on Antonio Hernández and if she invoked the devil to do so. Magdalena denied both accusations.

Baños y Sotomayor questioned her again, asking how she could deny it since she had confessed before the Indian justices from her town. Magdalena again denied causing the illness. What really happened, she claimed, was that when Antonio Hernández became sick, he accused her of bewitching him, and the Indian justices arrested her because of their "ill-will" toward her.[92] The officials then whipped her on four occasions, and she said she finally confessed because she was afraid and wanted to stop the whipping. Magdalena added that Joaquín confessed for the same reason, even though he was also not guilty.

Questioned separately, Joaquín, about forty years old and the legitimate son of Indian parents, also recanted. Joaquín told the judge that he had confessed only to stop the whipping he received at the hands of the Indian justices, who had also arrested Joaquín's wife and children, probably to use as leverage against him. Both Magdalena and Joaquín denied that they shape-changed into animals, though both allowed that they may have hissed or growled like cats and tigers during their interrogations as the Indian officials charged, because of their fear and pain during the whippings.

Baños y Sotomayor asked both of the accused the same questions, indicating that he took the charges of their supernatural powers seriously, as in the precolonial and colonial periods the ability to shape-change was reserved only for the most powerful and important Maya leaders.[93] The Indian officials and Baños y Sotomayor also treated both of the accused similarly. Indian justices whipped both of them until they confessed and then jailed them. Baños y Sotomayor then accused them of acting as sorcerer-witches and imprisoned them in the city jail. The final outcome of the case, however, was not recorded in the documents.

A major difference in Baños y Sotomayor's interrogation of the accused curanderos was the last question he asked Magdalena but which he did not ask Joaquín—if she bewitched the infants and children of San Miguel Milpas Dueñas, causing their deaths, a charge that Magdalena also denied. The judge's question and the Indian justices' accusations speak to one area of women's healing powers that men did not participate in: midwifery and the care of mothers, newborns, and young children. And if female healers and midwives had the power to care for and heal children, many believed they also had the power to cause their illness and death.

Midwives in colonial society, and even to the present day, were both practical and religious specialists who mediated between the natural and supernatural worlds.[94] Supernatural signs, interpreted by ritual specialists in local communities, such as birth signs, omens, dreams, illness, and the appearance of strange objects around the chosen woman, recruited Maya midwives to their calling.[95] As guardians of maternal and child health, midwives played a socially critical role, especially in colonial Guatemala, where Maya populations had suffered devastating population losses due to violence and epidemic disease. The rumors and community perceptions that Magdalena used supernatural means to kill the town's infants and children appear to reflect continued experiences of suffering and dislocation in rural Maya communities under Spanish rule as well as an apprehension about women's roles as healers and midwives in community life.

"It Is Not the Word of God": Midwives and Magical Healing

Popular beliefs about certain women's ability to cure as well as cause harm and even death left popular healers, especially female healers and midwives, open to suspicion, persecution, and arrest. A number of the more graphic and fantastic descriptions of supernatural illness center on pregnancy, labor, and the birth of a child, a particularly dangerous time for mother and baby.[96] Children were important to the economic well-being of the family, as well as to the cultural and ritual maintenance of community life. Female healers and midwives often became the target of blame for difficult pregnancies, bizarre births, and births of deformed or dead children. In addition, pregnancy was a time when the husband or lover could not protect the woman. The health of the mother and child was left in the hands of a midwife, a ritual specialist who possessed authority and power to bring new life into the community. Supernatural illness accounts having to do with pregnancies reveal the danger midwives faced if a pregnancy went wrong, for whatever reason.

Many community members described pregnant women as especially vulnerable to supernatural intervention. Doña María Cecilia Paniagua, the twenty-nine-year-old wife of don Luis de Aguilar, *escribano público* (public scribe) of Santiago, described how she gave birth to a half-human, half-toad baby.[97] Both she and the local priest suspected that the strange birth resulted from some sort of sorcery or witchcraft. Doña María Cecilia regularly consulted a number of women in the capital for spells to gain wealth and status, for love magic, and for protection from evil, including María Savina, an unmarried mestiza from the barrio of El Tortuguero.

For reasons not described, María Savina became angry with doña María Cecilia. A few days later, María Savina brought over some meat stew as a gift, which doña María Cecilia said she suspected was bewitched. Despite this belief, she ate one mouthful. She also reported that she saved the stew and that two days later it was full of worms. At that point, doña María Cecilia, who was five months' pregnant, further claimed that each night as she slept in her bedroom, she and others in the household heard a toad chirp from midnight until 4:00 A.M., and the noise continued for the rest of her pregnancy, even when she changed rooms.

Four months after eating the bewitched stew, doña María Cecilia gave birth to *el monstruo* (the monster or freak) whose lower half of the body was a human baby, but from the waist up was a toad, with arms like a frog's and the head of a toad, and the arms were so long that they almost reached the baby's feet, with very rough skin.

The baby was born dead. According to doña María Cecilia, the afterbirth "was not natural blood [but] like mud from a lake."[98] When Padre Fray Tomás Serrano of the Dominican order saw the monstrous baby, he told her that it must be the result of sorcery.

A common theme of supernatural illness accusations was the belief in and fear of women's power to interfere in a pregnancy to deform a baby, cause a miscarriage, or cause the death of the mother. Inhabitants of the capital were not unacquainted with strange births, nor did colonial officials and family members always deem such births the result of sorcery. The chronicler Francisco Antonio de Fuentes y Guzmán, for example, noted that in 1675 an Indian woman from the pueblo of Santo Domingo Sinacao near the capital gave birth to conjoined twins.[99] Calling the twins, joined at the abdomen, "un monstruo natural" (a natural monster), Fuentes y Guzmán noted that the parish priest baptized them. He then brought the twins to the capital, probably to be viewed by the curious. When the babies died a few days later, they were buried along with their mother, who had died in childbirth, in the parish church in Santo Domingo Sinacao.

The birth accounts suggest that inhabitants of the capital shared symbolic categories that defined, or at least strongly suggested, when a midwife had disrupted a pregnancy supernaturally. Fuentes y Guzmán labeled the conjoined twins "natural" monsters, and the parish priest baptized them and gave them a Christian burial. He made no mention of possible supernatural intervention. In the case of Doña María Cecilia, her claims that a toad chirped continually at night throughout her pregnancy, that her dead baby's skin was toadlike, and that the afterbirth was like mud supported the belief in supernatural intervention. In addition, in Mayan society, toads, snakes, and frogs were often associated with sorcery and death.[100] Similar beliefs about supernatural intervention in pregnancies can also be found in Africa.[101] Such descriptions illustrate community fears that female healers and midwives had the necessary knowledge of women's bodies as well as the supernatural power to disrupt a pregnancy.

In 1660 two husbands denounced a midwife, the wife of a former pueblo official, for using sorcery to subvert the pregnancies of their wives.[102] As a result of the denunciations, Indian officials from the pueblo of Santa Catalina Pinula arrested and punished Marta de la Figueroa, a married Indian midwife, for casting spells. Five members of the community came forward to denounce her for causing a number of illnesses and deaths, which they linked to conflicts with Marta or her husband, revealing a town divided. Each person who accused the midwife used the phrase "no era palabra de Dios" (it was not the word of God) to indicate the supernatural origin of the illnesses and deaths.

In an effort to extract a confession from Marta, town officials hung her up and publicly punished her with *humaso de chiles* (dense smoke from burning spicy red chile peppers). Then they covered her face and body with the chiles "until she was in danger of losing her life." Marta confessed and told the town officials that a married Indian woman who spun cotton taught her how to use spells. Marta's husband brought the case to the attention of the alcalde ordinario in the capital, Captain Zelesón de Santiago, complaining that the alcaldes of Pinula had illegally punished his wife. Captain Santiago ordered the Indian alcaldes from Pinula to bring him the original testimonies so he could judge for himself and imprisoned María in the jail in the capital. When the alcalde ordinario questioned María, she recanted her previous confession, saying she confessed only "because I was terrified because the [Indian officials] tortured me."

Andrés Yos had charged that Marta de la Figueroa cast a spell on his pregnant wife after the two women argued.[103] Andrés claimed that Marta mixed earth with animal fat and formed the mixture into little balls. She then passed the balls between her legs and partes bajas four times. Marta then threw the bewitched dirt balls at the pregnant woman so that somehow they entered her body, while she chanted, "Stamp on the earth and enter the body of the Indian woman so that the devil takes her."[104] Soon after, the pregnant woman became very ill, and Andrés asked Marta to return and cure Juana of the curse. Andrés claimed that when Marta returned to heal his pregnant wife, she screamed at Marta, "For the love of God take this evil that is in my body, because it is not the word of God, this evil that you are killing me with."

Marta reportedly replied, "You are drunk, do not tell me that I am a sorcerer."[105] Soon after, Andrés's wife died from her illness.

Andrés García, who lived in the same town, charged that Marta also caused his pregnant wife to fall ill after the two women had a series of arguments. His wife, Catalina, pregnant and sick in bed, complained to him that Marta repeatedly visited her and asked to be her midwife. Catalina refused, explaining that she already had one and that she did not want Marta to treat her. Andrés told colonial authorities that from that moment on, Catalina fell ill, and "worms came out of her genitals and her stomach became swollen, and it was not possible to cure her."

In addition, each night Catalina dreamed that Marta wanted to smother her.[106] Catalina's husband charged that the "evil" that had killed Andrés Yos's wife also killed his wife. The illness accounts in the criminal case against Marta focus on her alleged use of sorcery against various women in the community while they were pregnant and on the subversion of her role as community midwife and guardian of the health of mother and child. Three other Indian men from Pinula, all prominent members of the community, also came forward with charges that Marta de la Figueroa used sorcery to cause supernatural illnesses. Regidor Lorenzo Perez told authorities that one day he went to Marta's house to purchase a chicken, but she refused to sell him one. When Lorenzo pressed her, saying that she had many, Marta responded by yelling *mil disparates* (a thousand insults) and *muchas desvergüenzas* (many shocking things), showing public disrespect for him and his political office. Lorenzo entered Marta's house to arrest her but was persuaded not to by another official. Lorenzo then charged that on his way out of Marta's house, she caused a *ronrón* (beetle) to bite him on the leg so fiercely that "he fell to the ground from the pain, and from that time on . . . had a sore on his leg that swelled up and filled with many worms."[107]

Cristobal Silva, a town elder, charged that Marta killed one of his sons and caused the other to become incurably paralyzed after a series of arguments. When Cristobal's first son became ill, the son told Cristobal that every night he saw Marta in his dreams and that she wanted to smother him. He died soon after. Cristobal complained that when his other son became ill, he had to look for someone from outside the pueblo "to take out the *demonios* [demons] that [Marta] placed in [his] body." The Indian curandero extracted wood chips and sawdust from his son's joints in an effort to cure him. Despite the ritual extractions, the son remained paralyzed.

Matias Vicente, the father-in-law of one of Marta's children, told colonial authorities that Marta used spells to make him ill as well: "I am very sick and it is not words of God, but [instead] she bewitched me." One day Matias felt ill and decided to take a traditional indigenous steambath to cure himself. He lit the fire and entered the temascal. Marta offered to help and followed him inside. Matias claimed that Marta then cast a spell on him with her touch:

[She] began to put her finger in my anus and thus began my illness; it felt like chile, it felt like ants, and my body ached [so I could not] drink nor eat nor sleep since I went into the temascal and [Marta] put her finger in my anus, and since then she has been above my body when I go to sleep.[108]

The use of the steambath played both a hygenic-therapeutic and a magico-religious role in Mayan culture. In preconquest and colonial Mesoamerica, a sick person who entered a steambath came into contact with various supernatural beings, especially female goddesses associated with the earth, healing, and midwifery. As a result, colonial religious authorities remained suspicious of its use.[109] Matias's account shows that he thought of the temescal as a ritual place that enhanced Marta's supernatural powers.

As we have seen, local rivalries, thought to be the root cause of supernatural illness, could lead to a community-wide denunciation of midwives as sorcerers, first to local Indian officials and then to colonial authorities in Santiago de Guatemala. In the case of Marta de la Figueroa, Marta's husband, the former regidor, as well as Lázaro de Verganza, the public scribe from Casaguastlán, attempted to appeal to colonial authorities to intervene in her maltreatment by Indian justices and to protest her innocence of the charges. Captain Santiago, however, ultimately convicted Marta of using sorcery and superstitions to cause "enfermedades incurables" (incurable illnesses) and the deaths of the women. She was punished with one hundred lashes "por las calles de su pueblo" (in the streets of her town).

Supernatural illness accounts reveal the ways in which colonial officials attempted to capitalize on the suffering of local populations, to act as official arbiters of community conflicts, and to intervene at both the individual and community levels. Women's informal participation in healing cultures challenged colonial and patriarchal authority, as religious and political officials deemed their activities not only as disorderly but also as having the potential to corrupt other women and men in the capital. Supernatural illness accounts, however, also highlight the role of local cultural practices in criticizing and reshaping experiences of poverty, physical violence, and illness in daily life and how those roles were gendered. In many instances, female healers threatened to cause supernatural illness as a way to gain revenge, intimidate others, and demonstrate their power in daily life.

5

Female Sorcery, Material Life, and Urban Community Formation

She has tarnished [the reputation of] many honorable and elite women, and so has been banished only six *leguas* from [Santiago], and when the authorities released her, she returned to her house and continued with much brazenness with her sorcery to acquire money.

— LETTER FROM NICOLÁS RESIGNO DE CABRERA, HEAD OF GUATEMALA'S INQUISITION, TO THE MEXICAN OFFICE OF THE INQUISITION, 13 MARCH 1693[1]

Female Sorcery and the Local Economy

In seventeenth- and eighteenth-century Guatemala, narratives of women's use of "sorcery" covered a broad range of religious-cultural practices, including magical healing, spell-casting, placing and removing curses, and using incantations to locate stolen objects. Narratives of women's sorcery in Inquisition records, however, not only provide evidence of alternative religious-magical cultures, they also reveal the difficulties women faced supporting themselves and those in their care. Women's sorcery practices, viewed through their use of spell-casting and sorcery that had explicit moneymaking goals, were intimately intertwined with economic and material life in the capital.

Women in colonial Guatemala who needed to work faced a narrow set of legal and illegal options. Sorcery represented one viable economic option for some women, especially during this period, when men and women of all social and ethnic groups participated in the extralegal economy through cattle rustling, hoarding, black market sales of regulated foodstuffs, clandestine alcohol sales, and smuggling.[2] Women's use of illegal religious-magical practices, described as "sorcery" in Inquisition records, represented the transformation of accepted women's social roles: they became magical healers and midwives, sexual witchcraft practitioners, and leaders of clandestine religious cults, attracting clients and followers willing to pay in cash or material goods for their services. Successful female sorcerers supported their children and ex-

FIGURE 3. Image of the Crucified Christ from a prayer book celebrating the Blood of Christ, published in 1762. Courtesy of the John Carter Brown Library at Brown University.

tended families, and some even prospered, owning homes and luxury goods.

Sorcery as a career possibility often comprised one part of an overall economic strategy wherein women pursued multiple occupations to support themselves and their families.[3] In Santiago, women sometimes combined sorcery with such occupations as market selling or domestic service. Gerónima de Barahona, the twice-widowed mulata mother of six and widely known sorcerer, had the nickname "La Carnicera" because she also sold beef from a shop in her home. María Manuela, also a widowed mulata sorcerer, had the nickname "La Cecinera," suggesting that she either made or sold dried beef.[4] María de Santa Inéz, the mulata sorcerer from Amatitlán who spent much of her time in the capital, sold rosaries and corn grinding stones to supplement her income.[5] Petrona Mungía, the married Indian woman, worked as a sorcerer and as a domestic servant in a Spanish household.[6] Women's strategies of combining sorcery with other kinds of economic activities such as market selling allowed them to move about the city and surrounding countryside legitimately and brought them into contact with potential clients.

Some women chose to target a particular subpopulation or specialized in specific types of sorcery. Pasquala, who was sometimes described as Spanish and sometimes as mestiza, peddled her sorcery services specifically to Indians and became known as "the healer of Indians," which set her apart from other magical healers in the capital.[7] In addition, Pasquala located lost or stolen objects by means of divination, also for Indian clients. The mestiza magical healer María García specialized in curing stomach ailments and attracted patients from the capital and surrounding countryside.[8] Through specialization in a particular subpopulation or in a narrowly defined specialty, female sorcerers could carve out a niche and distinguish themselves from other local practitioners.

Female sorcerers charged their clients for spells, curses, and rituals, underlining the fact that sorcery was in part an economic transaction. Nicolasa de Torres paid a female sorcerer two reales for some packets of powders to use to bewitch her employer.[9] Two reales represented no small sum of money in late-seventeenth-century Guatemala. For two reales, one could purchase a pound of salted fish and twelve tamales, which would go far in feeding a woman and her children.[10] Gertrudes de San José, a free mulata married to a muleteer, paid four or six reales for love magic (she could not remember the exact price). The service included the burial of chewed cacao beans and doctored bathwater under the door of the target's house.[11]

Petrona Mungía charged Antonia Martínez twelve pesos for spells designed to keep a man from pursuing her daughter.[12] Antonia implied that there was violence, or the threat of it, in the man's pursuit of her daughter. Antonia, listed as a single woman, appeared not to have had a male partner or a relative that she could ask to restrain the man's inappropriate behavior, so she consulted Petrona for a spell. Petrona charged another woman three pesos for a spell designed to bring wealth. The price covered all the necessary sorcery materials, including two human umbilical cords and ritual incensing of her home to drive away evil.[13]

Female sorcerers were not necessarily poor.[14] When Santiago's Inquisition proceeded against the sorcerer–meat seller Gerónima de Barahona, it decided to confiscate her house and belongings. In the process, officials found that Gerónima owned at least one and probably two houses, both in the barrio of Santo Domingo. They also confiscated strings of coral and pearls.[15]

Cecilia de Arriola carried a wide array of clothing and other material goods when Guatemalan officials sent her from Santiago to the Inquisition jail in Mexico City. These goods can be roughly divided into three categories: clothing, jewelry, and bedding. Among her clothing items, she had at least five linen blouses, two of them from Europe and decorated with lace and silk thread; more than twenty pairs of embroidered stockings, some blue, some white, and others dark red; two pairs of leather shoes; and a green veil from Spain, adorned with a red silk border. Her bedding consisted of a mattress, a new violet-colored blanket, a wool blanket, and two sheets, one cotton and one linen. Among her jewelry were four silver rings, one copper ring, one silver and four copper religious medals, and a pair of gold earrings. It is possible that Cecilia intended to sell or trade these goods for food or better conditions in her jail cell. Such a wide array of European and New World material goods, decorated with high-status silk and intricate embroidery, indicates that Cecilia led a fairly comfortable life in the capital.[16] Gerónima and Cecilia may have been exceptional; it is likely that not all female sorcerers had so much wealth. However, it suggests that the Inquisition did not necessarily target only poor women for practicing sorcery.

Community members and colonial authorities sometimes used economic categories to distinguish the most powerful and notorious female

sorcerers from other sorcerers in Santiago. Official letters and witness testimony described Gerónima as both a "maestra" (master) and
a "gran maestra" (great master).[17] Guilds in Santiago divided workers
into the following hierarchy: apprentices, journeymen, and masters.
Formal rules existed for how one progressed from apprentice to master,
which included examinations given by the notary public of the city government, the head official of the guild, and other masters in the same
occupation.[18]

The use of the term "master" in reference to Gerónima suggests that
an informal hierarchy existed among local female sorcerers based on
their abilities and experience, at least in terms of how outsiders and
their clients perceived them, and that within this hierarchy Gerónima
ranked among the top local sorcerers. Characterizations of a few female
sorcerers as "masters" were usually accompanied by descriptions of
their reputations as powerful and successful as well as by accusations
that they taught others sorcery, as a master instructs an apprentice.

Not only can sorcery be viewed as a cultural and economic activity,
"economic sorcery," rituals designed to bring wealth or material gain or
to take away the wealth of others were closely connected to material
life in the capital. Sorcery often occurred in women's places of business, especially in small shops that sold food and drink, operated out
of the front of their homes. Local authorities regulated shop owner-
ship through licensing, set official prices for goods offered for sale, and
prohibited casta, Black, and Indian women from owning shops in the
capital. Only a small percentage of women officially owned shops in
seventeenth-century Santiago. In 1632, of the forty-five licensed shop
owners in the capital, seven were women; in 1650, nine out of thirty-six;
and in 1681, six out of forty-nine.[19] Nevertheless, Inquisition records
show that some women ran neighborhood stores out of their houses
informally, without an official license.

Shops functioned not only as places to sell food and other items
but also as semipublic gathering spaces where women and men socialized and gossiped, and they also became a prime space for practicing
sorcery. Juana de Arrate, a mestiza baker, sold bread from a shop in
her house, where she came into conflict with the sorcerer Gerónima
de Barahona.[20] Juana claimed that Gerónima cursed her daughter by
giving her a supernatural illness that lasted for six months and caused
severe pain in her genitals. One day while in her bakery, Juana saw
Gerónima pass by outside. Juana ran out to confront her, but Gerónima escaped. Juana claimed that a short time later, a large black ani-

mal entered her store and stole all the bread she had for sale. The event reportedly left the store smelling of sulfur and brimstone, indicating to Juana that Gerónima used sorcery to steal the bread.

Street vendors and shopkeepers sometimes purchased the services of female sorcerers to protect their businesses from "evil," increase their sales, and ensure their success. Many of those active in the local economy depended on the small amounts of money they earned each day to pay for their daily expenses. A few bad days or weeks could cause serious difficulties in men's and women's lives, and some chose supernatural strategies to address this. In 1704 Catalina Francisca de Paz, a twenty-year-old mulata doncella, described how her mother, Teresa de Paz, and her friends—among them three mulatas, a Black woman, and an Indian woman, all women of *mal crédito* (evil reputations) — conducted ritual cleansings of her shop. Teresa and her friends socialized at the shop and also carried out the "strange rituals," including burning incense in the four corners of the shop to protect it from evil.[21]

Francisca de Fuentes, a mulata street vendor who sold pastries in the capital, also used supernatural means to increase her business. She reportedly bought two packets of doctored powders from Antonio de Larios, one for the "buena venta de los pasteles" (strong sales of her pastries). Francisca then placed the powders in the pastries and food she sold. She used the other packet of powders for love magic. Francisca's daughter-in-law remarked that the powders Francisca used to bewitch her lover "had such a strong effect that even though she is old and without teeth . . . nevertheless he returned."[22]

Economic Witchcraft and the Formation of Multiethnic Social Networks

Although some women developed strategies that combined various economic activities, such as market selling and sorcery or domestic service and magical healing, as a hedge against potential difficulties, fear of economic hardship and a slide into poverty was ever present. And many of those who consulted female sorcerers did so for economic reasons. Women's concern for making ends meet is especially apparent in sorcery to bring wealth or material gain. Through an examination of women who either practiced economic witchcraft themselves or consulted others for economic witchcraft, one can identify lines of multiethnic social networks designed to help them through difficult times.[23] Women drew on relationships with relatives and neighbors to share their experiences with economic hardship, identify economic witchcraft practitioners, and share material resources to get them through short-term difficulties.

An unexpected illness, for example, especially for those women who could not rely on family or social networks, often caused great concern. In March 1698 Fray Domingo de Los Reyes, vicar of the Candelaria parish, administered the last rites to a dying mulata woman named Nicolasa de Avedaño. According to Fray Domingo, Nicolasa "found herself in poverty, and to cure it she spread the word of her miseries to another [female] friend."[24] This friend knew of Petrona Mungía, who had a reputation for using remedios to "cure" poverty and bring wealth. Nicolasa located Petrona and contracted her services. Petrona prescribed spells for wealth and good fortune, and Nicolasa paid her three pesos.

Elite women also took advantage of economic witchcraft designed to bring wealth. In 1695 Sebastiana de Aguilar, a thirty-year-old Spanish widow, consulted a sorcerer named Chita de Agreda for economic witchcraft.[25] Chita sold her a ritual stick that came from the coast and told her the stick would bring her good luck because a mulata named Chana Lucrecia had given it to her "to bring her money." Sebastiana added that one day while visiting Chita de Agreda in her home, she met an unmarried mulato named Antonio de Larios. Antonio made his living as a peddler, traveling between the coast and the capital, selling amulets, powders, incense, and other goods. Sebastiana, a widowed Spanish woman, decided to allow Antonio to stay at her house for fifteen days. In return, he offered to teach her all he knew about sorcery. He also gave her a small bag of incense to perfume her clothing "to attract men and to have money." Antonio also used incense to perfume the four corners of her home, designed to ritually cleanse the home and protect it from evil.

Doña María Cecilia de Paniagua, the twenty-nine-year-old wife of don Luis de Aguilar, consulted a number of women in the city for various types of economic sorcery.[26] One was María Manuela, a widowed mulata from the barrio of Chipilapa. In one instance, María Manuela showed doña María Cecilia fifteen small stones and explained that each had different supernatural "properties." María Manuela chose a triangular stone and gave it to doña María Cecilia, telling her "with this one she would have much silver and much respect." María Manuela instructed her to incense the stone three days a week (Mondays, Wednesdays, and Fridays) so that it would retain its magical properties. Doña

María Cecilia should then give the stone to men with whom she had sexual relations "so that the men will give her all the reales and precious jewels that she wants." Doña María Cecilia also purchased from María Manuela "two very smelly monkey hands," amulets designed to bring wealth. Finally, doña María Cecilia had María Manuela cast a spell on some of her money, so that when she used the "bewitched pesos" to play card games and dice, she would win.

A number of the women used their social networks to identify sorcerers for a spell designed to simultaneously attract a male sexual partner and "cure" their poverty. This aspect of economically motivated sorcery highlights the connections women made between economic survival and stable relations with men, as well as the precariousness of women's economic situations on a day-to-day basis, whether or not they had children to support. María, a Spanish seamstress, purchased a spell from a female sorcerer "so that they [men] desire you, and do not leave you for another woman, and that they give you presents and money."[27] Another woman, María Mauricia, a mulata, consulted a female sorcerer for ritual feathers designed to bring her wealth and men. The sorcerer sold her herbs and *zacate verde* (green hay or fodder) and told her to cook with them and bathe in the doctored water to gain wealth.[28]

Having a husband did not guarantee an economically stable life, however, and married couples also consulted sorcerers for economic witchcraft. One couple bought powders that were supposed to bring them wealth if on the night of San Juan they walked through the city and sprinkled the powders on the streets of the capital.[29]

Female slaves also relied on social networks to identify female sorcerers for economic witchcraft. María Luisa, a twenty-seven-year-old *negra criolla* (Black woman born in the Americas), was the slave of don Juan Antonio Dignero.[30] In 1694 she found herself destitute when she was abandoned by the man who supported her. Apparently her master, don Juan, did not provide for María Luisa's basic needs. She consulted a sorcerer named Francisca de Avedaño who gathered the herb *zintuli,* which she ground up and used to wash María Luisa's face, arms, and the rest of her body "so money would come." Francisca also took an amberlike stone, wet it with water, and rubbed it over María Luisa's body "so that when she left the house she would [sexually] provoke men."

Women also linked economic witchcraft goals with counteracting curses believed to have brought poverty and economic ruin. In 1693 Francisca González, a single mulata blanca, described how her sister

Nicolasa injured herself in an accident. She did not heal but remained ill from *espantos y miedos* (terrors and fears), suggesting to those involved that the injury had a supernatural origin. Nicolasa became desperate because she had no one to support her or her children after her male partner left her. When Nicolasa consulted a mulata sorcerer, the sorcerer told her that someone had cursed her to cause her to become "so poor that she would have to beg for alms." Nicolasa purchased some special herbs to bathe in and cook with to counteract the curse.[31]

The informal networks that linked female sorcerers who practiced economic witchcraft with potential clients allowed women to discuss their economic difficulties and potentially procure food, clothing, temporary housing, and other resources. Women thus developed informal and fluid social relationships with family members, neighbors, comadres, and friends across ethnic, class, and geographic divisions in urban society.[32]

While resource sharing and gift-giving was a common strategy that women used to establish social ties and maintain friendships, women's social networks could also appear suspicious to the men in their lives.[33] When Juan de Fuentes, a mulato construction worker, denounced his mulata blanca wife, Cecilia, to the Inquisition for practicing sorcery, he highlighted Cecilia's ritual ties to and suspicious friendship with her comadre Gerónima de Barahona.[34] Juan claimed that Gerónima gave Cecilia gifts of food, clothing, and candles each day, and the women constantly gossiped together. Inquisition records report:

> Gerónima [de Barahona] is publicly known to be a sorcerer. Gerónima is continuously locked in with [Juan's] wife, and gives her many presents, so that everyday Gerónima sends food, candles, chocolate rolls, and clothes to Cecilia, and [Juan] just became aware that the spells and curses that [Juan's] wife casts are with the counsel and help of Gerónima.

The close friendship between the two women and the fact that they shared food and clothing made Juan suspicious that they also practiced sorcery together.

Mother-daughter sorcery networks were not uncommon in Santiago. Gerónima de Barahona had ritual ties to three of her four daughters and her mestiza daughter-in-law. All apparently had such reputations as sorcerers that when they stopped together at the threshold of a neighbor's door holding large leaves, the neighbor, a Spanish woman, became suspicious and reported the incident to Inquisition authorities.[35] The mulata slave of a priest characterized Gerónima's mestiza daughter-in-law as a witch and charged that she learned her trade in San Juan Amatitlán, a mainly indigenous town close to the capital.[36] Another neighbor characterized Gerónima's daughter Bernarda "as notorious a witch and sorcerer as her mother."

Gerónima also had ties to an elite Spanish widow named doña Magdalena de Medrano, whom she allegedly had trained in sorcery. One neighbor claimed that Gerónima visited doña Magdalena's house at all hours of the day and night and that they appeared to have "great friendship and communication," implying that their closeness was inappropriate and therefore suspicious, perhaps because of their social differences. Doña Magdalena also sent her servants to Gerónima's house two or three times a day. And at one point during their friendship, Gerónima lived in doña Magadalena's home for three months.

Social ties between rich and poor women, such as those between Gerónima and doña Magdalena, might have had strategic benefits for both parties. Gerónima gained temporary housing and a wealthy, high-status patron for her sorcery services, which enhanced her reputation and probably increased her business. For doña Magdalena, publicly linking herself to Gerónima despite the risk of prosecution by the Inquisition may have helped her to establish her own reputation as a sorcerer due to Gerónima's informal status as a maestra. A public alliance with Gerónima, whose reputation as a powerful sorcerer was recalled in an Inquisition testimony fifteen years after her death, could also help doña Magdalena to intimidate a neighbor or an enemy.[37] In addition, social practices dictated who could walk in the streets of the city at certain times in certain neighborhoods. By day, an elite woman could go out in the street and perhaps only risk her reputation if she spoke to a man who was not a close relative. If she were to go out at night alone, however, she might be taken for a woman of ill repute or even a witch.[38] Gerónima, a mulata and a meat seller, did not risk her reputation by being out and about at all hours.

Women's use of multiethnic networks in economic witchcraft practices suggests new ways to think about community and identity in Santiago de Guatemala and other Spanish colonial cities.[39] Women's attempts to "cure" their poverty, bring wealth, and increase business with economic witchcraft were more than symbolic expressions of the difficulties of life in a colonial city. Through informal community networks, the multiracial urban poor, women in particular, drew on neighborhood and community ties for assistance in dealing with hunger, disease, spousal abandonment, and other difficulties in daily life. These informal alliances suggest that colonial inhabitants of urban Guatemala formed their communities based not only on colonial institutions but also on shared cultural practices and the social experiences of ethnicity, status, and gender.

Community Conflicts and Multiethnic Social Networks

Narratives of economic sorcery reveal women's shared concerns about economic survival and their fears of becoming poor. They provide evidence of multiethnic material networks that linked female sorcerers with potential clients and allowed women to discuss their economic difficulties and share resources. Female sorcerers and their clients also used economic sorcery to punish those who refused to repay debts, to curse someone who would not extend credit, and to exact revenge against competitive family members, neighbors, and business rivals. As a result, economic sorcery accounts reveal community fault lines and fluid, competing social networks centered on economic and material concerns in Santiago de Guatemala.

Men and women combined various supernatural strategies of conflict resolution with the court system or appeals to political and religious authorities and community elders.[40] Many of those who went on their own to denounce others to the Inquisition and other colonial institutions, calling for their intervention in local conflicts, did so months or years after an event occurred, suggesting that the use of official avenues of redress was only one of many strategies pursued for community conflict resolution.

There is a time lag in many denunciations to colonial civil and religious authorities. In 1695 a forty-one-year-old widow named Magdalena Delgado, a lay Franciscan, told Inquisition authorities that she had known about Gerónima de Barahona's sorcery activities for thirty-five years and that during that time Gerónima was widely known as a witch and a sorcerer.[41] Juan de Fuentes, who attributed his inability to have sexual relations with his wife to her use of sorcery against him, only denounced her after she had an affair with his coworker and she tried to stab him with a knife during the ensuing argument.[42]

Lending small amounts of money to family members, neighbors, and customers was a common practice in daily life in colonial society.[43] Also, women who worked as shopkeepers, peddlers, and market sellers sometimes sold goods on credit. In 1693 a Spanish woman named Choma de Alguero owed a debt for some meat she bought on credit from Gerónima de Barahona. When Choma could not or would not re-pay the money, Gerónima reportedly cursed Choma so that she fell ill, suffered for many years, and finally died.[44] As a businesswoman who sold beef in a shop from her home, it may have made sense for Gerónima to cultivate a reputation as someone who took strong measures against those who refused to repay their debts so as to intimidate others.

Gerónima even went so far as to curse a shop owner who refused to extend credit to her. One day Gerónima went into a shop and asked the shopkeeper for credit to buy some goods. When the shopkeeper re-fused, Gerónima reportedly reached into her "bag of spells" that she carried on a belt tied around her waist and took out some powders. Then, in front of the shopkeeper and other witnesses, Gerónima placed her hands on the counter and scattered the powders "to take away the wealth" of the shopkeeper.[45] From this description of Gerónima's ac-tivities and the rumors surrounding her supernatural abilities, it is not surprising that the head of Guatemala's Inquisition called her "la carni-cera mujer de mala fama en esta ciudad" (the female beef seller of evil reputation in this city).[46]

Others consulted female sorcerers to counteract the spells their ene-mies used against them. One night María de la Aruburu, an eighteen-year-old unmarried mulata, visited the house of her friend, a mestiza named María de la Natividad, commonly known as "La Soltera" (the Spinster).[47] Antonio de Larios, the mulato peddler, was also present. María de la Aruburu claimed that a Spanish woman, with the coopera-tion of an "intimate [female] friend," threw something suspicious on the door of her house "to do evil to her and to cause her misfortune."

La Soltera ordered Antonio to incense María's house to drive the evil away. Antonio used rosemary, an herb associated with good luck in Spanish culture, along with copal, associated with ritual cleansing in indigenous practices. María complained that the incense was not strong enough to counteract the curse, however, and that "the misfortunes and evil events that followed her did not cease." In this case a young un-married mulata, worried that an acquaintance cursed her to cause her to become poor, went to a mestiza friend's house to discuss her prob-lems and at the house met a mulato sorcerer. The mulato sorcerer sold her spells to counteract the curse perpetrated by her rival, a Spanish woman, with the help of her female accomplice.

Men and women in colonial Santiago gave accounts of how female sorcerers intervened in local rivalries to cause others to become poor. In 1698 Andrés Miranda, a twenty-three-year-old minor sexton in San Sebastián parish, complained that a married mulata woman named Juana de Castellanos put a curse on him that caused him to have many arguments with the bishop and the priests in his parish, and so he became poor, implying that he lost his job as a result.[48] He suspected that Juana, who had a citywide reputation as a sorcerer, might have cast a spell on him through food and told her that he would no longer eat any food she served him, nor would he allow anything from her into his house. Juana taunted him, saying "that with only an old shoe she could [magically] seize him and do him harm." Andrés claimed that Juana cursed him anyway by sprinkling the doors of his house with "foul-smelling waters." That a lay religious official in the church felt threatened by a mulata sorcerer suggests local fears that certain women had the power to cast spells and curses to bring poverty and disgrace to their enemies or the enemies of their clients.

Sometimes community members who felt they were targets of women's curses, spells, or love magic took revenge through direct violent attacks against those involved instead of going to Inquisition authorities or parish priests. Juana de Arrate, a forty-year-old married mestiza baker, related some gossip to Inquisition authorities that she heard from a mulato tailor named Francisco García.[49] Apparently María de la Natividad cursed Pedro Ordóñez, a mestizo from Chiapas, by sending him some bewitched hot chocolate. Josefa Rosa, María's mestiza servant, warned Pedro that María had bewitched the chocolate and advised him not to drink it. Pedro did not drink the chocolate, and the next day he found the cup full of worms, which indicated to him that María had indeed bewitched the chocolate. The next day he went to María's home and beat her. Juana heard the blows and María's cries, as did Francisco, who lived across the street from María, but neither intervened.

The stories men and women told and retold about certain women's ability to cast spells, curse, and even murder their enemies reveal competing social networks in everyday life. A major element of these networks is the fact that women often denounced other women for supernatural activities, pointing to emerging class differences among men and women in the capital, conflictive servant-master relations, and economic and social competition between community members.

Women denounced women if the spells they purchased did not bring the desired result, which is what happened to Inéz González, a free mulata widow who practiced sorcery in Santiago in the 1720s.[50] María de la Concepción, a forty-two-year-old mulata and widow of a shoemaker, accused Inéz of practicing love magic and economic witchcraft after the spell she paid Inéz for failed to work. María explained that "she found herself poor" and had consulted Inéz for an appropriate spell. Inéz asked María "if she wanted to have a house with a tiled roof, wealth, and rest from labor," which María did, and so she purchased the spell ingredients. Inéz instructed María to grind two red-colored roots with some powders and then add to the mixture some "small animals that looked like *ronroncitos* [tiny beetles]." Then María was to throw the mixture on the cloak of the first wealthy man she met. Or, if this was not possible, she should approach the man, "pretend to remove lice from his head," and then sprinkle the mixture into his hair.

A month passed, but María remained poor. She returned to Inéz's house and confronted her about the spell's failure, and the two women argued over the payment, since María had trouble coming up with the two pesos. In addition, Inéz asked María if she had performed the spell as instructed and speculated that the spell failed because the beetles had died. Inéz then sent an Indian man to the countryside for more ritual ingredients. He traveled to the town of Jumay to procure more beetles and roots and to the town of Masagua to purchase a *zihuamonte*, a type of animal, which "women use[d] to acquire wealth."[51] Apparently this did not work either, and María became disgruntled enough to go on her own to denounce Inéz to the Inquisition.

Women also denounced other women as a result of master-servant conflicts, as when a female slave denounced an elite woman after she threatened her friend in the aftermath of a theft. In 1668, Dionisia de Castellanos, the sixteen-year-old mulata slave of Guatemala's first printer, José Pineda de Ibarra, and his wife, María Monte Ramírez, denounced doña Lorenza de Gálvez, an elite widow, to the Inquisition.[52] Dionisia described how a month earlier, she and some of the slaves and servants from neighboring households gathered in doña Lorenza's house. Doña Lorenza told them that someone had recently stolen a number of things that were "very precious" to her, including a cloak, a shawl, a petticoat, and a woman's head covering, and that she would cast a spell to determine who among them was guilty.

This conflict reveals extensive social interaction among different ethnic groups. Doña Lorenza, an elite woman, conducted the spell, aided by her mulata and Black servants, in the presence of a female Black slave, a mulata slave, two Indian servants, and two free mulata servants. Doña Lorenza and her servants fixed a thread to a finger ring and attached the other end to a pair of scissors. Present to witness the ritual, in addition to Dionisia, were Ana María, the Black slave of doña Francisca de Castellanos; the servants and slaves of her neighbors, José de Pineda Ibarra and María Monte Ramírez; Lorenza de la Concepción, a twenty-two-year-old single Indian servant; Francisca, an Indian servant; Magdalena, a mulata servant; and María Ramona, a single free mulata servant. As the women swung the silk thread, they chanted, "By San Pedro and San Pablo and all the apostles, tell me who has stolen the items," and then said the names of those they suspected. When doña Lorenza chanted the name of her neighbor's servant Magdalena, the thread began to spin, indicating that Magdalena committed the crime. According to Dionisia, doña Lorenza then began to threaten the woman, her friend and a servant in the same household.

Employers and servants often clashed over property, and theft was one form of resistance open to angry slaves and servants. Clothing was an easily transportable item, and if it was in good condition, servants could easily sell it or pawn it for cash.[53] The theft of her clothing represented not only a loss of material goods but a challenge to doña Lorenza's household authority as well. As a widow and head of household, doña Lorenza exercised her power through a supernatural ritual invoking various saints. She drew on her own network to help her in this endeavor, her two servants, a Black woman and a mulata. The ritual elaborately legitimated doña Lorenza's accusation that Magdalena stole the clothing.

Dionisia then denounced doña Lorenza to the Inquisition after she threatened Magdalena about the theft. The Inquisition took Dionisia's accusations against doña Lorenza seriously, despite doña Lorenza's elite status. This suggests that Inquisition officials needed to legitimate a slave's denunciation in order to prosecute elite women. In this case, they privileged a female slave's word over an elite Spanish woman's word. Dionisia's charges were probably buttressed by her mistress, María Monte Ramírez, a wealthy woman who had a number of slaves and servants, who also denounced doña Lorenza after she became angry that doña Lorenza tried to intimidate her servants. Women's competing social networks come into play here, and at the root of the conflict lay doña Lorenza's inappropriate interference with her neighbor's servants.

Doña Lorenza's elite status, however, protected her in ways that casta and Black accused sorcerers could not appeal to. Inquisition officials did not arrest doña Lorenza and put her in jail, nor did they place her in a casa de recogidas. Officials did not search her house for further evidence of sorcery or confiscate her house and material possessions. Instead, the Inquisition judge conducted another round of questioning to evaluate doña Lorenza's public reputation, particularly her reputation as a good Catholic and as a virtuous woman. Authorities interviewed two priests who vouched for doña Lorenza, including Fray Juan Alarcón, a forty-four-year-old Dominican, who said he had known her since she was a child in her parents' house and that she was a good and virtuous Catholic. Again, doña Lorenza continued to draw on her social relationships, in this case two priests who knew her and her family and who were willing to vouch for her reputation.

With that, the Inquisition concluded that another woman or group of women must have led doña Lorenza astray, and they conducted a third round of questioning to root out suspected women's sorcery networks. Six men testified—a city councilman, an Inquisition notary, a Dominican priest, a parish priest, a captain, and a choirmaster—but none knew of any female sorcery networks. By the end of this round of questioning, which ended in 1681, thirteen years after Dionisia's original denunciation, the head of Santiago's Inquisition let doña Lorenza off with a reprimand.

Contesting Urban Spaces: Gossip, Rumor, and Community Discourses on Women's Power

Social relations in community life were characterized by multiple if uneven exercises of authority and power in daily life. Men in Santiago often asserted their power through their roles in formal colonial institutions, that is, as militia members, priests, tradesmen in guilds, and members of religious brotherhoods. Women in colonial cities often claimed authority and power in noninstitutional realms of community life by drawing on their gendered social roles and re-creating and extending these roles through the integration of Mayan, African, and Spanish ideas about religion and the supernatural.

While women played central roles in social networks that structured community relations, there also existed a fear of and anxiety about women's roles. Guatemala's Inquisition and other colonial institutions attempted to root out such networks, especially networks of casta, Indian, and Black female sorcerers, magical healers, clandestine cult leaders, and their accomplices and clients. Colonial officials and men and women in the local community linked fears of female sorcerers and their roles in networks to their public displays of supernatural power.

Through gossip and rumor, female sorcerers' activities entered the public realm and reflected not only the perceived powers of certain women but also community discourses regarding local social relations as community members talked about, manipulated, retold, and embellished various supernatural events and women's roles in them. Gossip and rumor in Santiago functioned as competing community discourses surrounding the perceived power of female sorcerers in the politics of daily life.

Scholars have had a tendency to see women as the primary vehicles of gossip and rumor, acting on the margins of male authority and power. Serge Gruzinski, for example, analyzed indigenous male authority and power in community life in colonial Mexico. He cited the importance of rumor and gossip, arguing that women played key roles in spreading stories of the powers and feats of Indian "Man-Gods," which legitimated and enhanced male ritual authority and power in indigenous communities.[54] While not widely acknowledged in the literature, men clearly gossiped as well. In colonial Santiago de Guatemala, men and women of all ethnic and social groups gossiped, discussed, and critiqued the reputations and practices of female sorcerers, creating, in the process, vibrant descriptions of community life. Such gossip served to enhance the power and reputation of female ritual specialists. But it could also attract the attention of colonial authorities.

Residents of Santiago often included the phrase "por pública voz y fama," literally, "by public voice and reputation," in describing the activities of female sorcerers. Community-generated gossip, however, was not separate from official discourses of colonial power but instead interacted and intersected with it. Religious and political officials searched out and collected these accounts and cataloged them in testimonies written down by Inquisition scribes. Officials retold accounts of community relations, women's supernatural powers in these relations, and their own roles in the ensuing dramas through correspondence and official records of the Inquisition court.

The Inquisition cases pursued against Gerónima de Barahona, during the years 1682 to 1702, provide an interesting glimpse of the dual role of gossip as both legitimizing women's power and providing the basis for the intervention of colonial authorities and her eventual arrest and imprisonment.[55] One woman described Gerónima as having "the ability and aptitude" to deprive others of their health, their lives, and their belongings. Rumors abounded regarding Gerónima's exploits and supernatural powers, including everything from curses and causing and curing magical illnesses to love magic and economic witchcraft. Nicolás Resigno de Cabrera, head of Guatemala's Inquisition in the 1680s, related a series of details about Gerónima's life in a letter to Mexican Inquisition authorities in order to justify further actions against her:

> [This] accusation [is made] against a mulata named Gerónima de Barahona, who is commonly known as "La Carnicera" because she sells meat from her home. [She] is the same [woman] who has been imprisoned in the public jail by the *justicia ordinaria* of this city, and she has tarnished [the reputation of] many honorable and elite women.[56]

Resigno de Cabrera noted her nickname and her job and described her as a bad influence on honorable and elite women in the capital. He also reported that she already had been punished various times but nevertheless continued her activities. José de Baños y Sotomayor, head of Guatemala's Inquisition for much of the 1690s, added to these descriptions, writing that "Gerónima de Barahona, alias 'La Carnicera,' is a sorcerer and a liar, and is publicly known as such." Baños y Sotomayor thus legitimized Gerónima's reputation as a sorcerer while simultaneously attempting to counteract this reputation by calling her a liar.

Women's colorful nicknames added to their notoriety and reputations in the capital. Some nicknames revolved around a woman's employment, such as La Carnicera, the Meat Seller. Other nicknames spoke to women's violent reputations. Doña Luisa de Gálvez, a Spanish widow from the barrio of Santo Domingo, was known as "La Machete." According to testimony, she was called this "because she can cut out a tongue with a machete."[57] And María de Santa Inez was known as "La Panesito" because she had reputedly bewitched men and women with chocolate pastries that caused them to become ill and die.[58]

Some aliases described women in terms of their marital status or in relation to their husbands. Community members more commonly knew Sebastiana de Aguilar, a Spanish woman, as "La Viuda del Peinero," the Widow of the Man Who Makes Combs.[59] María de la Natividad went by the nickname "La Soltera," the Spinster.[60] Residents of Santiago knew doña Magdalena de Medrano, an elite Spanish widow, as "La Fiscala," in reference to her husband's occupation as an Audiencia official.

Women's nicknames also referred to their places of origin. Juana de

Arrate, a married mestiza, had the alias "La San Salvador." She lived in
Santiago but originally hailed from San Salvador.[61] Lorenza de Molina,
the mestiza widow of a barber, had the alias "La Perulera" because
she had left Peru to settle in Guatemala.[62] Women's nicknames sometimes commented on their physical appearance, as in the case of a Black
woman named María de la Candelaria, known as "María Gorda," Fat
María.[63]

While nicknames captured community descriptions and reputations
of local women, including their use of violence, supernatural events that
took place in public and were discussed through gossip and storytell-
ing left stronger impressions and more detailed accounts of women's
powers, as in the case of Gerónima's daughter and her bewitched stomach. Rumors circulated among community members about Gerónima's
daughter's accidental consumption of bewitched food, destined for a
love magic concoction, that resulted in her physical transformation. The
event, and the community recounting of it, served to enhance Gerónima's reputation as a powerful sorcerer while at the same time it attracted the Inquisition's attention. Cecilia de Arriola, Gerónima's married mestiza comadre, mentioned the event first. One day Gerónima
cooked some bewitched food, among them a chicken, for a spell for
a female client to use to cast a spell on her lover. At one point Gerónima left the kitchen to wash up, and while she was gone, her daughter Francisca returned home. Francisca, who saw the chicken cooking,
thought it was her dinner and ate it. When Gerónima returned to the
kitchen and realized that Francisca ate the food, the two women argued.
Soon after, Francisca became ill, and Cecilia claimed that "[Francisca's]
belly swelled so much that to this day she appears to be pregnant with
twins."[64]

Two years later, in September 1695, María de Lorenza, a forty-year-
old mulata married to a mulato tailor, told of a similar rumor. One day
Gerónima prepared bewitched food in her kitchen for sorcery. When
her daughter Francisca returned home unexpectedly and ate the doctored food "it caused her abdomen to become distorted like a very pregnant woman's, which has remained to this day." A month later, Catalina del Castillo, the thirty-year-old unmarried slave of Captain Gaspar
Viteri, related virtually the same story that Francisca accidentally ate
some bewitched food that caused her stomach to swell "like a very pregnant woman."

A variation on this rumor contended that Gerónima wreaked supernatural violence on a female enemy, who exhibited the same symp-

toms as her daughter who accidentally ate bewitched food. Teresa de Solorzano, a thirty-year-old single mulata, told about how after Gerónima fought with a woman named Nicolasa from Panama, Gerónima cursed Nicolasa with an illness that caused her stomach to swell until she died.[65]

Many rumors reaffirmed Gerónima's reputation as a murderer but gave no specific details. Cecilia de Arriola, Gerónima's comadre, claimed that if anyone dared cast a spell or curse on Gerónima, she would place a ritual item in the street to cause that person to slip and fall on their chest "expelling blood from their mouth" that could not be cured. Three sisters, Francisca, Nicolasa, and María González, all described as light-skinned mulatas, also related general rumors of Gerónima's violent reputation as a sorcerer. Nicolasa claimed that she knew of Gerónima's reputation for about ten years and that "it was public knowledge" that Gerónima, along with one of her daughters, "used spells and curses to kill people." María added that Gerónima lived in the barrio of Santo Domingo, where she also lived, and that she had heard "for many years" that Gerónima practiced sorcery and cast spells and that "all of those in the barrio live in suspicion and fear of Gerónima and her spells."

Others told stories of Gerónima's reputation by naming specific occasions on which she used sorcery to murder someone. Gerónima reportedly cursed a woman who publicly called her a witch, causing her to become ill and die. Rumors spread that Gerónima cursed an Augustinian priest at the behest of a mulata named Francisca de Agreda, by causing a pain in his leg, from which he later died. Gerónima also took supernatural revenge against Gerónima de Alguero, the woman with whom she feuded. She first cast a spell that "disgraced" her son, a priest of the Bethlemite order who worked in a hospital. According to Lucía de Cuellar, a thirty-year-old unmarried mulata, Gerónima later cursed the mother as well, adding: "It is public knowledge that when Gerónima de Alguero died, all of the neighbors threw insults at Gerónima for having killed [the woman] with spells."[66]

Women's Public Displays of Power and the Intervention of the Colonial State

The colonial state, through the Inquisition and other legal institutions in Spanish America, capitalized on the most violence-laden, notorious, and exotic accounts of women's authority and power described in gos-

sip and rumor to intervene in local social relations. Gossip, then, became a double-edged sword: it enhanced the agency and public reputations of certain women as powerful in the community and at the same
time brought the scrutiny of political and religious officials, who used
it as grounds to intervene in community life.

Competing public performances of power were manifested in a particularly striking way in an illegal religious movement, directed by a
widowed mulata, Sebastiana de la Cruz, and centered on her thirteen-
year-old mulato son, Bartolomé Catalán, who she claimed was the son
of Christ. Community discourses regarding the intersection of gender, religion, power, and community life came into play through this
movement, as well as through the response of the colonial state and
its allies on multiple levels: the cooperation of selected local residents,
local parish priests, and Guatemalan and Mexican Inquisition officials
in the investigation of the illegal religious cult.

In June 1694 Santiago's Inquisition received a letter from Fray José
Delgado, parish priest of San Juan Amatitlán, charging Sebastiana de
la Cruz "for giving her son adoration and worshiping him as a son of
God."⁶⁷ Sebastiana had lived for many years in the town of Amatitlán but two years earlier had moved to the capital, where she lived
with Bartolomé in a house along the aptly named *callejones de Belén*, the
alleys of Bethlehem. Bartolomé had become gravely ill in Santiago and,
according to Sebastiana, was miraculously healed "when Our Lord
[Jesus Christ] entered his body." Bartolomé confirmed this, claiming
that "his father, Our Lord" healed him. When he felt well enough to
travel, Sebastiana brought Bartolomé from the capital to convalesce in
her home in Amatitlán, among her grown children and their families
and the neighbors and friends she had known for twenty years or more.
From Sebastiana's home in Amatitlán, Bartolomé began to *hacer milagros* (perform miracles) in front of family members and neighbors.⁶⁸

After reading the priest's letter, José de Baños y Sotomayor appointed the priest Sebastián de Arroyo to question witnesses in San
Juan Amatitlán about the charges made against Sebastiana and her son.
The witnesses described Sebastiana as fifty years old and noted she had
been married twice, first to a mestizo named Nicolás Sazo and then to a
mulato, Pascual Catalán. Twice widowed, she had seven living children,
five boys and two girls ranging in age from ten to thirty.

Sebastiana's social network crossed rural-urban divisions, as she had
family and social ties in the city, where she lived with her four young-
est children and where her eldest daughter, María Sazo, lived with her

husband and their children. In addition, Sebastiana continued to maintain social ties to her family and neighbors in Amatitlán, among them her two eldest sons, Lorenzo Sazo and Sebastián Sazo, and their families and her comadre María Mendoza, a fifty-year-old widowed mestiza. In addition to her house in the capital, Sebastiana also maintained a house in Amatitlán, where they returned in the aftermath of Bartolomé's illness.

Immediately after their return, gossip and rumor spread through the town about Bartolomé's special status as a saint. Don Juan de Estrada, a forty-four-year-old elite farmer, remarked that he heard that Bartolomé "could do things that appeared to be more like things done with the light of God than things from this life or other natural things."

When Domingo Alesío, a widowed rancher and father of four, talked one day with three other men, he heard that Sebastiana "venerates Bartolomé . . . as a son of God" and that he "performs miracles" and says mass every night in Sebastiana's home. Sebastiana also told her comadre María Mendoza that she kissed Bartolomé's feet and hands "because God has protected him [from the illness] to be a bishop."

To legitimate her and her son's authority and power in the eyes of her peers, Sebastiana produced an elaborate genealogy and creation myth declaring that her son was holy, that his "father is Jesus Christ, the Holy Trinity his grandfather, and the Holy Spirit his brother," and that the archangel Gabriel baptized him and brought him from heaven to earth. On another occasion, Sebastiana proclaimed that Bartolomé's father was Jesus Christ and the Holy Virgin his mother. By using religious language and symbols to construct Bartolomé's creation myth, she gave her own perspective on the importance of lineage and legitimate birth in Spanish colonial society based on her experiences and beliefs.

During 1694–95, eight community members, five men and three women separated by ethnicity and social status, testified about the illegal religious cult. Although the Inquisition held the investigation in secret, community members nevertheless told similar stories regarding Bartolomé's performance of miracles, which they had either seen for themselves in Sebastiana's house or heard about from other men and women of Amatitlán.

They described Sebastiana's actions in detail, along with the rituals she performed and the miracles attributed to Bartolomé. Six of them recounted versions of the following miraculous rosary account, including Don Juan, a married elite farmer, Domingo Alesío, a widowed ranch owner, Juan Chrisostomo, an illegitimate widowed farmer, María Men-doza, a mestiza widow and mother of five, and Lorenzo Sazo, a married mulato. One day Lorenzo went to visit his mother, Sebastiana, and his brother Bartolomé in their home. Bartolomé told his brother to take the rosary from his neck and "put it in his [Bartolomé's] power." Lorenzo gave Bartolomé the rosary and left the house.

When Lorenzo returned to find out what happened to the rosary, Bartolomé asked Sebastiana to look for it on the altar they had in their home, but she could not find it. Sebastiana told Bartolomé that the rosary was not on the altar, and Bartolomé reportedly replied, "It does not matter, soon my father [Jesus Christ] will send it to me." Suddenly the rosary fell from the air. Bartolomé caught it and returned the rosary, saying, "This rosary came from the side of Our Savior Jesus Christ."

Bartolomé declared that the rosary would protect Lorenzo "from the demons who harassed him" and told him to worship it as a holy relic. In Catholicism, the side of Christ is associated with one of his crucifixion wounds, and Bartolomé implied that he somehow sent the rosary to Christ who bathed it in the blood from the wound, blessing the object. Sebastiana aided in the drama of the public miracle.

Community members asserted that Bartolomé had direct communi-cation with Jesus Christ through the altar in Sebastiana's home and through the image of the Crucified Christ in the parish church. One day Bartolomé told Lorenzo to pray and give thanks to the Christ image in the church. When Lorenzo entered the church, the statue of Christ, whose altar stood next to the entrance, nodded his head to him. Bar-tolomé also gave the impression that he spoke to the image of the Virgin Mary, located on their home altar. Juana saw Bartolomé pray at the altar before the image and said that many times he would return hor-rified after looking at the image and tell everyone to kneel "because Our Lady was coming," and so they all knelt. Bartolomé's brother Lorenzo asserted that Bartolomé spoke to Jesus Christ and the Vir-gin Mary and that once he saw him kneel down before the home altar and make it appear that the image spoke to him. Lorenzo asked Bar-tolomé what the Virgin Mary said, and he said that she asked him "if the people in the house were being cared for, and if they had enough to eat." Bartolomé's assertion provides a glimpse of the more general con-cerns Sebastiana and her family and neighbors shared about poverty that may have fueled the movement.

Bartolomé's miracles, including the creation of the holy rosary and speaking directly with Christ and the Virgin Mary, attracted the faithful and the curious to Sebastiana's home. Among them were representatives of all ethnic groups in the vicinity. Every night Bartolomé went into a trance and said mass in "ecstatic rapture" in front of those gathered. Bartolomé reportedly "floated in the air" while he said mass and called on San Rafael, San Miguel, and San Gabriel, while Juana Jiménez, a widowed mestiza, and María Candelaria, a Black woman, walked around him carrying crosses. Martín García, a free mulato, added that it was "public knowledge" that Bartolomé "se ponía en cruz," (put himself up on the Cross). Sebastiana, her children, three of her female friends, a Black woman, a Spanish woman, and a mestiza knelt before Bartolomé while he was on the cross.

While it was thirteen-year-old Bartolomé who performed the public miracles, Sebastiana became central to the maintenance of the cult. Her home became the focal point of the religious movement, both as a public space for people to gather and as a sacred space. In this space domestic and public boundaries of colonial life became blurred.

Some community members viewed Sebastiana's house as a holy space that repelled demons and remarked that "it was public knowledge" that anywhere from two demons to "a thousand legions of demons" pursued Lorenzo, Bartolomé's brother, and that Bartolomé's powers included the ability to protect Lorenzo from those demons. First, Bartolomé called on San Francisco to intercede and protect Lorenzo. He also "invoked the sweet name of Jesus" to expel the demons from Lorenzo's house. On another occasion, Lorenzo entered Sebastiana's house, and when Bartolomé saw him enter, he rose and prayed to the Santíssimo Sacramento (the Holy Sacrament), so that when Lorenzo came through the door, the "five thousand demons" pursuing him could not follow.

Sebastiana, taking on a public role in her home, actively encouraged and even pressured family and neighbors to watch her son perform the miracles. When Lorenzo went to visit his mother and brother in their house, Sebastiana scolded him, and said, "why haven't you come to visit before this? We returned [from Santiago de Guatemala to San Juan Amatitlán] three days ago." Immediately Bartolomé began to preach to Lorenzo, "extolling the hardships of hell, and how Our Lord Jesus Christ suffered for him, and that he [Bartolomé] saw Jesus Christ with the cross on his shoulder." After Bartolomé finished, Sebastiana reportedly told Lorenzo, "Now you have seen what the boy has done, kneeling and speaking with the Holy Virgin and trying to make you a good Christian."

Sebastiana also chastised her daughter-in-law Bernardina de Guzmán, her second son's wife. One night when Bartolomé was up on
the cross and the faithful gathered around, Bernardina did not participate and instead sat and ate some chicken. Sebastiana became angry
and told Bernardina "that she should not spend her time nourishing
her body, but that [instead] she should try to nourish her soul," and
pushed her to go watch Bartolomé "perform miracles" in the front
room. Sebastiana pressured those who may have been content to watch
to actively participate in the rituals.

Sebastiana's role in the what colonial authorities considered an illegal religious cult, then, became an extension of her gendered social role
as a woman and as a mother, re-created through her son's local status
as a saint. Legitimating Bartolomé as a saint involved in part his public
presentation; he had to look like a saint, not a sickly thirteen-year-old
boy. Sebastiana clothed him sometimes as the Christ child and other
times as the figure of the crucified Christ with a crown of thorns and
placed the boy in a niche in the wall of the house. María Mendoza
claimed that on most of the days she visited Sebastiana at her home,
she found Bartolomé dressed as Christ with a palm frond in his hand.

In addition, implicit in her son's status as a saint and the son of Christ
was that she, a twice-widowed mulata mother of seven, had a special
status as the mother of a saint. Sebastiana underlined the importance
of mysticism and ritual in her actions, which reinforced her community power as the mother of the son of Christ. Her activities also reflect
her beliefs about the importance of church symbolism and ritual but
refashioned based on her lived experiences.

Women enhanced their power through public displays, gossip, and
reputation, but at same time, the crucial public aspects of women's activities that attracted more customers, or in this case, more followers,
also invited the state into community relations. The public miracles,
nightly ecstatic masses, and widespread gossip surrounding Sebastiana
and Bartolomé attracted the attention of the parish priest. The state,
through the Inquisition, began a public performance of colonial authority, and officials in San Juan Amatitlán and in Santiago seized
the opportunity to intervene in local community relations. María de
la Candelaria, a Black woman, remembered that when Sebastiana and
Bartolomé returned to San Juan Amatitlán from Santiago after Bartolomé's illness, Sebastiana began to proclaim that Bartolomé's father
was Christ and his mother the Virgin Mary. This attracted "such a great
crowd of people" to Sebastiana's house to see the boy that an unnamed

priest, probably Fray Delgado, also came to the house and told every-one present that Sebastiana "was lying."

The face-to-face, local and personal intervention of the parish priest publicly denouncing Sebastiana as a liar set in motion colonial net-works of social control, as well as counterdiscourses of colonial au-thority. When women's actions invited the state in, the state enacted a public performance of its own through formal and informal policing at the local, Audiencia, and colonial level, a process that depended on both the freely given and the coerced cooperation of some residents.

In June 1694, when Fray Delgado, a Dominican priest in San Juan Amatitlán, wrote to José de Baños y Sotomayor, head of Santiago's Inquisition, denouncing Sebastiana de la Cruz and her son, he stated that in his sermons he tried with great care to tell the Indians and gente ladino of Amatitlán about their obligation to denounce "sacrile-gious cults." A number of these people, however, had been carrying on "superstitions" for a number of years, and "the first and principal" among them was the mulata Sebastiana de la Cruz. Fray Delgado noted that Sebastiana had lived in San Juan Amatitlán until a few years be-fore when she moved to Santiago and that she called Bartolomé a son of God, implying that she not only adored and worshiped him in Ama-titlán but also in Santiago.

The town of San Juan Amatitlán, located close to the capital, was surrounded by the largest concentration of sugar estates in colonial Guatemala, worked by large numbers of slaves, along with a sizable free Black and mulato population.[69] In the late seventeenth century, colonial officials considered Amatitlán a disorderly place and launched an investigation and held hearings about the many Spaniards and castas who had settled in what had previously been a mainly indigenous town. Spanish and Indian witnesses, legal residents of the town, testified that many other Spaniards, mestizos, and mulatos had settled there illegally. They added that there were many that the Indian justices did not recog-nize, *vagabundos* (vagrants) who caused disturbances.[70] Because Indian justices did not have the authority to police and punish non-Indians, and there was no other colonial political authority present in the town, the illegal Spanish and casta residents reportedly "live[d] without con-trol, committing many crimes."[71]

When Fray Delgado denounced Sebastiana in his letter to the In-quisition, he charged that she was the "first and principal" actor within a larger problem of "superstitions and other things detrimental to our Sainted Catholic Faith" occurring in Santiago and the surrounding towns. The priest's letter suggests that he worried that Sebastiana's move back to Amatitlán, and her illegal activities there, would not only show his lack of control over his parishioners, but could also lead to wider instability. Fray Delgado's denunciation demonstrates the importance of local, personal relations along with the bureaucratic apparatus of Spanish rule in maintaining the hegemony of the colonial state.

In the capital, José de Baños y Sotomayor deemed the charges of an illegal religious cult serious enough to begin an investigation, formalizing the colonial state's intervention in the affair. He appointed Sebastián de Arroyo, a Dominican, to conduct a round of questionings in Amatitlán. In the questions Arroyo asked in the first round, he was not concerned about Sebastiana's sexuality or her public sexual reputation, a lack of concern that suggests ethnicity and economic status played a role in the expectations regarding women's "virtue" and the state's notion of order.

Arroyo asked witnesses if Sebastiana was married, if she had any marks on her body, and her occupation. While those questioned had known Sebastiana for from fifteen to thirty-five years and could often name her two deceased husbands and at least three or four of her seven children, none could recall what, if any, occupation Sebastiana practiced. The question about her occupation again speaks to how social expectations for women differed by ethnicity and economic status. Elite Spanish women, for example, were not expected to have an occupation other than that of wife or widow.

In the course of its investigation, the state enacted a public performance of its own. Fray Arroyo conducted two rounds of questioning, in the summer 1694 and in 1695, and it must have been well known among the residents of the small town that an official representative of the Inquisition had come to conduct an investigation. Also, while the two rounds of questioning gave later witnesses a chance to get their stories straight, it also provided time for local priests to put pressure on those involved.

María Candelaria, Sebastiana's friend and considered a major participant, confessed to a priest from the nearby town of Petapa. The priest told María that if Sebastiana and her son returned to Amatitlán, the authorities would punish them for what they did. He also reminded her of her responsibility to denounce Sebastiana if she did return to Amatitlán. Fray Arroyo called María during the second round of questioning, during which she argued that Sebastiana and her son were observant Catholics, probably in an attempt to do what she could to protect Sebastiana, despite the priest's admonitions and in the face of Inquisition questioning.

María asserted that Sebastiana went to confession every week and that she always brought Bartolomé with her to hear mass and sermons, instructing him on how to be a good Catholic. María also provided an alternative version of why Bartolomé was dressed like Christ: Maria claimed that what really happened was that she, Sebastiana, Juana Jiménez, and Sebastiana's second son and his wife made flower garlands in Sebastiana's house for the upcoming Easter celebrations. She said that after that, she began to hear gossip that they had practiced "idolatries" by making flower garlands to put on Bartolomé's head and that they adored and incensed Bartolomé and carried him on a cross around the house and around the town. Whether truthfully or not, in the face of Inquisition questioning, María attempted to protect Sebastiana and her son with an alternative account while at the same time directly responding to some of the "secret" accusations made in the first round of questioning. The case against Sebastiana and her son stops there; there is no evidence of its ultimate resolution.

Inhabitants of Santiago drew on different aspects of their social experiences in daily life, including ethnicity, gender, status, and religion, to create and re-create themselves and their communities under Spanish colonial rule. Female sorcerers, magical healers and midwives, and clandestine cult leaders maintained power in Santiago and the surrounding towns through the formation of informal social networks among family, friends, and neighbors, ties that often crossed ethnic, status, and rural/urban divisions in late-seventeenth- and early-eighteenth-century society. Women's cultural agency, revealed through practices of magical healing, sorcery, and popular expressions of religious faith, became performances in public spaces of the city, in the shops, homes, city plazas, fountains, and streets, and through gossip and reputation about these events, performances that continuously sought to explain, critique, and reshape colonial social relations in Santiago de Guatemala.

While the public component of certain women's supernatural activities—the rituals, spells, and miracles that took place in front of witnesses and were designed to be discussed and talked about—reinforced women's power to intervene in community conflicts and attracted more clients and followers, they also attracted the attention of colonial authorities. Word of women's public displays of violence, healing, and devotional acts, witnessed by family members, neighbors, and friends and spread through the city por pública voz y fama, created the opportunity for the colonial state to intervene in community life.

Parish priests, Indian town government members, political officials, and community elders, along with angry, competitive, or fearful community members, formally denounced the rumors and gossip to colonial authorities, the Inquisition tribunal, or the criminal courts. In other instances, colonial authorities in Santiago took it upon themselves to investigate what they deemed particularly strange rumors of women's illegal magical-religious behavior and intervened to reinscribe colonial authority and power in local social relations. Inquisition cases, other legal proceedings, and all that went along with them, including the interrogations, searches, and confiscation of the homes and material goods of women under suspicion, physical punishments, and the rumors surrounding them, became competing public displays. As a result, the actions of the colonial state became, in effect, a performance of colonial power, as representatives of the colonial state pushed their way into the households, sick rooms, and marriage beds of community life.

Conclusion

The history of women in Guatemala and elsewhere in colonial Latin America has become an important part of the discipline, as scholars have uncovered information about women's roles in politics, economics, religion, and society. More than just documenting women's lives, however, recent work on women's history has forced scholars to grapple with its historical significance and how it has reframed questions, ideas, and arguments about ethnicity, culture, and power during Spanish colonial rule.[1]

How, then, do we weigh the historical significance of "women who live evil lives"—female sorcerers, witches, magical healers, and leaders of clandestine religious devotions—in seventeenth- and eighteenth-century Santiago de Guatemala? These women and their male and female clients, family members, and friends continuously contested colonial authority through the cultural relations of power in daily life. In this context, Spanish colonial rule in Santiago de Guatemala can be seen, not as static, but as continuously in process. In response to a wide variety of religious and cultural challenges, colonial institutions, and the men who administered them, attempted to exploit divisions among the multiethnic population in the capital, to intervene in community relations by reinscribing Spanish colonial power at the local level.

Work by Irene Silverblatt and Inga Clendinnen has highlighted the importance of indigenous women's cultural roles, especially those tied to religious beliefs in preconquest indigenous societies. They have argued that Spanish colonialism and patriarchy subordinated women to men, pushing them to the margins of indigenous religious cultures.[2] In seventeenth- and eighteenth-century Guatemala, culture and religion continued to be of central importance to the social relations of colonial rule, and women from all ethnic and social groups participated in rich cultures of ritual authority and power, even in urban centers such as Santiago de Guatemala. Women and men re-formed and re-created religious-magical practices in the context of the city's multiethnic social milieu of Indians, Blacks, Europeans, and castas, reinforced through the movement of people in and out of the capital and through ties of kinship, sexual relations, trade, and healing shrines that crossed urban-rural boundaries.

The expansion of local and regional economies in the Audiencia of Guatemala in the late seventeenth and early eighteenth century seemed to increase economic opportunities for women, though more work needs to be done on this topic. It does appear that even in the context of economic expansion, however, women tended to work on the margins of the colonial economy in dangerous, socially stigmatized employment—as market sellers, street peddlers, healers, midwives, bakers, tortilla makers, butchers, and meat sellers.

In this historical context, Santiago de Guatemala witnessed a significant amount of community conflict, not unlike what Steve Stern found in late colonial Mexico.[3] Stern highlighted codes of honor and shame, as well as patriarchy, as the historical and cultural foundations of authority and power in gender relations in colonial Mexico.[4] The analysis of gender, culture, and state formation in Santiago de Guatemala reveals that the honor/shame complex and patriarchy as ideologies that structured gender relations of power were not yet fixed. Women seen as sorcerers, magical healers, and leaders of popular religious devotions played key cultural roles as brokers of social relations in community life, consulted by men and women from all social and ethnic groups and paid for their services. Women's public displays of power—causing a supernatural illness, casting spells on rival shopkeepers, using sexual witchcraft to tame unruly husbands—provided counterdiscourses of female power designed to be seen, to be discussed, and to attract more clients.

Christopher Lutz has documented how the Spanish were able to exploit divisions among the urban poor through the use of mulato militias and Indian justicia officials to police the capital.[5] Inquisition and criminal records reveal the strategies by which institutions of colonial rule, including the Catholic Church and the Inquisition, asserted themselves in attempts to silence competing religious practices and interpretations.

In late-seventeenth-century Guatemala the Inquisition made examples of the women associated with the most notorious and exotic supernatural events. As one Inquisition comisario put it, "If we punished all of them [the women], Illustrious Sir, there would not be enough jails to put them in. But I believe . . . that it is necessary to punish some of them, so that the others see it and are warned."[6]

What having a multiethnic society means in this historical context in Santiago de Guatemala is the breakdown of the colonizer/colonized dichotomy at the community level. The breakdown occurred when male and female Indians, Blacks, and castas denounced female sorcerers to colonial authorities, whether by personal choice or because of the threat of punishment, arrest, or excommunication. The breakdown between colonizer and colonized also occurred when Spaniards consulted female sorcerers to obtain love magic, cures for supernatural illness, and curses against business rivals or became magical-religious practitioners themselves.

In her work on gender and sexual witchcraft in colonial Mexico, Ruth Behar found that many women denounced themselves to the Inquisition and argued that by the late eighteenth century, women had internalized religious prescriptions for appropriate female behavior and denigrated sorcery practices and their roles in them.[7] By comparison, in Santiago de Guatemala, self-denunciation formed one part of women's strategies when faced with prosecution by Inquisition authorities. In particular, elite Spanish women, hearing that the Inquisition had begun an investigation, might adopt a preemptive strategy and put themselves at the mercy of the Inquisition court.

Elite Spanish women seemed to expect, and for the most part received, relatively lenient responses from the Inquisition, such as penitence, promises not to engage in such behavior in the future, and the like. Other women, especially indigenous, Black, and casta women, could not expect the same kinds of responses from the Inquisition and criminal courts and more often faced economic punishments such as the confiscation of their homes and belongings, imprisonment in the city jail or casa de recogidas, and, in extreme cases, physical punishment or transportation to and imprisonment in the Inquisition jail in Mexico City. As a result, these women used other strategies to deflect the Inquisition's glare, such as flight, counterdenunciations, contracting the services of other sorcerers for spells to bewitch colonial officials or intimidate witnesses, and blaming dead persons, especially "dead Indians," as those responsible for their introduction into the arts of sorcery.

Inquisition records and the testimonies contained in them, then, re-flected and reshaped colonial hierarchies of power in multiethnic cities such as Santiago de Guatemala. The tensions and contradictions within the documents provide evidence for the characterization of Spanish rule as a process of continuous reinscription of colonial authority, in this case in the face of competing magical-religious cultures. Inquisi-tion officials and witnesses often belittled the practices and beliefs as superstitious and "women's gossip" and generally denigrated accounts of women's power. At the same time, by bringing these accusations to the Inquisition, and through conducting investigations, interrogat-ing witnesses, and enacting public punishment, colonial authorities and male and female accusers also validated such practices as dangerous and powerful. What becomes important, then, for an analysis of the gender and ethnic relations of power in colonial Latin America is how colonial officials, as well as men and women of all ethnic and social groups in the capital, drew on the discourses, representations, and sym-bolism of women's use of supernatural power in the conflicts and con-frontations of daily life.

Local practices of devotional acts, curing, and magic showed op-portunities for women's cultural and symbolic authority and power in everyday life in Santiago de Guatemala. On the one hand, women's public roles in local religious cultures left them open to sorcery accu-sations and became opportunities for the Spanish state to reinscribe colonial rule at the community level through institutions such as the In-quisition. On the other hand, however, women's continued use of ritual practices to intervene in community conflicts and earn money despite the dangers reveals the crucial but often overlooked gender dynamics of power within the broader framework of ethnic and cultural resistance to colonial rule.

Notes

Chapter 1

1. Archivo General de la Nación (México), Ramo de Inquisición (hereafter AGN, Inq.), vol. 695, exp. 78, fs. 330–490 (November 1695).

2. AGN, Inq., vol. 727, exp. (none), fs. 560–75 (1704), and vol. 727, exp. 26, fs. 576–92 (1704). For more on racial and ethnic designations in colonial Guatemala, see W. George Lovell and Christopher H. Lutz, eds., *Demography and Empire: A Guide to the Population History of Spanish Central America, 1500–1821* (Boulder: Westview Press, 1995).

3. Both Padre Quevedo and the barber who examined him suggested that the size, shape, and location of the priest's wounds resembled those of the crucified Christ. For more on stigmata in Inquisition testimonies, see Richard L. Kagan, "Politics, Prophecy, and the Inquisition in Late-Sixteenth-Century Spain," in Mary Elizabeth Perry and Anne J. Cruz, eds., *Cultural Encounters: The Impact of the Inquisition in Spain and the New World* (Berkeley: University of California Press, 1991).

4. While my interpretations of gender and ethnic resistance to colonial rule differ from the important works of Ruth Behar for Mexico and Irene Silverblatt for Peru, much of my understanding of the connections between witchcraft and women's power is indebted to their scholarship. See Ruth Behar, "Sexual Witchcraft, Colonialism, and Women's Powers: Views from the Mexican Inquisition," in Asunción Lavrin, ed., *Sexuality and Marriage in Colonial Latin America* (Lincoln: University of Nebraska Press, 1991); and Irene Silverblatt, *Moon, Sun, and Witches: Gender Ideologies and Class in Inca and Colonial Peru* (Princeton: Princeton University Press, 1987).

5. See, for example, Irene Silverblatt, "Interpreting Women in States: New Feminist Ethnohistories," in Micaela di Leonardo, ed., *Gender at the Crossroads of Knowledge: Feminist Anthropology in the Postmodern Era* (Berkeley: University of California, 1991); William B. Taylor, "Between Global Processes and Local Knowledge: An Inquiry into Early American History, 1500–1900," in Oliver Zunz, ed.,

The World of Social History (Chapel Hill: University of North Carolina Press, 1985); Steve J. Stern, "Feudalism, Capitalism, and the World-System in the Perspective of Latin America and the Caribbean," *American Historical Review* 93 (1988), 829–72.

6. For an analysis of everyday peasant resistance to colonial rule in southeast Asia, see James C. Scott, *Weapons of the Weak: Everyday Forms of Peasant Resistance* (New Haven: Yale University Press, 1985). For indigenous societies in Spanish America, see Nancy M. Farriss, *Maya Society under Colonial Rule: The Collective Enterprise of Survival* (Princeton: Princeton University Press, 1984); Karen Spalding, *Huarochirí: An Andean Society under Inca and Spanish Rule* (Stanford: Stanford University Press, 1984); and Steve J. Stern, "Approaches to the Study of Peasant Rebellions and Consciousness in the Andean Peasant World," in Steve J. Stern, ed., *Resistance, Rebellion and Consciousness in the Andean Peasant World, Eighteenth to Twentieth Centuries* (Madison: University of Wisconsin Press, 1987). For multiethnic urban societies in colonial New Spain, see Christopher H. Lutz, *Santiago de Guatemala, 1541–1773: City, Caste, and the Colonial Experience* (Norman: University of Oklahoma Press, 1994); and R. Douglas Cope, *The Limits of Racial Domination: Plebeian Society in Colonial Mexico City, 1660–1720* (Madison: University of Wisconsin Press, 1994).

7. Here I build on Carol Smith's work on state formation in contemporary Guatemala, specifically, her argument that local processes simultaneously shaped and were shaped by regional and national structures. See Carol A. Smith, "Local History in a Global Context: Social and Economic Transitions in Western Guatemala," *Comparative Studies in Society and History* 26 (1984): 193–228; and Carol A. Smith, ed., *Guatemalan Indians and the State: 1540–1988* (Austin: University of Texas Press, 1990).

8. I address this in detail in chapter 2.

9. Padre Quevedo, however, had a troubled career in the church. The Inquisition brought charges against him for solicitation in the confessional. See AGN, Inq., vol. 530, exp. 3, fs. 120–225 (1695).

10. See, for example, Serge Gruzinski, *Man-Gods in the Mexican Highlands: Indian Power and Colonial Society, 1520–1800*, trans. Eileen Corrigan (Stanford: Stanford University Press, 1989); Victoria R. Bricker, *The Indian Christ, the Indian King: The Historical Substrate of Maya Myth and Ritual* (Austin: University of Texas Press, 1981); Kevin M. Gosner, *Soldiers of the Virgin: The Moral Economy of a Colonial Maya Rebellion* (Tucson: University of Arizona Press, 1992); Kevin M. Gosner, "Women, Rebellion, and the Moral Economy of Maya Peasants in Colonial Mexico," in Susan Schroeder, Stephanie Wood, and Robert Haskett, eds., *Indian Women of Early Mexico* (Norman: University of Oklahoma Press, 1997), 217–30; Martha Few, "Women, Religion, and Power: Gender and Resistance in Daily Life in Late-Seventeenth-Century Santiago de Guatemala," *Ethnohistory* 42:4 (fall 1995): 627–37; Mario Humberto Ruz, "Sebastiana de la Cruz, alias 'la Polilla': Mulata de Petapa y Madre del Hijo de Dios," *Mesoamérica* 13:23 (1992): 55–66; and Irene Silverblatt, "Political Memories and Colonizing Symbols: Santiago and the Mountain Gods of Peru," in Jonathan D. Hill, ed., *Rethinking History and Myth: Indigenous South American Perspectives on the Past* (Urbana: University of Illinois Press, 1988).

11. See, for example, James C. Scott, *Domination and the Arts of Resistance: Hidden Transcripts* (New Haven: Yale University Press, 1989); Scott, *Weapons of the*

Weak; E. P. Thompson, "The Moral Economy of the English Crowd in the Eighteenth Century," *Past and Present* 50 (1971): 76–136; E. P. Thompson, *Customs in Common* (New York: New Press, 1991). For indigenous resistance to Spanish colonial rule, see Inga Clendinnen, "Yucatec Maya Women and the Spanish Conquest: Role and Ritual in Historical Reconstruction," *Journal of Social History* 15 (1982): 427–42; Ramón A. Gutiérrez, *When Jesus Came, the Corn Mothers Went Away: Marriage, Sexuality, and Power in New Mexico, 1500–1846* (Stanford: Stanford University Press, 1991); and Silverblatt, *Moon, Sun, and Witches.* For colonial New France, see Karen L. Anderson, *Chain Her by One Foot: The Subjugation of Women in Seventeenth-Century New France* (New York: Routledge, 1991).

12. For colonial Latin America, see, for example, Silvia M. Arrom, *The Women of Mexico City, 1790–1857* (Stanford: Stanford University Press, 1985); Asunción Lavrin, "'Lo feminino': Women in Colonial Historical Sources," in Francisco Javier Cevallos-Candau, Jeffrey A. Cole, Nina M. Scott, and Nicomedes Suárez-Araúz, eds., *Coded Encounters: Writing, Gender, and Ethnicity in Colonial Latin America* (Amherst: University of Massachusetts Press, 1994); Patricia Seed, *To Love, Honor, and Obey in Colonial Mexico: Conflicts over Marriage Choice, 1574–1821* (Stanford: Stanford University Press, 1988); Steve J. Stern, *The Secret History of Gender: Women, Men, and Power in Late Colonial Mexico* (Chapel Hill: University of North Carolina Press, 1995); and Ann Twinam, *Public Lives, Private Secrets: Gender, Honor, Sexuality, and Illegitimacy in Colonial Spanish America* (Stanford: Stanford University Press, 1999). For the late nineteenth and early twentieth century, see Donna J. Guy, *Sex and Danger in Buenos Aires: Prostitution, Family, and Nation in Argentina* (Lincoln: University of Nebraska Press, 1991).

13. As Irene Silverblatt explained, "[Female] witches, manipulating structures and ideologies introduced by the Spanish, formed crucial links in an underground politico-religious movement that was emerging in response to colonialism. From the indigenous point of view, women became identified as the upholders of traditional Andean culture, defenders of pre-Columbian lifeways against an illegitimate regime." Silverblatt, *Moon, Sun, and Witches,* 195. Also see Clendinnen, "Yucatec Maya Women."

14. Cope, *The Limits of Racial Domination;* Elizabeth Kuznesof, *Household Economy and Urban Development: São Paulo 1765 to 1836* (Boulder: Westview Press, 1986); Lutz, *Santiago de Guatemala;* Ann Zulawski, "Social Differentiation, Gender, and Ethnicity: Urban Indian Women in Colonial Bolivia, 1640–1725," *Latin American Research Review* 25:2 (1990): 93–113. Work on cities and towns in early modern Europe has been done on this topic; see, for example, David Warren Sabean, *Power in the Blood: Popular Culture and Village Discourse in Early Modern Germany* (New York: Cambridge University Press, 1984).

15. Stern's *Secret History of Gender* is an exception to this, as part of his analysis has to do with gender relations in eighteenth-century Mexico City. See also Linda Gordon, *Heroes of Their Own Lives: The Politics and History of Family Violence, Boston, 1880–1960* (New York: Viking, 1988); Deborah Gordon, "Writing Culture, Writing Feminism: The Poetics and Politics of Experimental Ethnography," *Inscriptions* 3:4 (1988): 7–24; Kamala Visweswaran, "Defining Feminist Ethnography," *Inscriptions* 3:4 (1988): 27–46; Karen Anderson, "Work, Gender, and Power in the American West," *Pacific Historical Review* 6:14 (1992): 481–99, and Karen Anderson, *Changing*

Woman: The History of Racial Ethnic Women in Modern America (New York: Oxford University Press, 1996).

16. See, for example, Chandra Mohanty, "Under Western Eyes: Feminist Scholarship and Colonial Discourses," in Patrick Williams and Laura Crisman, eds., *Colonial Discourses and Post-Colonial Theory: A Reader* (New York: Columbia University Press, 1994); Ruth Behar and Deborah A. Gordon, eds., *Women Writing Culture* (Berkeley: University of California Press, 1995); bell hooks, *Yearning: Race, Gender, and Cultural Politics* (Boston: South End Press, 1990).

17. Belinda Bozzoli, "Marxism, Feminism, and South African Studies," *Journal of South African Studies* 9:2 (April 1983): 139–71.

18. Michel Foucault, *Discipline and Punish: The Birth of the Prison*, trans. Alan Sheridan (New York: Pantheon, 1977), 23, passim.

19. Lois Paul, "The Mastery of Work and the Mystery of Sex in a Guatemalan Village," in Michelle Zimbalist Rosaldo and Louise Lamphere, eds., *Woman, Culture, and Society* (Stanford: Stanford University Press, 1974), 282.

20. A number of scholars of Europe have focused on the importance of the body in relations of power in a variety of contexts. See, for example, Lyndal Roper, *Oedipus and the Devil: Witchcraft, Sexuality, and Religion in Early Modern Europe* (New York: Routledge, 1994); Barbara Duden, *The Woman Beneath the Skin: A Doctor's Patients in Eighteenth-Century Germany*, trans. Thomas Dunlap (Cambridge, Mass.: Harvard University Press, 1991); and Caroline Walker Bynum, *Fragmentation and Redemption: Essays on Gender and the Human Body in Medieval Religion* (New York: Zone Books, 1991). For contemporary Guatemala, see Diane M. Nelson, *A Finger in the Wound: Body Politics in Quincentennial Guatemala* (Berkeley: University of California Press, 1999).

21. Interest in Indian community formation in colonial Latin America began, in part, from Eric Wolf's classic model of the "closed corporate peasant community" as the central paradigm to explain how rural indigenous peoples organized to reinforce their identity and defend indigenous culture under Spanish colonial rule. This model has been revised with the work of Farriss, *Maya Society under Colonial Rule;* Charles Gibson, *The Aztecs under Spanish Rule: A History of the Indians of the Valley of Mexico, 1519-1810* (Stanford: Stanford University Press, 1964); and William B. Taylor, *Drinking, Homicide and Rebellion in Colonial Mexican Villages* (Stanford: Stanford University Press, 1979).

22. John M. Watanabe, *Maya Saints and Souls in a Changing World* (Austin: University of Texas Press, 1992), 15; John Monaghan, *The Covenants with Earth and Rain: Exchange, Sacrifice, and Revelation in Mixtec Society* (Norman: University of Oklahoma Press, 1995).

23. Farriss, *Maya Society under Colonial Rule.* Farriss argued that one reason Mayan cultural survival was possible in colonial Yucatán was geographic mobility and the proximity of the frontier to Maya communities.

24. Scholars of early modern Europe have long pointed to Inquisition records, and their concern with magic, religion, and gender, as important historical sources about relations of power. See Mary E. Giles, ed., *Women in the Inquisition: Spain and the New World* (Baltimore: Johns Hopkins University Press, 1999); Carlo Ginzburg, *The Cheese and the Worms: The Cosmos of a Sixteenth-Century Miller*, trans. John Tedeschi and Anne Tedeschi (Baltimore: Johns Hopkins University Press, 1980);

and Guido Ruggiero, *Binding Passions: Tales of Magic, Marriage, and Power at the End of the Renaissance* (New York: Oxford University Press, 1993).

25. See Ruggiero, *Binding Passions;* and Ginzburg, *The Cheese and the Worms.*

26. For more on the Inquisition in the sixteenth century in New Spain, see Solange Alberro, *Inquisición y sociedad en México, 1571-1700* (México, D.F.: Fondo de Cultura Económica, 1988); Ernesto Chinchilla Aguilar, *La Inquisición en Guatemala* (Guatemala: Editorial del Ministerio de Educación Pública, 1953); Richard E. Greenleaf, *The Mexican Inquisition of the Sixteenth Century* (Albuquerque: University of New Mexico Press, 1969); Richard E. Greenleaf, *Zumárraga and the Mexican Inquisition, 1536-1543* (Washington, D.C.: Academy of American Franciscan History, 1961); and Julio Jiménez Rueda, *Herejías y supersticiones en la Nueva España: Los heterodoxos en México* (México, D.F.: Imprenta Universitaria, 1946).

27. See Richard E. Boyer, *Lives of the Bigamists: Marriage, Family and Community in Colonial Mexico* (Albuquerque: University of New Mexico Press, 1995), 17.

28. For a useful discussion of the periodization of the Inquisition in Spain and the New World, see Mary E. Giles, introduction to Giles, ed., *Women in the Inquisition,* 1-15.

29. According to Solange Alberro, among the 2,401 procesos dated from 1571 to 1700, 380 targeted Judaism.

30. Jacqueline Holler, "'More Sins than the Queen of England': Marina de San Miguel before the Mexican Inquisition," in Giles, ed., *Women in the Inquisition,* 212-23.

31. Solange Alberro, *La actividad del Santo Officio de la Inquisición en Nueva España, 1571-1700* (México, D.F.: INAH, 1981).

32. Holler, "'More Sins than the Queen of England,'" 213, n. 10. For more on bigamy cases, see Boyer, *Lives of the Bigamists,* 232. Boyer found 684 bigamy cases in the seventeenth century. For witchcraft cases in eighteenth-century Mexico, see Behar, "Sexual Witchcraft." According to Kathryn Joy McKnight, blasphemy was the most common charge that brought slaves before the Mexican Inquisition at the turn of the seventeenth century. She found that 101 slaves were denounced for or accused of blasphemy from between 1590 and 1620, comprising 80 percent of the slaves whose prosecutions are recorded for those years. See McKnight, "Blasphemy as Resistance: An African Slave Woman before the Inquisition," in Giles, ed., *Women in the Inquisition,* 229-53.

33. AGN, Inq., vol. 680, exp. 1, fs. 1-16, August 1694.

Chapter 2

1. AGN, Inq., vol. 497, exp. (none), fs. 313-20 (14 March 1695-11 April 1695).

2. For indigenous-language accounts of the Spanish conquest of Guatemala, see *Memorial de Sololá, Anales de los Cakchiqueles, y Título de los Señores de Totonicapán,* 2d ed., trans. Adrián Recinos (Guatemala: Editorial Piedra Santa, 1991); and Adrián Recinos, *Crónicas indígenas de Guatemala* (Guatemala: Editorial Universitaria, 1957). For sixteenth-century Spanish accounts, see Pedro de Alvarado, *An Account of the Conquest of Guatemala in 1524,* ed. Sedley J. Mackie (Boston: Longwood Press, 1978); and Bernal Díaz del Castillo, *Historia verdadera de la conquista de la Nueva España. Monumenta Hispano-Indiana V Centenario del Descubrimiento de Amé-*

rica 1 (Madrid: Instituto Gonzalo Fernández de Oveido, 1982). A small part of this chapter contains a reworked version of my essay "Women, Religion, and Power: Gender and Resistance in Daily Life in Late-Seventeenth-Century Santiago de Guatemala," *Ethnohistory* 42:4 (fall 1995): 627–37.

3. The K'iche' capital of K'umarcaah was called Utatlán, "place of the giant cane," by Alvarado's Nahuatl-speaking allies. K'umarcaah was located near the present-day town of Santa Cruz del Quiché. For more on the K'iche', see Robert M. Carmack, *Quichean Civilization: The Ethnohistoric, Ethnographic, and Archaeological Sources* (Berkeley: University of California Press, 1973). Unlike Cortés's conquest of Mexico, the Spanish conquest of Guatemala took nearly twenty years and involved a series of campaigns against other indigenous groups such as the Kaqchikel, Tz'utujil, Mam, and Ixil. Other Maya groups such as the Lacandón and the Itzá actively opposed the Spanish colonial state into the seventeenth century.

4. Juan Rodríguez, *Relación del espantable terremoto que agora nuevamente ha acontesido en las Yndias en vna ciudad llamada Guatimala* [Valladolid? Mexico? 1542?] (Boston: Massachusetts Historical Society, 1940).

5. Lutz, *Santiago de Guatemala,* 7–8, 210.

6. Santiago de Guatemala remained the capital of the Audiencia of Guatemala until 1773, when it too was destroyed in a major earthquake. Colonial authorities then moved the capital to its present-day site in Guatemala City. For an account of the 1773 destruction of Santiago de Guatemala, see Felipe Cadena, *Breve descripción de la noble ciudad de Santiago de los Caballeros de Guatemala, y puntual noticia de su lamentable ruina ocasionada de un violento terremoto el día veinte-nueve de julio de 1773* (Guatemala: Impresa de Luna, 1858). For more on the establishment of the capitals, see, for example, Lutz, *Santiago de Guatemala;* Jorge Luján Muñoz, "El processo fundacional en el Reino de Guatemala durante los siglos XVII y XVIII: Una primera approximación," *Anales de la Academia de Geografía e Historia de Guatemala* 53 (1980): 236–56; and Sidney David Markman, *Colonial Architecture of Antigua Guatemala* (Philadelphia: American Philosophical Society, 1966).

7. The territory of the diocese included Guatemala and El Salvador except for the Petén region, which belonged to the bishopric of Yucatán. In 1743–44, a papal bull and a royal directive accorded the diocese of Guatemala archdiocese status, in charge of the bishoprics of Chiapas, Honduras, and Nicaragua.

8. J. Joaquín Pardo, *Efemérides para escribir la historia de la muy noble y muy leal ciudad de Santiago de los Caballeros del Reino de Guatemala* (Guatemala: Tipografía Nacional, 1944).

9. Cited in Robert M. Carmack, *Rebels of Highland Guatemala: The Quiché-Mayas of Momostenango* (Norman: University of Oklahoma Press, 1995), 45.

10. For more on native religions and the Spanish conquest, see David Brading, "Images and Prophets: Indian Religion and the Spanish Conquest," in Arij Ouweneel and Simon Miller, eds., *The Indian Community in Colonial Mexico: Fifteen Essays on Land Tenure, Corporate Organizations, Ideology, and Village Politics* (Amsterdam: CEDLA, 1990), 184–204; Inga Clendinnen, *Ambivalent Conquests: Maya and Spaniard in Yucatán, 1517–1570* (New York: Cambridge University Press, 1987); Kenneth R. Mills, *Idolatry and Its Enemies: Colonial Andean Religion and Extirpation, 1640–1750* (Princeton: Princeton University Press, 1997); Ronaldo Vainfas, *A heresia dos indios: Catolocismo e rebeldia no Brasil colonial* (São Paulo: Companhia das Letras,

1995); Kevin M. Gosner, "Caciques and Conversion: Juan Atonal and the Struggle for Legitimacy in Post-conquest Chiapas," *Americas* 49:2 (October 1992): 115–29; and Nicholas Griffiths, *The Cross and the Serpent: Religious Repression and Resurgence in Colonial Peru* (Norman: University of Oklahoma Press, 1996).

11. The *Patronato Real* was promulgated in the papal bull *Universalis ecclesiae* of 1508. Adriaan C. Van Oss, *Catholic Colonialism: A Parish History of Guatemala, 1524–1821* (New York: Cambridge University Press, 1986), 52; and W. George Lovell, *Conquest and Survival in Colonial Guatemala: A Historical Geography of the Cuchumatán Highlands* (Montreal: McGill-Queen's University Press, 1992), 90–91.

12. The Jesuits did not come to Guatemala until 1580 and were not active in religious conversion there.

13. *Memorial de Sololá*, 153. Religious visions occurred elsewhere in early colonial New Spain. In 1531, a Nahua speaker named Juan Diego reportedly also saw a vision of the Virgin Mary outside of Mexico City that came to be known as Nuestra Señora de Guadalupe. For more on the recent debates about the Virgin of Guadalupe in colonial and national Mexico, see Stafford Poole, *Our Lady of Guadalupe: The Origins and Sources of a Mexican National Symbol, 1531–1797* (Tucson: University of Arizona Press, 1995); and William B. Taylor, "The Virgin of Guadalupe: An Inquiry into the Social History of a Marian Devotion," *American Ethnologist* (1986): 9–33.

14. Magnus Mörner, *Race Mixture in the History of Latin America* (Boston: Little, Brown, 1967), 45–46. For more detail on the establishment of two republics in Guatemala, see Murdo J. MacLeod, *Spanish Central America: A Socioeconomic History, 1520–1720* (Berkeley: University of California Press, 1973), 120–42; Lutz, *Santiago de Guatemala*, 19–78; and Christopher H. Lutz, "Evolución demográfica de la población no indígena," in Jorge Luján Múñoz, gen. ed., *Historia general de Guatemala*, Tomo II: "Dominación española: Desde la Conquista hasta 1700" (Guatemala: Asociación de Amigos del País, Fundación para la Cultural y el Desarollo, 1993), 249–58.

15. Markman, *Colonial Architecture*, 21–30. For more on the architecture of Santiago de Guatemala and the physical layout of the city, see J. Joaquín Pardo, Pedro Zamora Castellanos, and Luis Luján Muñoz, *Guía de Antigua Guatemala*, 2d ed. (Guatemala: Editorial "José de Pineda Ibarra," 1968); and Verle Lincoln Annis, *The Architecture of Antigua, Guatemala, 1543–1773* (Guatemala: University of San Carlos of Guatemala, 1968). For more on the political organization of colonial Guatemala, see especially Lovell, *Conquest and Survival in Colonial Guatemala*; Miles L. Wortman, *Government and Society in Central America, 1680–1840* (New York: Columbia University Press, 1982); Oakah L. Jones, *Guatemala in the Spanish Colonial Period* (Norman: University of Oklahoma Press, 1994); and Ralph Lee Woodward, Jr., *Central America: A Nation Divided*, 2d ed. (New York: Oxford University Press, 1985).

16. Pardo, Zamora Castellanos, and Luján Muñoz, *Guía de Antigua*, 40.

17. Lutz, *Santiago de Guatemala*, 19–44.

18. Pardo, *Efemerides*, 20, 37. For more on confession and Indian populations, see Serge Gruzinski, "Individualization and Acculturation: Confession among the Nahuas of Mexico from the Sixteenth to the Eighteenth Century," in Asunción Lavrin, ed., *Sexuality and Marriage in Colonial Latin America* (Lincoln: University of Nebraska Press, 1989). For more on the Inquisition in New Spain, see Alberro, *In-*

quisición y sociedad en México; Greenleaf, *Zumárraga and the Mexican Inquisition;* and Greenleaf, *The Mexican Inquisition of the Sixteenth Century.*

19. Chinchilla de Aguilar, *La Inquisición en Guatemala,* 25, 33. For more on the Inquisition for Indians, see Richard Greenleaf, "The Inquisition and the Indians of New Spain: A Study in Jurisdictional Confusion," *Americas* 34:3 (1978): 315–44; Roberto Moreno de los Arcos, "New Spain's Inquisition for Indians from the Sixteenth to the Nineteenth Century," in Perry and Cruz, eds., *Cultural Encounters;* and J. Jorge Klor de Alva, "Colonizing Souls: The Failure of the Indian Inquisition and the Rise of Penitential Discipline," in Perry and Cruz, eds., *Cultural Encounters.*

20. Pardo, *Efemerides,* 22–24; and *Miscelanea histórica: Guatemala, siglos 16 a 19: Vida, costumbres, sociedad* (Guatemala: Universidad de San Carlos de Guatemala, 1978), 36–40. In 1730 the convent contained 103 nuns, 104 pupils (*educadas*), 700 servants, and 12 *beatas.* By 1742 the convent contained only 80 nuns and one novitiate.

21. For an in-depth study of the first encomiendas in colonial Guatemala, see Wendy Kramer, *Encomienda Politics in Early Colonial Guatemala, 1524–1544: Dividing the Spoils* (Boulder: Westview Press, 1994).

22. Lutz, *Santiago de Guatemala,* 5–6.

23. Lovell, *Conquest and Survival in Colonial Guatemala,* 95–117, 193. Lasting from 1592 until the eighteenth century, the *servicio del tostón* was first instituted to pay the cost of the Spanish armada.

24. Lutz, *Santiago de Guatemala,* 21–23, 32, 262; and "Evolución demográfica," 252.

25. Murdo J. MacLeod, "Ethnic Relations and Indian Society in the Province of Guatemala, ca. 1620–ca. 1800," in Murdo J. MacLeod and Robert Wasserstrom, eds., *Spaniards and Indians in Southeast Mesoamerica: Essays on the History of Ethnic Relations* (Lincoln: University of Nebraska Press, 1983), 192–94; Lutz, *Santiago de Guatemala,* 22–23, 144–45; Lovell, *Conquest and Survival in Colonial Guatemala,* 104–6, 194; and William L. Sherman, *Forced Native Labor in Sixteenth-Century Central America* (Lincoln: University of Nebraska Press, 1979), 313–14, 322–23. For one of the only analyses of Indian women and forced labor in colonial Central America, see Sherman's chapter devoted to that topic. On the practice of Indian slavery in Brazil, see Stuart B. Schwartz, "Indian Labor and New World Plantations: European Demands and Indian Responses," *American Historical Review* 83:1 (February 1978): 43–79; and John Hemming, *Red Gold: The Conquest of the Brazilian Indians* (London: Papermac, 1978).

26. Gibson, *The Aztecs under Spanish Rule,* 226.

27. Lutz, *Santiago de Guatemala,* 96–97.

28. Lovell and Lutz, *Demography and Empire,* 12–17; Pardo, *Efemerides,* 8; and Lutz, "Evolución demográfica," 250. Also see Robinson Antonio Herrera, "The People of Guatemala, 1538–1587" (Ph.D. diss., University of California, Los Angeles, 1997).

29. Lutz, *Santiago de Guatemala,* 85–86, 281–82.

30. Lutz, "Evolución demográfica," 252; and *Santiago de Guatemala,* 209–32; MacLeod, *Spanish Central America,* 298. Lutz used *asientos* and marriage records to reconstruct African slave populations in the capital. He estimates that 20 to 30 percent of Santiago's slave population formally married in the seventeenth and eigh-

teenth centuries, many marrying free or freed spouses. From 1593 to 1769 in Santiago, approximately 56 percent of Black slaves and 80 percent of mulato slaves
married spouses of free status.

31. For a comparative look at African slavery and manumission in Brazil, see
Mary C. Karasch, "Anastacia and the Slave Women of Rio de Janeiro," in Paul E.
Lovejoy, ed., *Africans in Bondage: Studies in Slavery and the Slave Trade* (Madison: Uni-
versity of Wisconsin Press, 1986), 79–105; and Stuart B. Schwartz, "The Manu-
mission of Slaves in Colonial Brazil: Bahia, 1684–1745," *Hispanic American Historical
Review* 54:4 (1974): 603–35.

32. Lutz, *Santiago de Guatemala*, 19–21; MacLeod, *Spanish Central America*, 109–
11; Pardo, *Efemerides*, 11; and Lovell, *Conquest and Survival in Colonial Guatemala*, 102.

33. Lutz, *Santiago de Guatemala*, 32, 41.

34. Ibid., 35, 41–42.

35. Lutz, in *Santiago de Guatemala*, outlined the rise of *mestizaje* (race mixture)
in the sixteenth and seventeenth centuries and the emergence of a multiethnic
population in the capital. See esp. pp. 48–51, 63.

36. Lutz, *Santiago de Guatemala*, 106–8; and "Evolución demográfica," 253. For
more on multiethnic populations in seventeenth-century Mexico City, see Cope,
The Limits of Racial Domination.

37. Lutz, *Santiago de Guatemala.*

38. MacLeod, *Spanish Central America*, esp. pt. 3, "The Seventeenth-Century
Depression and the First Signs of Recovery, c. 1635–1720"; Murdo J. MacLeod,
"An Outline of Central American Colonial Demographics," in Robert M. Carmack,
John Early, and Christopher H. Lutz, eds., *The Historical Demography of Highland
Guatemala* (Albany: Institute for Mesoamerican Studies, State University of New
York at Albany, 1982), 14.

39. Lutz, "Evolución demográfica," 253.

40. Members of all social groups participated in illicit economic activities, including some wealthy Spaniards and various political and religious officials in Santiago. Lutz, *Santiago de Guatemala*, 141–42.

41. For an analysis of the daily working life of Maya women in colonial Yuca-
tán, see Marta Espejo-Ponce Hunt and Matthew Restall, "Work, Marriage, and
Status: Maya Women in Colonial Yucatan," in Schroeder, Wood, and Haskett, eds.,
Indian Women of Early Mexico.

42. Lutz, *Santiago de Guatemala*, 146–47; Pardo, *Efemerides*, 84, 112–13.

43. Archivo General de Centroamérica, Guatemala City, Guatemala (hereafter AGCA), A3-2357-34.714; Lutz, *Santiago de Guatemala*, 149–51, 305; and Pardo,
Efemerides, 130.

44. Markman, *Colonial Architecture*, 12–14, 27–28, 31, 35.

45. Pardo, Zamora Castellanos, and Luján Muñoz, *Guía de Antigua Guatemala*,
149–55, 290, 380.

46. MacLeod, "Ethnic Relations," 192; William L. Sherman, "Abusos contra
los indios de Guatemala (1602–1605): Relaciones del Obispo," *Cahiers du Monde Hispanique et Luso-Brésilien Caravelle* 11 (1968): 4–28; and Severo Martínez Peláez, "Los
motines de indios en el período colonial guatemalteco," in Germán Romero Vargas et al., eds., *Ensayos de historia centroamericana* (San José, Costa Rica: CEDAL,
1974).

47. MacLeod, "Ethnic Relations," 192, 430; Pardo, *Efemerides,* 113, 123, 137; and *Miscelanea histórica,* 65–67. Also see AGCA A1-23-4588.9 (1605), A1-23-4568.21 (1646).

48. Lutz, *Santiago de Guatemala,* 44.

49. MacLeod, *Spanish Central America,* 190–91; Pardo, *Efemerides,* 43. Also see Archivo General de Indias, Seville, Spain (hereafter AGI), Guatemala 13: Conde de la Gómera to the Crown, 14 November 1611; and AGI, Guatemala 14: "Sobre la reducción y prision de negros cimarrones," 2 July 1618. For an interesting approach to rebellion in early-nineteenth-century Bahia, Brazil, in which free, freed, and slave groups solidified their rebellion along religious lines, see João José Reis, *Slave Rebellion in Brazil: The Muslim Uprising of 1835 in Bahia,* trans. Arthur Brakel (Baltimore: Johns Hopkins University Press, 1993).

50. I have not been able to find any studies of this rebellion. Francisco Ximénez briefly mentions the rebellion in *Historia de la provincia de San Vicente de Chiapa y Guatemala de la orden de Predicadores,* 3 vols. [ca. 1700] (Guatemala: Sociedad de Geografia e Historia de Guatemala, 1920–31). Pardo also mentions it briefly in *Efemerides,* 120.

51. For more on how fear of slave rebellion in colonial Mexico motivated Inquisition prosecutions of black and mulato slaves at the turn of the seventeenth century, see McKnight, "Blasphemy as Resistance," 234–35.

52. Antonio de Molina, *Antigua Guatemala: Memorias del M.R.P. Maestro Fray Antonio de Molina continuadas y marginadas por Fray Agustín Cano y Fray Francisco Ximénez, de la orden de Santo Domingo,* trans. Jorge del Valle Matheu (Guatemala: Unión Tipográfica, 1943), 131–32.

53. Agustín Estrada de Monroy, *Datos para la historia de la iglesia en Guatemala* (Guatemala: Sociedad de Geografia e Historia de Guatemala, 1972–79), 1:299–300.

54. AGN, Inq., vol. 530, exp. 35, fs. 547–53 (1695).

55. AGN, Inq., vol. 497, exp. (none), fs. 313–20 (14 March 1695)

56. Ibid.

57. These are legajos that I located at AGN in Mexico. From 1650 to 1750 a total of 117 legajos are listed for the Audiencia of Guatemala, and so legajos targeting women made up just over 36 percent.

58. Guatemalan Inquisition records are currently housed in the Archivo General de la Nación, Ramo de Inquisición, in Mexico City, Mexico. I have supplemented my use of Inquisition records from 1650 to 1750 with criminal records from the same period for context and comparison. For the only contemporary history of the Inquisition in Guatemala, see Chinchilla Aguilar, *La Inquisición en Guatemala.*

59. Chinchilla Aguilar, *La Inquisición en Guatemala,* 25, 33; AGN, vol. 536, exp. 70, fs. 279–80.

60. A more systematic study would need to be undertaken to see if this bears out.

61. Chinchilla Aguilar, *La Inquisición en Guatemala,* 221; AGN, Inq., vol. 706, exp. 11, fs. 81–89 and vol. 531, exp. 50. fs. 327–43. For more on the term *indio ladino,* see Lutz, *Santiago de Guatemala.*

62. Chinchilla Aguilar, *La Inquisición en Guatemala,* 221. Guatemala's criminal records can be found in AGCA, Actuaciones Civiles y Criminales (A1.15) and

Denuncias y Processos (A4.1). The Inquisition in Mexico, Peru, and Brazil also prosecuted cases of witchcraft and sorcery. For Mexico, see Behar, "Sexual Witchcraft"; and "Sex, Sin, Witchcraft, and the Devil in Late-Colonial Mexico," *American Ethnologist* 14 (1987): 35–55. For Peru, see Silverblatt, *Moon, Sun, and Witches;* María Emma Manarelli, *Inquisición y mujeres: Las hechiceras en el Perú durante el siglo XVII* (Lima: Centro de Documentación sobre la Mujer, 1987); and Paulino Castaneda Delgado, *La Inquisición de Lima* (Madrid: Deimos, 1989). For Brazil, see Luiz R. B. Mott, *Escravidão, homosexualidad e demonologia* (São Paulo: Icone, 1988), and *O sexo prohibido: Virgens, gays e escravos nas garras da Inquisição* (Campinas, São Paulo: Papirus Editora, 1988), and *Rosa Egipciaca: Uma santa africana no Brasil* (Rio de Janeiro: Bertrand Brasil, 1993); Laura de Mello e Souza, *O Inferno atlântico: Demonologia e colonização, séculos XVI–XVIII* (São Paulo: Companhia das Letras, 1993), and *O diabo e a Terra de Santa Cruz: Feiticaria e religiosidade popular no Brasil colonial* (São Paulo: Companhia das Letras, 1986); Ronaldo Vainfas, *Trópico dos pecados: Moral, sexualidade e Inquisição no Brasil* (Rio de Janeiro: Editora Campus, 1989); Sonia A. Siquiera, *A Inquisição portuguesa e a sociedade colonial* (São Paulo: Editora Atica, 1978).

63. Chinchilla Aguilar, *La Inquisición en Guatemala*, 44–45.

64. Pardo, *Efemerides*, 97, 99, 103.

65. Lutz, *Santiago de Guatemala*, 100; Pardo, *Efemerides*, 13.

66. Pardo, *Miscelanea histórica*, 110–12; and Pardo, Zamora Castellanos, and Luján Muñoz, *Guía de Antigua Guatemala*, 128–29.

67. Pardo, *Efemerides*, 110, 124, 127.

68. The term *comadre* expressed a ritual kinship between a mother and godmother. I have constructed a narrative of the events surrounding the activities of Cecilia de Arriola and Gerónima de Baharona from a series of Inquisition cases prosecuted during the years 1680 and 1702. While many cases from the late seventeenth and early eighteenth century touch on or relate to the women's activities, the major sources are AGN, Inq., vol. 497, exp. (none), fs. 297–303; vol. 644, exp. 2, fs. 196–347; vol. 680, exp. 1, fs. 1–16, and col. 684, exp. 44, fs. 288–96; vol. 695, exp. 78, fs. 330–490 and vol. 695, exp. 78, fs. 491–582.

69. Las Salinas del Mar was one of a number of towns along the edge of the Pacific Ocean. Because it was an informal town in an out-of-the-way place, Las Salinas del Mar and the settlements around it generally had neither clergy nor representatives of the Spanish crown present and so made a good place to hide out. Christopher H. Lutz, personal communication, 1997.

70. Sabean, *Power in the Blood*, 3.

71. I have found various references to Gerónima's other brushes with the law but have not yet located these documents in the archive.

72. AGN, Inq., vol. 644, exp. 2, fs. 196–347.

73. AGN, Inq., vol. 684, exp. 44, fs. 288–96.

74. Murdo MacLeod defines *fiscal* as a "Crown attorney, the oidor charged with financial matters." MacLeod, *Spanish Central America*, 469.

75. Josefa's master is listed as don Félix de Zamora.

76. The annual pilgrimage to this site occurred on February 2. For more on this shrine and the other important pilgrimage sites in colonial Guatemala, see Van Oss, *Catholic Colonialism*, 103–5.

Chapter 3

1. AGN, Inq., vol. 831, exp. 2, fs. 214–352 (25 June 1733).

2. For an analysis of the centrality of the indigenous body in politics in nine-teenth-century Canada, see Michael Harkin, "Contested Bodies: Affliction and Power in Heiltsuk Culture and History," *American Ethnologist* 21:3 (1994): 586–605.

3. See, for example, Kenneth M. George, *Showing Signs of Violence: The Cultural Politics of a Twentieth-Century Headhunting Ritual* (Berkeley: University of California Press, 1996); Sharon E. Hutchinson, *Nuer Dilemmas: Coping with Money, War, and the State* (Berkeley: University of California Press, 1996); Nelson, *A Finger in the Wound;* Guido Ruggiero, *Violence in Early Renaissance Venice* (New Brunswick, N.J.: Rutgers University Press, 1980); Elaine Scarry, *The Body in Pain: The Making and Unmaking of the World* (New York: Oxford University Press, 1985); and Kay B. Warren, ed., *The Violence Within: Cultural and Political Opposition in Divided Nations* (Boulder: Westview Press, 1993).

4. Kay B. Warren explored and analyzed what she called the "cultural con-struction of terror" in contemporary Guatemala—how Mayans made sense of their understandings of state violence in everyday life—by analyzing Kaqchikel narra-tives of the *rajav a'a*, certain members of the community, usually women, believed to have the power to transform themselves into supernatural beings to do evil. Kay B. Warren, "Interpreting *La Violencia* in Guatemala: Shapes of Mayan Silence and Re-sistance," in Warren, ed., *The Violence Within*, 25–56. For other analyses of the effects of La Violencia in the 1970s and 1980s on cultural and material intracommunity relations in Guatemala, see the essays in Robert M. Carmack, ed., *Harvest of Vio-lence: The Maya Indians and the Guatemalan Crisis* (Norman: University of Oklahoma Press, 1988); and Nelson, *A Finger in the Wound.*

5. I build on David Arnold's argument that the colonial body became "sym-bolic of wider fields of contention between indigenous and colonial perceptions, practices, and concerns." See his essay "Touching the Body: Perspectives on the Indian Plague, 1896–1900," in Ranajit Guha and Gayatri Chakravorty Spivak, eds., *Selected Subaltern Studies*, foreword by Edward Said (New York: Oxford University Press, 1988); and *Colonizing the Body: State Medicine and Epidemic Disease in Nineteenth-Century India* (Berkeley: University of California Press, 1993).

6. See Stephanie Camp's insight into the personal and public aspects of physi-cal bodies in women's resistance to African slavery in the U.S. South. Stephanie M. H. Camp, "Viragos: Enslaved Women's Everyday Politics in the Old South" (Ph.D. diss., University of Pennsylvania, 1998).

7. For interesting discussions of this process in colonial New Mexico, see Gutiérrez, *When Jesus Came, the Corn Mothers Went Away;* for the Andes, Silverblatt, *Moon, Sun, and Witches;* and for the Audiencia of Guatemala, Sherman, *Forced Native Labor.*

8. See Susan Brownmiller, *Against Our Will: Men, Women, and Rape* (New York: Simon and Schuster, 1975). For recent work on gender, sexuality, and honor in colonial Latin America, see Lyman L. Johnson and Sonya Lipsett-Rivera, eds., *The Faces of Honor: Sex, Shame, and Violence in Colonial Latin America* (Albuquerque: University of New Mexico Press, 1998); and Twinam, *Public Lives, Private Secrets.*

9. Jacquelyn Down Hall, "'The Mind That Burns Each Body': Women,

Rape, and Racial Violence," in Ana Snitow, Christine Stansell, and Sharon Thompson, eds., *Powers of Desire: The Politics of Sexuality* (New York: Monthly Review Press,
1983), 328-49; Jenny Sharpe, "The Unspeakable Limits of Rape: Colonial Violence and Counter-Insurgency," in Patrick Williams and Laura Chrisman, eds.,
Colonial Discourse and Post-Colonial Theory: A Reader (New York: Columbia University
Press, 1994), 221-43.

10. Asunción Lavrin, "Introduction: The Scenario, the Actors, and the Issues,"
10-11, and "Sexuality in Colonial Mexico: A Church Dilemma," in Lavrin, ed.,
Sexuality and Marriage.

11. For discussions of rape and sexual violence in colonial Latin America, see
Sonya Lipsett-Rivera, "The Intersection of Rape and Marriage in Late-Colonial
and Early National Mexico," *Colonial Latin American Historical Review* 6:4 (fall 1997):
559-90; Asunción Lavrin, "Sexuality in Colonial Mexico," in Lavrin, ed., *Sexuality
and Marriage,* 69-92; Sherman, *Forced Native Labor,* 305-24; and Silverblatt, *Moon,
Sun, and Witches,* esp. 138-55.

12. I drew information about this conflict from three Inquisition legajos involving Padre Quevedo: AGN, Inq., vol. 530, exp. 3, fs. 120-225; vol. 727, exp. 26, fs.
560-75; vol. 727, exp. 26, fs. 576-92.

13. The word *coyol* came from the Nahuatl word *coyolli,* a type of palm tree that
produced fruit. People made rosaries, buttons, rings, and other items from this tree.

14. In her essay "Woman as Source of Evil," María Helena Sánchez Ortega
argued that in Spain, men in particular feared falling under the influence of powerful women and so played a large role in denunciations against women for witchcraft: "The masculine fear of falling under the influence of a powerful woman,
one capable of keeping a man against his will, is frequently in evidence in the
testimonies and accusations made against both sorceresses and their clients." See
her essay in Anne J. Cruz and Mary Elizabeth Perry, eds., *Culture and Control in
Counter-Reformation Spain* (Minneapolis: University of Minnesota Press, 1992).

15. In seventeenth-century Guatemala and elsewhere, barbers performed medical procedures.

16. For an analysis of the Inquisition and beliefs about female witches' Sab-
baths and practices of sorcery in Italy, see Carlo Ginzburg, *The Night Battles: Witchcraft and Agrarian Cults in the Sixteenth and Seventeenth Centuries,* trans. John Tedeschi
and Anne Tedeschi (Baltimore: Johns Hopkins University Press, 1992).

17. Alison Weber, "Santa Teresa, Demonologist," in Cruz and Perry, eds., *Culture and Control,* 172.

18. See chapter 5 for an analysis of women's public displays of supernatural
power in the context of community social relations.

19. AGN, Inq., vol. 689, exp. 7, fs. 189-201.

20. A *huipil* is a traditional embroidered blouse worn by indigenous women in
Guatemala.

21. This is the feast of Corpus Christi, Solemnity of the Body and Blood of
Christ, celebrated on the Sunday following Trinity Sunday. This feast celebrates
the body and blood of Jesus Christ and highlights the redemptive effects of the
sacrament. Richard P. McBrien, gen. ed., *The HarperCollins Encyclopedia of Catholicism* (New York: HarperCollins, 1995), 369.

22. The *tercera orden de San Francisco* or Third Order of San Francisco, a Francis-

can lay religious order, was established in Santiago de Guatemala in 1613. Originally designed for men, the order began to accept women in 1615. See Pardo, Zamora Castellanos, and Luján Muñoz, *Guía de Antigua Guatemala*, 226–27; and Domingo Juarros, *Compendio de la historia del Reino de Guatemala, 1500–1800* (Guatemala: Editorial Piedra Santa, [18–?] 1981), 140–41.

23. This holy oil was generally consecrated by the bishop on Holy Thursday but could be blessed by a priest in an emergency. Mcbrien, gen. ed., *The Encyclopedia of Catholicism*, 931.

24. While the language here is ambiguous, it appears that María dragged Michaela by the hair during their argument.

25. No surname for Teresa is listed in the documents.

26. AGN, Inq., vol. 644, exp. 2, fs. 196–347 (17 September 1695).

27. Bynum, *Fragmentation and Redemption.*

28. Ibid., 194.

29. For more on sexual witchcraft in Mexico, see Alberro, *Inquisición y sociedad*; Behar, "Sexual Witchcraft"; Noemí Quezada, *Amor y magia amorosa entre los aztecas: Supervivencia en el México colonial* (México, D.F.: UNAM, 1975); and *Sexualidad, amor, y erotismo: México prehispánico y México colonial* (México, D.F.: UNAM, 1996). For Peru, see Silverblatt, *Moon, Sun, and Witches.*

30. In an examination of testimonies made against male witches in Santiago from 1680 to 1700, I found little corresponding belief in the power of male body parts. There is one reference to a mulato peddler who threatened to use his semen in a magic ritual against a woman in an attempt to regain a small loan, though it is unclear from the testimony exactly how he did so. See AGN, Inq., vol. 644, exp. 2, fs. 196–347 (11 September 1695).

31. Robbie E. Davis-Floyd and Carolyn F. Sargent, eds., *Childbirth and Authoritative Knowledge: Cross-Cultural Perspectives* (Berkeley: University of California Press, 1997); Linda Gordon, "What's New in Women's History," in Teresa di Laurentis, ed., *Feminist Studies/Critical Studies* (Bloomington: Indiana University Press, 1986), 20–30.

32. The use of the female body and sexuality as critical elements in love magic practices, along with the frequent use of food and drink as supernatural agents in Santiago, resonates with themes in the literature on European witchcraft. See, for example, Sabean, *Power in the Blood*; Roper, *Oedipus and the Devil*; and Cruz and Perry, eds., *Culture and Control.*

33. Ruth Behar has written on women's love magic practices in colonial Mexico in which women forced men to eat their ritual body parts. In particular, she analyzed women's use of menstrual blood in love magic. I have not come across any descriptions in Inquisition records of the use of menstrual blood in women's practices of sexual magic in late-seventeenth- and early-eighteenth-century Santiago de Guatemala. Behar, "Sexual Witchcraft."

34. See Gayle Rubin, "The Traffic in Women," in Rayna Reiter, ed., *Toward an Anthropology of Women.*

35. AGN, Inq., vol. 644, exp. 2, fs. 196–347 (11 October 1694).

36. AGN, Inq., vol. 644, exp. 2, fs. 196–347 (10 September 1695).

37. AGN, Inq., vol. 706, exp. 11, fs. 81–89.

38. AGN, Inq., vol. 729, exp. 12, fs. 406–24 (4 March 1705 and 6 June 1715).

39. See, for example, William A. Christian, *Local Religion in Sixteenth-Century Spain* (Princeton: Princeton University Press, 1981).

40. Pardo, *Efemérides*, 28.

41. AGCA, A3-1624-26688: List of ship's contents (named *El Pajaro*), dated 26 February 1770; received 4 August 1770.

42. Manuel Lobo, *Relación de la vida y virtudes del V. hermano Pedro de San Joseph de Betancur* (Guatemala, 1677).

43. AGN, Inq., vol. 497, exp. (none), fs. 291–303 (1694).

44. For more on this, see my unpublished paper, "Chocolate, Sex, and Disorderly Women in Seventeenth-Century Guatemala," presented at the fall 1999 meetings of the American Society for Ethnohistory, Mashantucket, Conn.

45. AGN, Inq., vol. 644, exp. 2, 196–347 (10 April 1682).

46. Ibid. Anita's surname is not listed in the documents.

47. Because of her illegal activities, colonial officials placed the Indian woman Anita in the Beaterio de Nuestra Señora de Rosario, also called Beatas Indias. This beaterio, run by religious officials and designated exclusively for Indian women, effectively functioned as a jail. The Beaterio de Santa Rosa de Lima, also called Beaterio de Gentes Blancas, housed white women. The Beaterio de Belen housed poor sick women. Pardo, Zamora Castellanos, and Lujan Muñoz, *Guía de Antigua Guatemala*, 223–27.

48. AGN, Inq., vol. 644, exp. 2, fs. 196–347 (8 September 1695). It was not uncommon in colonial Latin America for couples who planned to marry to engage in premarital sex. For more on this, see Lipsett-Rivera, "The Intersection of Rape and Marriage," 559–90.

49. AGN, Inq., vol. 540, exp. 33, fs. 585–94 (Guatemala, 1701).

50. AGN, Inq., vol. 727, exp. (none), fs. 560–75; vol. 727, exp. 26, fs. 576–92.

51. AGN, vol. 644, exp. 2, fs. 196–347.

52. L. Musgrave-Portilla, "The Nahualli or Transforming Wizard in Pre- and Postconquest Mesoamerica," *Journal of Latin American Lore* 8:1 (1982): 3–62; Warren, "Interpreting *La Violencia* in Guatemala"; and Edward E. Calnek, "Highland Chiapas before the Spanish Conquest" (Ph.D. diss., University of Chicago, 1962).

53. Musgrave-Portilla, "The Nahualli," 11.

54. *The Popul Vuh: The Definitive Edition of the Mayan Book of the Dawn of Life and the Glories of Gods and Kings*, trans. Dennis Tedlock (New York: Touchstone, 1985), 212–13.

55. See Fernando Cervantes, *The Devil in the New World: The Impact of Diabolism in New Spain* (New Haven: Yale University Press, 1994); Christian, *Local Religion*; Musgrave-Portilla, "The Nahualli," 21–23; Sabine MacCormack, *Religion in the Andes: Vision and Imagination in Early Colonial Peru* (Princeton: Princeton University Press, 1991); and Mills, *Idolatry and Its Enemies*.

56. María Helena Sánchez Ortega, "Sorcery and Eroticism in Love Magic," in Cruz and Perry, eds., *Culture and Control*, 211.

57. Musgrave-Portilla, "The Nahualli," 4.

58. John Thornton, *Africa and Africans in the Making of the Atlantic World, 1400–1680* (New York: Cambridge University Press, 1992), 239.

59. Carmack, *Rebels of Highland Guatemala*, 43–45. This is Carmack's English translation. The full text can be found in Recinos, *Crónicas indígenas de Guatemala*.

60. *Isagoge histórico apologético general de todas las Indias y especial de la provincia de San Vicente Ferrer de Chiapa y Goatemala* [1700–11] (Guatemala: Tipografía de Tomás Minuesa e los Ríos, 1892).

61. See Cecilia Klein, "Wild Women in Colonial Mexico: An Encounter of European and Aztec Concepts of Other," in Claire Farago, ed., *Reframing the Renaissance: Visual Culture in Europe and Latin America, 1450–1650* (New Haven: Yale University Press, 1995).

62. Warren, "Interpreting *La Violencia* in Guatemala," 45; Ana Erice, "Reconsideración de las creencias Mayas en torno al nahualismo," *Estudios de Cultura Maya* 16 (1985): 255–70; George Foster, "Nahualism in Mexico and Guatemala," *Acta Americana* 2 (1944): 85–103; Benson Saler, *Nagual, brujo, y hechicero en un pueblo quiché* (Guatemala: Ministerio de Educación, 1969); Alfonso Villa Rojas, "Kinship and Nagualism in a Tzeltal Community, Southeastern Mexico," *American Anthropologist* 49 (1947): 578–87; and Richard Wilson, "Machine Guns and Mountain Spirits: The Cultural Effects of State Repression among the Q'eqchi' of Guatemala," *Critique of Anthropology* 11:1 (1991): 33–61.

63. Musgrave-Portilla, "The Nahualli," 46.

64. AGN, Inq., vol. 735/1a. parte, exp. 16, fs. 149–54.

65. AGN, Inq., vol. 831, exp. 2, fs. 214–352 (1730).

66. No surname is listed for Rosa in the documents.

67. I have defined *evangelio* here as a prayer used in exorcisms to drive demons from the body.

68. *Manual para administrar los santos sacramentos, conforme al reformado de Paulo V.P.M.* [1665] (Guatemala, 1756).

69. Ibid.

70. Ibid.

Chapter 4

1. AGCA A1-4929-42045 (Pinula, 1660).

2. Female healers and midwives provided their services to men and women in Santiago de Guatemala for a fee. This did not mean that the women had any university training, nor did they have an official license.

3. See the essays in Davis-Floyd and Sargent, eds., *Childbirth and Authoritative Knowledge*. For more on the intersections of African, indigenous, and European religious and supernatural beliefs in colonial Latin America, see Gonzalo Aguirre Beltrán, *La población negra de México, 1519–1810: Estudio etno-histórico*, 3d ed. (México, D.F.: Fondo Cultura Económica, 1990); Patrick James Carroll, *Blacks in Colonial Veracruz: Race, Ethnicity, and Regional Development* (Austin: University of Texas Press, 1991); Freire Gomes, *Um Herege Vai ao Paraíso*; Mello e Souza, *O Inferno atlântico*; Mott, *Rosa Egipciaca*; Nicolás Ngou-Mve, *El África Bantú en la colonización de México (1595–1650)* (Madrid: Consejo Superior de Investigaciones Científicas, 1994); and "El cimarronaje como forma de expresión del África Bantú en la América colonial: El Ejemplo de Yangá en México," *América Negra* 14 (1997): 27–51; and Colin A. Palmer, *Slaves of the White God: Blacks in Mexico, 1570–1650* (Cambridge, Mass.: Harvard University Press, 1976).

4. This chapter is based in part on my essay "Illness Accusations and the

Cultural Politics of Power in Colonial Santiago de Guatemala, 1650–1750," Harvard University, Working Paper 98-10, International Seminar on the History of the Atlantic World, August 1998. I published a revised version of the essay in "'No es la palabra de Dios': Acusaciones de enfermedad y las políticas culturales de poder en la Guatemala colonial, 1650–1720," *Mesoamérica* 20:38 (December 1999): 33–54.

5. For an analysis of the links between ritual healing and identity politics in contemporary Navajo society and between Navajo society and Euro-American society, see Thomas J. Csordas, "Ritual Healing and the Politics of Identity in Contemporary Navajo Society," *American Ethnologist* 26:1 (1999): 3–23.

6. See Jean Comaroff's argument that healing is an important way to analyze "the structural features of changing contexts and between the symbolic and material dimensions of such change" (p. 638). Jean Comaroff, "Healing and the Cultural Order: The Case of the Barolong boo Ratshidi of Southern Africa," *American Ethnologist* 7:4 (1980): 637–57. See also Harkin, "Contested Bodies."

7. Here I draw on Comaroff, who linked illness and experiences of instability, alienation, and suffering under colonial rule in southern Africa in her essay "Healing and the Cultural Order." Linda Green argued that certain illnesses reflected the effects of the violence of military rule experienced in Maya communities in contemporary Guatemala, characterizing those illnesses as "a moral response, an emotional survival strategy, to the political repression they [the Maya] have experienced and in which they continue to live." Linda Green, "Fear as a Way of Life," *Cultural Anthropology* 9:2 (1994): 227–56.

8. For example, a typhus or pneumonic plague epidemic hit Santiago in 1686 and killed at least one-tenth of the population of the capital, mostly Indians and the poor. In the wake of the epidemic, Santiago's city council asked the Audiencia, the religious orders, and the council itself to contribute to a fund to pay the salary of a doctor from Mexico City. The Audiencia notified local authorities that it contracted the services of a physician named Bartolomé Sánchez Parejo for a salary of 600 pesos per year. See MacLeod, *Spanish Central America*, 99; and Pardo, *Efemérides*, 60.

9. The use of combinations of medical paradigms is common today, even in the United States. For a good introduction to the official practice of medicine in Spain and New Spain, see Guenter B. Risse, "Medicine in New Spain," in Ronald L. Numbers, ed., *Medicine in the New World: New Spain, New France, and New England* (Knoxville: University of Tennessee Press, 1987), 12–63; and John Tate Lanning, *The Royal Protomedicato: The Regulation of the Medical Professions in the Spanish Empire*, ed. John TePaske. (Durham: Duke University Press, 1985). For more on folk healers, see Noemí Quezada, "The Inquisition's Repression of Curanderos," in Perry and Cruz, eds., *Cultural Encounters*, 37–57; and *Enfermedad y maleficio: El curandero en el México colonial* (México, D.F.: UNAM, 1989).

10. For recent work on epidemic disease in colonial Latin America, see W. George Lovell, "Las enfermedades del Viejo Mundo y mortandad amerindia: La viruela y el tabardillo en la sierra de los Cuchumatanes de Guatemala (1780–1810)," *Mesoamérica* 9:16 (1988): 239–85; Noble David Cook and W. George Lovell, eds., *Secret Judgements of God: Old World Disease in Colonial Spanish America* (Norman: University of Oklahoma Press, 1992); and David Cook, *Born to Die: Disease and New World Conquest, 1492–1650* (New York: Cambridge University Press, 1998).

11. Sandra L. Orellana, *Indian Medicine in Highland Guatemala: The Pre-Hispanic and Colonial Periods* (Albuquerque: University of New Mexico Press, 1987), 148.

12. In November 1527, Jorge de Alvarado, brother of the conquistador Pedro de Alvarado, founded the first hospital in colonial Guatemala in Santiago de Almolonga. Construction probably did not begin until 1535, and the hospital opened in 1541. In the same year, a flood and mudslide from a nearby volcano destroyed the city. Julio Roberto Herrera S., "Anotaciones y documentos para la historia de los hospitales de la ciudad de Santiago de los Caballeros de Guatemala," *Anales de la Sociedad de Geografía e Historia* 8:8 (March 1942): 225–72.

13. Ibid., 228, 231. The hospital was originally founded as Nuestra Señora de los Remedios, but in 1559 a royal decree changed the name to the Hospital Real de Santiago.

14. AGI, Guatemala 28 (1683); and AGCA A1-1826-12043 (1693).

15. AGCA A1-7205-314299, "Fundación del hospital de San Lázaro, en la ciudad de Santiago de Guatemala, 23 de enero de 1638," transcribed and published in *Boletín del Archivo General del Gobierno* 10:4 (December 1945): 270–76.

16. Pardo, Zamora Castellanos, and Luján Muñoz, *Guía de Antigua Guatemala*, 191–99. In 1714 Francisco Vásquez noted that the priests of San Juan de Dios, who administered the Hospital de San Alejo for Indians, did not know *la lengua*, which meant that they did not speak or understand any of the Maya languages. The members of the order depended on priests from the monastery of San Francisco to interpret while they treated the sick and heard confessions. Francisco Vásquez, *Crónica de la provincia del Santísimo Nombre de Jesús de Guatemala de la orden de n. seráfico padre San Francisco en el reino de la Nueva España* [ca. 1714], 4 vols., 2d ed. (Guatemala: Sociedad de Geografía e Historia de Guatemala, 1937–44), vol. I, 79.

17. Christopher Lutz noted that in the one-hundred-year period from 1650 to 1750, the time span covered in this study, twenty-four serious epidemics swept the capital, approximately one every four years. See Lutz, *Santiago de Guatemala*, 246–49.

18. Ibid., 247.

19. AGCA A1-1783-11777, Libro de Cabildos 21 (17 January 1687), fs. 192–192v.

20. Sidney David Markman, *Architecture and Urbanization of Colonial Central America: Primary Documentary and Literary Sources* (Tempe: Center for Latin American Studies, Arizona State University, 1993), 1:38.

21. AGCA A1-1783-11777, Libro de Cabildos 22 (21 January 1687), fs. 190v–191.

22. Molina, *Antigua Guatemala*, 44–45.

23. Lutz, *Santiago de Guatemala*, 247; Pardo, *Efemérides*, 118; AGCA A1-1784-11778, Libro de Cabildos 22 (20 April 1694), fs. 290–290v.

24. AGCA A1-1781-11778, Libro de Cabildos 22 (27 April 1694), fs. 292v–293.

25. There is a large body of work that addresses the binary framework of illness causation and explanation in Mesoamerica. See, for example, Azzo Ghidinelli, "El sistema de ideas sobre la enfermedad en Mesoamerica," *Tradiciones de Guatemala* 26 (1986): 69–89. In his ethnographic work among the Ixil Maya in Chajúl, Alfredo Méndez Domínguez (p. 276) found that Chajuleños distinguished between two types of illness, "con contenido," or with supernatural intervention, and "sin

contenido," without supernatural intervention. See his essay, "Illness and Medical Theory Among Guatemalan Indians," in Carl Kendall, John Hawkins, and Laurel Bossen, eds., *Heritage of Conquest Thirty Years Later,* preface by Sol Tax (Albuquerque: University of New Mexico Press, 1983), 267-98.

26. Sheila Cosminsky, "Medical Pluralism in Mesoamerica," in Kendall, Hawkins, and Bossen, eds., *Heritage of Conquest Thirty Years Later,* 160; Linda Schele and Mary Ellen Miller, *The Blood of Kings: Dynasty and Ritual in Maya Art* (New York: Braziller, 1986), 54.

27. *Popul Vuh,* 136 passim.

28. Orellana, *Indian Medicine,* 42-43.

29. Schele and Miller, *The Blood of Kings,* 54.

30. This belief extends to the present day. Munro Edmunson, "The Mayan Faith," in Gary H. Gossen, ed., *South and Meso-American Native Spirituality: From the Cult of the Feathered Serpent to the Theology of Liberation* (New York: Crossroad, 1993), 79.

31. Richard N. Adams and Arthur J. Rubel, "Sickness and Social Relations," in *Handbook of Middle American Indians: Social Anthropology,* vol. 6 (Austin: University of Texas Press, 1967), 333-55.

32. Robert Hill II also noted that the extraction of supernatural items from a sick person's body played a central role in colonial Kaqchikel Maya healing rituals. See his article "Instances of Maya Witchcraft in the Eighteenth-Century Totonicapán Area," *Estudios de Cultura Maya* 17 (1988): 275-76.

33. Edward Geoffrey Parrinder, *Witchcraft: European and African* (London: Faber and Faber, 1963), 141.

34. Thornton, *Africa and Africans,* 243.

35. Alberro, *Inquisición y sociedad,* especially the section "Curanderos y hechiceros," 297-304.

36. Mary C. Karasch, *Slave Life in Rio de Janeiro, 1808-1850* (Princeton: Princeton University Press, 1987), 262-63.

37. See Christian, *Local Religion;* and Mary Elizabeth Perry, "Magdelens and Jezebels in Counter-Reformation Spain," in Cruz and Perry, eds., *Culture and Control.*

38. Perry, "Magdelens and Jezebels," 131.

39. Pedro de San José de Betancurt (1626-67), a lay brother of the Third Order of San Francisco and considered by many to be a saint, was a well-known figure in seventeenth-century Santiago de Guatemala. He dedicated himself to caring for the indigent poor and sick in the capital. For more on his life, see Lobo, *Relación de la vida.*

40. "Ay, Señor, Señor, ya veo que por entrar un tan grande pecador como yo, envías este castigo a esta ciudad." Ibid., 40.

41. Molina, *Antigua Guatemala,* 94. Worms found in sores and wounds were probably fairly common since without disinfectants, it was difficult to keep them clean. Maud Oakes, in a personal account of her experiences as an ethnographer in Todos Santos, Guatemala, described how one day a man came to her house and asked her to cure his father, Lauriano Pablo, who had run a planting stick through his leg three weeks earlier. The son claimed that his father's foot and leg had swollen to "three times their natural size." Oakes went to cure him and reported: "The leg

and foot were very swollen, but not three times their natural size. I syringed out the wound with hot water and a strong disinfectant, and to my horror out came a worm, a white worm. I almost threw up. The old man said: 'Señorita, I told you there was an animal in my leg.'" Maud Oakes, *Beyond the Windy Place: Life in the Guatemalan Highlands* (New York: Farrar, Straus, and Young, 1951), 258.

42. In his *arte*, Fray Delgado described the K'iche' vocabulary and how to learn the language.

43. Molina, *Antigua Guatemala*, 115–16.

44. Christian, *Local Religion*, 101–2.

45. Ibid., 93.

46. Vásquez, *Crónica*, vol. IV, 220.

47. Thomas Gage, *The English-American and His Travail by Sea and Land: or, A New Survey of the West-Indies* (London, 1648), 148; Orellana, *Indian Medicine*, 163; and Stephan F. Borhegyi, "Culto a la imagen del Señor de Esquipulas en Centro América y Nuevo México," *Antropología y Historia de Guatemala* 11:1 (1959): 44–49.

48. Persons involved in healing were often thought to be involved in sorcery as well. See Barbara Ann Kidd, "Maya Curing: An Analysis of Ethnohistorical Sources," *Human Mosaic* 2:2 (1977): 36; Charles Wisdom, "The Supernatural World and Curing," in Tax, *Heritage of Conquest*, 131; and Adams and Rubel, "Sickness and Social Relations," 342.

49. AGN, Inq., vol. 729, exp. 4, fs. 330–43 (1705). Felipa described herself as mestiza. Other witnesses described Felipa as both mestiza and mulata. During her blindness and at the time of her testimony, Felipa worked as a servant in the household of doña Juana de Aragón, and she seems to have worked much of that time as a laundress. Felipa gave her official occupation to Inquisition authorities, however, as *tejedora*, or weaver.

50. "Chocolate" referred to a hot chocolate beverage common in colonial Guatemala.

51. A *mantilla* is a type of women's veil; the color black suggests a mourning veil.

52. AGN, Inq., vol. 706, exp. 11, fs. 81–89 (1698). Petrona Mungía, also known as Petrona de Andujar, was also described in the documents as *india prieta* (Black Indian). She was married to a carpenter and lived in the barrio of Santo Domingo.

53. Tobacco had an important ritual role in preconquest Maya cultures. See Edmunson, "The Mayan Faith," 79. Fuentes y Guzmán noted that tobacco continued to have important uses in religious rituals and as an intoxicant in postconquest Mayan society. Francisco Antonio de Fuentes y Guzmán, *Historia de Guatemala ó Recordación Florida* [17th century] (Madrid: L. Navarro, 1882–83), vol. II, 281.

54. AGN, Inq., vol. 695, exp. 78, fs. 330–490 (17 October 1695). No surname is listed for Agustina.

55. Agustina was a servant of don José Montalvo. As a slave, Agustina seems to have had a fair amount of freedom to move about the city and conduct a personal life outside the control of her employer, in whose house she lived.

56. The wording here is vague and uses the phrase "they brought over some chocolate." From the context, however, doña Catarina appears to refer to Agustina

and Chana de don Jorge. No further details are given about Chana de don Jorge in the denunciation.

57. AGN, Inq., vol. 644, exp. 2, fs. 196–347 (28 September 1695).

58. "hallandose atarantada."

59. It is not clear from the testimony why Felipa found it necessary to do the washing in Ciudad Vieja and not in Santiago de Guatemala.

60. It appears that the woman who approached Felipa while she washed clothes was María García (who was later named in Felipa's testimony), but this is ambiguous in the various accounts.

61. Felipa's identification of the second woman is ambiguous at this point in her testimony.

62. Maud Oakes also noted the role of reputation in the practices of successful healers and midwives. According to Oakes, shamans in the Mam community were also healers, and some were brujos as well. Some shamans had a reputation for being more powerful than others, and if a person did not get well, he or she would consult another shaman. Oakes stated that everyone "knows" who the successful healers are in the area. Oakes, *Beyond the Windy Place*. Reputation also played a role in contemporary *finca* (plantation) medical practices in Guatemala. See Julia González Alonso y Jude Pansini, "El cuidado médico propio y los trabajadores de las fincas de Guatemala," *Mesoamérica* 32 (December 1996): 315–38.

63. I have not been able to locate a pueblo named Santa Lucia between Ciudad Vieja and Santiago. It is possible that Felipa referred to the Hermita de Santa Lucia in the southwest corner of the city whose name was, at times, associated with the barrio of Espíritu Santo. Christopher H. Lutz, personal communication, 1997.

64. Gloria Fraser Giffords, *Mexican Folk Retablos*, rev. ed. (Albuquerque: University of New Mexico Press, 1992), 118; McBrien, gen. ed., *Encyclopedia of Catholicism*, 798.

65. Though blood and the symbolism of blood played central roles in Catholic and Mesoamerican ritual life, it is rarely explicitly mentioned in supernatural illness accounts in colonial Guatemala. This is in contrast to Behar's findings of the central importance of blood in women's sorcery activities, especially in sexual witchcraft in late-colonial Mexico.

66. Lois Paul and Benjamin D. Paul noted that dreams or visions of women in white represented supernatural teachers of midwifery. Paul and Paul, "The Maya Midwife as Sacred Specialist," 712.

67. It is unclear exactly which herb or plant *tesumpate* referred to.

68. Sandra Orellana noted that women used a number of plants to induce abortions in colonial Guatemala. She states that in Cobán, leaves of Mexican giant thyssop were cooked with other plants and made into a drink; in Chajul, Ibannatto was cooked with five glasses of water and taken three times a day for five days; and in San Martín Sacatepéquez, branches of Southern maidenhair fern were cooked into a beverage and consumed at breakfast for nine days. Orellana, *Indian Medicine in Highland Guatemala*, 136.

69. AGN, Inq., vol. 695, exp. 78, fs. 330–490 (1695).

70. *Chile de chocolate* refers to a kind of chile pepper. Christa Little-Siebold and Todd Little-Siebold, personal communication, 1999.

71. No surname is listed for Mapola.

72. "La qual se movia sola."

73. AGN, Inq., vol. 695, exp. 78, fs. 330–490 (1695). There are scattered references to Antonio Álvarez and his activities by Inquisition authorities. See AGN, Inq., vol. 697, exp. 17, 204–15 (1695); and AGN, Inq., vol. 644, exp. 2, fs. 96–347 (1682).

74. AGN, Inq., vol. 692, exp. 4, fs. 329–66 (1694). The Guatemalan Inquisition began its investigation of Antonio de Larios in February 1694 and carried out a first round of questioning. Antonio died in June 1696, however, before the Inquisition could question him. Other descriptions of Antonio de Larios can be found in a number of legajos from the mid-1690s. See AGN, Inq., vol. 695, exp. 78, fs. 330–490 (1695); and AGN, Inq., vol. 697, exp. 17, fs. 204–15 (1695).

75. The word *chuntal,* and also the word *chumpipe,* refers to a type of turkey found in the Guatemalan highlands.

76. AGN, Inq., vol. 644, exp. 2, 196–347 (16 September 1693).

77. Adams and Rubel, "Sickness and Social Relations," 334–35.

78. Orellana, *Indian Medicine in Highland Guatemala,* 74–75; and George Simeon, *Illness and Curing in a Guatemalan Village: A Study in Ethnomedicine* (Honolulu: University of Hawaii Press, 1977).

79. More work needs to be done to see if this hypothesis bears out.

80. Today, Chinautla is located just north of Guatemala City.

81. AGCA A1-4060-3160 (1687). The Arrevillaga family was very wealthy and influential in this period and owned large sugar estates near Lake Amatitlán. Christopher H. Lutz, personal communication, 1997.

82. Given Padre Tomás's likely connection with the Arrevillaga family and their landholdings located near San Juan Amatitlán, he might have had a special interest in or knowledge of the sorcery activities described here.

83. ". . . que le fue tentado todo su cuerpo."

84. AGN, Inq., vol. 497, exp. (none), fs. 203–7 (1694). No surname is listed for Pasquala in the record.

85. Victorina de San Joseph was a member of a lay Franciscan order called Third Order of San Francisco.

86. Santa Isabel was a contiguous barrio on the southeastern edge of Santiago. Christopher H. Lutz, personal communication, 1997.

87. Archivo Histórico Arquidiocesano "Francisco de Paula García Peláez," A4-67 Inquisición (T1, 25).

88. While the documents describe the pueblo as San Juan Milpas Dueñas, it was known as San Miguel Milpas Dueñas, so I have changed the name of the town in the text. The pueblo was a mainly Kaqchikel-speaking town. Christopher H. Lutz, personal communication, 1999.

89. Note that both Magdalena Mendez and Joaquín Sánchez were Kaqchikel speakers and legally defined as Indians and so could not be prosecuted by the Inquisition.

90. The Indian justices who gave their testimonies in the case include don Antonio Felipe, gobernador of the district of Almolonga; Alejo Paredes, regidor of Tequantepeque and principal; Pablo Hernández, alcalde of San Miguel Milpas Dueñas; Mathias Hernández, principal and tributary Indian of San Miguel Mil-

pas Dueñas; and Pedro Hernández and Tomás Hernández, both tributary Indians from San Miguel Milpas Dueñas.

91. Magdalena did not know her age, however, and officials did not offer a guess. Santiago Zamora is a very small town between Dueñas, San Antonio Aguas Calientes, and Santa Catarina Barahona.

92. The details of this "ill-will" are not described in the documents, though it is suggestive of previous intracommunity conflicts.

93. Kidd, "Maya Curing," 40.

94. Paul and Paul, "The Maya Midwife as Sacred Professional," 707.

95. Sheila Cosminsky, "Childbirth and Change: A Guatemalan Study," in Carol P. MacCormack, ed., *Ethnography of Fertility and Birth* (London: Academic Press, 1982), 197–98. Paul and Paul, "The Maya Midwife as Sacred Professional," 707, note that in contemporary Tz'utujil society, a midwife-to-be is born with a "white mantle," a piece of the amniotic membrane, over her head.

96. Paul and Paul noted that in the Tz'utujil Maya community of San Pedro La Laguna inhabitants equated pregnancy with illness "because pregnancy was regarded as hazardous for mother and child." See "The Maya Midwife as Sacred Professional," 707.

97. AGN, Inq., vol. 830, exp. 7, fs. 100–28 (1729). Doña María Cecilia was probably an elite Spanish woman, given the honorific attached to her name and that her husband was a colonial official.

98. "La sangre que hecho del parto la Paniagua era lodo o como lodo de laguna."

99. Fuentes y Guzmán, *Historia de Guatemala ó Recordación Florida*, vol. 2, p. 978: "De un singular y admirable monstruo que nació de una india, natural y vecina del pueblo de Santo Domingo Sinacao." Today the town is called Santo Domingo Xenacoj.

100. Wisdom, "The Supernatural World and Curing," 128.

101. Parrinder, *Witchcraft*, 146.

102. AGCA A1-4929-42045 (Pinula, 1660). Marta de Figueroa was married to Pedro Luis, a former regidor of Pinula.

103. Andrés Yos is also called Andrés Maeda and Andrés González in the documents. Andrés's wife, Juana Candelera, was the sister of Juan Luis, Marta de la Figueroa's husband.

104. "Pisote la tierra y entra en el cuerpo, de aquella india para que la llebe el diablo."

105. The pregnant woman reportedly yelled, "Por amor de Dios saca esta mal que está en mi cuerpo porque no es palabra de Dios de este mal que me esta matando." Marta reportedly replied, "Estás borracha, no me digas que soy yo hechicera."

106. It is not clear from the testimony what this means. Perhaps Marta came to Catalina in her dreams and tried to smother her. Three other afflicted persons also reported seeing Marta at night and feeling as if she wanted to smother them.

107. Beliefs among the Ibo of Nigeria also reveal connections between insect bites and witchcraft, that witches "can turn into the smallest insect and so enter tightly closed houses and bite men as flies do at night." Parrinder, *Witchcraft*, 145–46.

108. Matias testified: "empeso a meter el dedo en mi culo alli empeso mi mal parece chile parece ormigas y duele en mi cuerpo ni beber ni comer ni dormir desde cuando me metio en el temescal y me metio su dedo en mi culo hasta que siempre esta sobre mi cuerpo cuando voy a dormir." Matias also apparently suffered from a cold sickness (frío).

109. Kevin P. Groak, "To Warm the Blood, to Warm the Flesh: The Role of the Steambath in Highland Maya (Tzeltal-Tzotzil) Ethnomedicine," *Journal of Latin American Lore* 20:1 (1997): 3-96.

Chapter 5

1. AGN, Inq., vol. 644, exp. 2, fs. 196-347 (13 March 1693).

2. Lutz analyzes the extralegal economy in the colonial period in *Santiago de Guatemala.*

3. Here I draw on the work of Sally Scully who analyzed witches as workers and characterized witchcraft as an employment option. See her article "Marriage or a Career? Witchcraft as an Alternative in Seventeenth-Century Venice," *Journal of Social History* 28:4 (summer 1995): 857-76.

4. AGN, Inq., vol. 830, exp. 7, fs. 100-28 (1729).

5. AGN, Inq., vol. 727, exp. (none), fs. 560-75 (1704); and vol. 727, exp. 26, fs. 576-92 (1704).

6. AGN, Inq., vol. 706, exp. 11, fs. 81-89 (1698).

7. Inquisition authorities did not record Pasquala's last name. AGN, Inq., vol. 497, exp. (none); fs. 203-7 (1694).

8. AGN, Inq., vol. 729, exp. 4, fs. 330-43 (1705).

9. AGN, Inq., vol. 531, exp. 50, fs. 327-43 (20 April 1698).

10. AGCA A1-2218-159.10: Prices listed in a 1674 inspection of Santiago's officially licensed shops.

11. AGN, Inq., vol. 644, exp. 2, fs. 196-347 (9 April 1682).

12. AGN, Inq., vol. 695, exp. 78, fs. 330-490 (1 October 1695). In this instance, Petrona worked with a male partner to carry out the sorcery.

13. AGN, Inq., vol. 706, exp. 11, fs. 81-89 (10 March 1698).

14. Alan Macfarlane and Keith Thomas argue that witchcraft prosecutions in Europe were connected to the decline of community responsibility for poor relief, especially the denial of poor relief to women. See Alan MacFarlane, *Witchcraft in Tudor and Stuart England: A Regional and Comparative Study* (New York: Harper & Row, 1970); and Keith Thomas, *Religion and the Decline of Magic* (New York: Scribner, 1971).

15. AGN, Inq., vol. 644, exp. 2, fs. 196-346 (17 September 1696).

16. For an analysis of the belongings that women brought with them from Spain and their cultural and social meanings in early colonial Mexico, see Amanda Angel, "Spanish Women in the New World: The Transmission of a Model Polity to New Spain, 1521-1570" (Ph.D. diss., University of California, Davis, 1997).

17. AGN, Inq., vol. 644, exp. 2, fs. 196-347 (2 October 1695 and 15 November 1695).

18. Héctor Humberto Samayoa Guevara, *Los gremios de artesanos en la Ciudad de Guatemala (1524-1821)* (Guatemala: Editorial Universitaria, 1962), 125-40.

19. I gathered the percentages of official licensed female shop owners in Santiago from selected *visitas* (inspections) by government officials. See AGCA A1-2217-15.903 (1632); A1-2217-15.905 (September 1650); A1-2218-15.910 (April 1681).

20. AGN, Inq., vol. 644, exp. 2, fs. 196–347 (28 September 1695).

21. AGN, Inq., vol. 727, exp. (none), fs. 508–13 (19 February 1704).

22. AGN, Inq., vol. 449, exp. 3, fs. 12–21 (19 February 1693).

23. Here I build on Mary Elizabeth Perry's outline of the possibility of historians uncovering "a female network" in which women helped each other by exchanging services and goods. Mary Elizabeth Perry, *Gender and Disorder in Early Modern Seville* (Princeton: Princeton University Press, 1990), esp. chap. 1.

24. AGN, Inq., vol. 706, exp. 11, fs. 81–89 (10 March 1698). In his testimony, Fray Domingo was unable to remember the name of the dying woman. Using evidence from the case, it seems she was Nicolasa de Avedaño, who appeared in a number of Inquisition testimonies from the 1690s.

25. AGN, Inq., vol. 497, exp. (none), fs. 313–20 (1695).

26. AGN, Inq., vol. 830, exp. 7, fs. 100–28 (1729).

27. AGN, Inq., vol. 644, exp. 2, fs. 196–347 (12 April 1682).

28. AGN, Inq., vol. 727, exp. (none), fs. 508–13 (9 April 1715).

29. AGN, Inq., vol. 644, exp. 2, fs. 196–347 (29 August 1695). Fernando Cervantes lists a number of cases in which men sought the assistance of the devil to procure wealth, physical prowess, and women. See his work *The Devil in the New World*, 77–97.

30. AGN, Inq., vol. 497, exp. (none), fs. 297–303 (1694). I have not been able to identify the herb zintuli.

31. AGN, Inq., vol. 644, exp. 2, fs. 196–347 (16 September 1693).

32. Perry, *Gender and Disorder in Early Modern Seville*, 14–32.

33. I use the long and richly detailed Inquisition case against Gerónima de Barahona that spanned a twenty-year period from the 1680s and 1690s, until her arrest and imprisonment in a city hospital, to trace her use of social networks.

34. AGN, Inq., vol. 644, exp. 78, fs. 330–490 (1695). I discuss the lives of both these women in some detail in chapter 2.

35. AGN, Inq., vol. 695, exp. 78, fs. 330–490 (17 September 1695).

36. AGN, Inq., vol. 695, exp. 78, fs. 330–490 (16 September 1695).

37. AGN, Inq., vol. 727, exp. 12, fs. 406–24 (19 February 1715). María Lucrecia de Utillo, a thirty-six-year-old mestiza doncella, commented in 1715, "Gerónima the meat seller who had a great reputation as a sorcerer," indicating that Gerónima's reputation survived years after her death.

38. Paul, "The Mastery of Work and the Mystery of Sex in a Guatemalan Village," 283.

39. Stern has also examined women's construction of social networks and alliance making in their efforts to control the misbehaving or abusive men in their lives. Stern, *The Secret History of Gender.*

40. Men's and women's use of the court system in colonial Latin America varied regionally. Susan Socolow, in an analysis of women and crime in late-colonial Buenos Aires, argued that elite and middle-class men and women were least likely to use the court system to find redress for sexual crimes against women

because it signaled the male's inability to protect the women under his care. See her essay "Women and Crime: Buenos Aires, 1757–97," in Lyman L. Johnson, ed., *The Problem of Order in Changing Societies: Essays on Crime and Policing in Argentina and Uruguay* (Albuquerque: University of New Mexico Press, 1990).

41. AGN, Inq., vol. 644, exp. 2, fs. 196–347.

42. AGN, Inq., vol. 695, exp. 78, fs. 330–490.

43. See especially Cope, *The Limits of Racial Domination*.

44. AGN, Inq., vol. 644, exp. 2, fs. 196–347 (19 February 1693).

45. Ibid.

46. AGN, Inq., vol. 644, exp. 2, fs. 196–347 (25 March 1687), letter from Nicolás Resigno de Cabrera, head of Guatemala's Inquisition, to the Mexican Office of the Inquisition.

47. AGN, Inq., vol. 695, exp. 78, fs. 330–490 (11 October 1695).

48. AGN, Inq., vol. 540, exp. 22, fs. 226–70.

49. AGN, Inq., vol. 644, exp. 2, fs. 196–347 (29 September 1695).

50. AGN, Inq., vol. 817, exp. 34, fs. 565–71 (1727).

51. I have not been able to determine the meaning of the word *zihuamonte*.

52. Doña Lorenza's ethnicity was not listed in the documents, though the head of Guatemala's Inquisition described her in a letter in the following manner: "This woman is one of the most noble women of this city." AGN, Inq., vol. 609, exp. 4, fs. 335–69 (1668). Dionisia gives her mistress's name as María de Castellanos, while María, in her own testimony before Inquisition authorities, lists it as María Monte Ramírez.

53. For more on servants stealing clothing from their employers and then pawning it, see Marie François, "When Pawnshops Talk: Popular Credit and Material Culture in Mexico City, 1775–1916" (Ph.D. diss., University of Arizona, 1998).

54. Gruzinski, *Man-Gods in the Mexican Highlands*, 12. John Beard Haviland also saw women as primary vehicles for the spread of rumor and wrote: "Women, on routine errands were the vehicles of this talk. Gathering firewood, tending sheep, carrying boiled corn to the mill to be ground into tortilla dough, women set aside time to exchange news with their friends and cousins." See *Gossip, Reputation, and Knowledge in Zinacantán* (Chicago: University of Chicago Press, 1977), 27. For an alternative analysis of indigenous women's community authority and power under colonial rule, see Ruth Behar, "The Visions of a Guachichil Witch in 1599: A Window on the Subjugation of Mexico's Hunter-Gatherers," *Ethnohistory* 34:2 (spring 1987): 115–38.

55. Secular authorities also charged Gerónima de Barahona with various crimes that are alluded to in the Inquisition documents, but I have not been able to locate these.

56. AGN, Inq., vol. 644, exp. 2, fs. 196–347.

57. AGN, Inq., vol. 644, exp. 2, fs. 196–347 (9 March 1682).

58. AGN, Inq., vol. 727, exp. (none), fs. 560–75 (1704).

59. AGN, Inq., vol. 497, exp. (none), fs. 313–20 (1694).

60. AGN, Inq., vol. 680, exp. 1, fs. 1–16 (1690).

61. AGN, Inq., 644, exp. 2, fs. 196–347 (28 September 1695).

62. AGN, Inq., vol. 727, exp. 26, fs. 560–75 (1704).

63. AGN, Inq., vol. 609, exp. 4, fs. 335–69 (1694).

64. AGN, Inq. vol. 695, exp. 78, fs. 330–490 (19 February 1693).

65. AGN, Inq., vol. 644, exp. 2, fs. 196–347 (1695).

66. Ibid.

67. AGN, Inq., vol. 609, exp. 4, fs. 335–69 (1694). I have published an earlier analysis of this case in a section of "Women, Religion, and Power: Gender and Resistance in Daily Life in Late-Seventeenth-Century Santiago de Guatemala," *Ethnohistory* 42:4 (fall 1995): 627–37. In the article I gave credit to Sebastián de Arroyo for writing the letter denouncing Sebastiana de la Cruz and her son; in fact, José Delgado, parish priest, wrote the initial letter. Neither Sebastiana de la Cruz nor Bartolomé Catalán were questioned, and after the initial two rounds of questioning that took place over a period of a year and a half, it is unclear from the documents how the Inquisition resolved the case. Mario Humberto Ruz has also written about this case in his essay "Sebastiana de la Cruz, alias 'la Polilla,'" 55–66.

68. It is unclear from the documentation whether Bartolomé practiced miracles in Santiago, though apparently the cult activities lasted for a few years before the local priest intervened. In any case, colonial authorities did not pick up on the illegal cult until he and his mother traveled back to Amatitlán.

69. Christopher H. Lutz, personal communication, July 1997.

70. AGI, Guatemala 77 (1675), "Hearings on the news that many Spanish and castas have moved to Petapa and San Juan Amatitlán."

71. AGI, Guatemala 26 (16 May 1678): "Letter from Guatemala to the King of Spain."

Chapter 6

1. For more on how the integration of women, especially Indian women, has reshaped historical studies of colonial Latin America, see Stephanie Wood and Robert Haskett, "Concluding Remarks," in Schroeder, Wood, and Haskett, eds., *Indian Women of Early Mexico*, 313–14; and Silverblatt, "Interpreting Women in States," in di Leonardo, ed., *Gender at the Crossroads of Knowledge*, 140–71.

2. Silverblatt, *Moon, Sun, and Witches*; and Clendinnen, "Yucatec Maya Women."

3. Stern, *The Secret History of Gender.*

4. Ibid., ix, 4.

5. Lutz, *Santiago de Guatemala.*

6. AGN, Inq., vol. 497, exp. (none), fs. 313–20 (14 March 1695/11 April 1695)

7. Behar, "Sexual Witchcraft."

Glossary

alcalde: mayor; the chief barrio official.
alcalde ordinario: city council member.
alguacil: constable.
alguacil mayor: chief constable.
asiento: contract for importing African slaves.
atarantada: dazed.
atole: indigenous-style corn drink.
auto: judicial decree.
ayuntamiento: town council.
barbas de chuntal: turkey wattles.
barrio: neighborhood; political jurisdiction within a city.
beata: lay holy woman.
bozal: slave recently arrived from Africa.
bruja, brujo: witch.
brujo-nahual: shape-changer.
cabildo: town or city council; see *ayuntamiento.*
capellán: priest of the city council.
cartas de instrucción: letters of instruction.
casa de recogidas: literally, "house of enclosed women," which could have a variety of functions including an orphanage, a school for young girls, and a place to effectively imprison women accused of various acts of social and religious deviance.
casta: mixed-race person.
chocolate: in colonial Guatemala, a hot beverage made with ground cacao beans mixed with water and/or ground corn and spiced with chile peppers, cinnamon, or vanilla. A very popular drink consumed by all sectors of Santiago society by the seventeenth century.
chumpipe: turkey; also *chuntal.*
cimarrón: escaped slave.
cofradías: religious sodalities.

comadre: expressed a ritual kinship between mother and godmother.
comisario: commissioner; head of Guatemala's Inquisition.
congregación: nucleated town.
conversos: baptized Jews and their descendants.
copal: type of incense; associated with ritual cleansing in indigenous practices.
corral: interior patio of a house.
curandera/curandero: healer.
curandero sangrador: healer-bleeder.
damas de sociedad: elite women.
daño: witchcraft; curse.
demonio: demon.
desenojar al hombre: to free a man of anger.
diabólica: diabolical.
doncella: maiden; virgin.
encomendero: encomienda holder.
encomienda: colonial institution in which the Spanish crown rewarded Spaniards with the rights to tribute and labor from Indian towns.
escote: low-cut dress.
escribano público: public scribe.
español: person of Spanish descent.
extramuros: literally, "outside the walls"; referred to Indian barrios.
fiesta: community celebration.
figurita: small religious figure.
fiscal: Audiencia official.
gallo de la tierra: turkey.
gente ladina: mixed-race people.
gente ordinaria: ecclesiastical term, used especially in parish registers, to differentiate Blacks, castas, and indios naboríos from tributary Indians and Spaniards.
gremio: guild.
hacer milagros: to perform miracles.
hechicera, hechicero: sorcerer.
hechicera-bruja: female sorcerer-witch.
hechizar: to bewitch, to cast a spell on.
hechizo: spell, charm, magic, sorcery.
hechizo antiguo: old spell.
huipil: traditional embroidered blouse worn by indigenous women.
india, indio: Indian; referred to indigenous men and women in colonial society. Can be considered a derogatory term.
indio ladino: hispanicized Indian.
indio natural: tributary Indian.
indio puro: "pure" Indian.
indios naboríos: hereditary Indian servants who worked for Spaniards in colonial cities.
jícara: gourd cup.
juez eclesiástico: ecclesiastical judge.
juicio: legal judgment.
justicia: justice official.

justicia real: secular royal justice.
lanceta: lance used in bloodletting.
legajo: file.
llaga: open sore.
locura: insanity.
maestra/maestro: master.
maestro nahualista: shape-changer.
mal aire: evil air.
mal crédito: evil reputation.
maleficio: spell; curse.
mal opinionado: not well thought of.
mestiza, mestizo: person of mixed Spanish and Indian descent.
mestizaje: race mixture.
ministro: calling.
mujeres de mal vivir: women who live evil lives.
mujersilla: worthless woman; strumpet, tart.
mulata, mulato: in colonial Central America, a person of mixed African, Spanish, and/or Indian descent.
mulata blanca: light-skinned mulata.
mulata prieta: Black mulata.
muñeco: doll.
negra, negro: person of African descent.
nuevo español: new Spaniard.
oidor: judge of the Audiencia.
panadera: baker.
partera: midwife.
partes bajas: literally, "lower parts"; genitals.
partes naturales: literally, "natural parts"; genitals.
patrón: patron.
patronato royal: royal patronage; an agreement made between Rome and the Spanish monarchy that confirmed the Spanish crown's authority over the church in the Americas.
perturbación: confusion, disquiet (of mind).
peste: plague.
plaza mayor: central plaza.
principal: town elder.
procesión de sangre: procession of blood.
proceso: legal proceeding; lawsuit.
protomédico: director of the Protomedicato, an institution that regulated medicine through examinations, licensing, and the courts.
pública voz y fama: public knowledge and reputation.
rabia: rabies.
real cédula: royal directive.
regidor: alderman.
reliquias: religious relics.
remedio: cure; remedy.
remedio espiritual: spiritual remedy.

repartimiento de indios: form of poorly paid forced labor imposed on tributary Indians in towns around Santiago; especially used to grow and harvest wheat for Spanish farmers and for certain urban labor, such as bread making and construction.

revendedoras: resellers of beef.

ronda: urban patrol.

ronrón: type of beetle.

sacate: hay; fodder.

sahumario: ritual incensing, often with rosemary or copal, to heal the sick, repel evil, or protect a person, home, or business.

santo oleo: holy oil, used for anointing the sick.

sapo: toad.

servicio del tostón: tribute in the form of an annual tax, equal to four reales or one-half peso.

servicio personal: part of early tribute obligation before the López de Cerrato reforms; forced tributary labor.

sirena: siren.

soltera: spinster.

sopa dorada: golden soup.

tameme: Indian bearer.

temescal: indigenous-style steambath.

tinajuela: earthenware container or jug.

título: native-language land documents; contained historical information.

tortillera: tortilla maker.

vagabundo: vagrant.

zopilote: turkey vulture.

Bibliography

Archives and Research Libraries

Archivo General de Centroamérica (AGCA), Guatemala City, Guatemala.
Archivo General de Indias (AGI), Seville, Spain.
Archivo General de la Nación (AGN), Mexico City, Mexico.
Archivo Histórico Arquidiocesano "Francisco de Paula García Peláez" (AHA),
   Guatemala City, Guatemala.
The John Carter Brown Library, Providence, Rhode Island.
The Newberry Library, Chicago, Illinois.

Published Primary Sources

Alvarado, Pedro de. *An Account of the Conquest of Guatemala in 1524.* Ed. Sedley J.
   Mackie. Boston: Longwood Press, 1978.
Álvarez de Toledo, Juan Bautista. *Sermon de la Dominica Sexagisima en la elección que
   hizo de ministro provincial la Santa Provicia del Santísimo Nombre de Jesús.* Guate-
   mala, 1694.
Boletín del Archivo General de Gobierno (Guatemala, Guatemala).
Boletín del Archivo Histórico Arquidiocesano "Francisco de Paula Garcia Peláez."
Compendio de la vida y muerte de San Juan Nepomuceno. Guatemala, 1767.
Cortés y Larraz, Pedro. *Por la gracia de Dios y la Santa Sede Apostólica Arzobispo de
   Guatemala.* Guatemala, 177-.
———. *El maestro de sagradas ceremonias de la Santa Metropolitana Iglesia de esta ciudad
   de Guatemala.* Guatemala, 1772.
———. *Instrucción pastoral sobre el methodo práctico.* Guatemala, 1773.
Cadena, Felipe. *Breve descripción de la noble ciudad de Santiago de los Caballeros de Guate-
   mala, y puntual noticia de su lamentable ruina ocasionada de un violento terremoto el día
   veinte-nueve de julio de 1773.* Guatemala: Impresa de Luna, 1858.
Devoción al Glorioso Patriarca Señor San Joseph. Guatemala, 1766.

Devoción para el día dies y nueve de cada mes a honra y gloria del Patriarca Señor San Joseph. Guatemala, 1768.

Díaz del Castillo, Bernal. *Historia verdadera de la conquista de la Nueva España. Monumenta Hispano-Indiana V Centenario del Descubrimiento de América 1.* Madrid: Instituto Gonzalo Fernández de Oviedo, 1982.

Fernández de la Caveda, Pedro. *Año sanctificado con la memoria de la passión de Christo Nuestro Redemptor.* Guatemala, 1716.

Figueredo y Victoria, Francisco Joseph de. *Carta pastoral exortatoria a penetencia . . . a la ciudad de Guatemala . . . con ocasion del terremoto . . . el dia 1 de noviembre . . . de 1755.* Guatemala, 1756.

———. *A nuestro muy ylustro venerable capítulo de esta nuestra Santa Yglesia Metropolitana.* Guatemala, 1759.

Fuentes y Guzmán, Francisco Antonio. *Historia de Guatemala o Recordación Flórida* [17th century]. Madrid: L. Navarro, 1882–83.

Gage, Thomas. *The English American and His Travail by Sea and Land; or, A New Survey of the West-Indies.* London, 1648.

García Peláez, Francisco de Paula. *Memorias para la historia del antiguo reyno de Guatemala.* 3d ed. 3 vols. Guatemala: Tipografía Nacional, 1968–73.

González Batres, Juan Joseph. *El triumpho de la sabiduria por debaxo de la sermón panegyrico.* Guatemala, 1758.

Herrera S., Julio Roberto. "Anotaciones y documentos para la historia de los hospitales de la ciudad de Santiago de los Caballeros de Guatemala." *Anales de la Sociedad de Geografía e Historia* 8:8 (marzo 1942): 225–72.

Hispanarium Ad Pias Serenissima Regis Catholici. Guatemala, 1729.

Isagoge histórico apologético general de todas las Indias y especial de la provincia de San Vicente Ferrer de Chiapa y Goatemala [1700–11]. Guatemala: Tipografía de Tomás Minuesa e Los Ríos, 1892.

Iturriga, Manuel Mariano de. *El dolor rey. Sentimiento de N. Catholico Monarch el Señor D[on] Fernando VI.* Guatemala, 1759.

Jesús, Brother Lucas de. *Novena al Glorioso Principe, Sagrado Archangel San Raphael.* Guatemala, 1775.

Juarros, Domingo. *Compendio de la historia del Reino de Guatemala, 1500-1800.* Guatemala: Editorial Piedra Santa, [18—?] 1981.

Lascano, Francisco Xavier. *Indice practico moral, para los sacerdotes que auxilian moribundos.* Guatemala, 1754.

Leal, Raimundo. *Guatemalensis ecclesiæ monumenta.* Madrid, 1744.

Lobo, Manuel. *Relación de la vida y virtudes del V. hermano Pedro de San Joseph de Betancur.* Guatemala, 1677.

The Malleus Maleficarum of Heinrich Kramer and James Sprenger. Trans. Montague Summers. New York: Dover, 1971.

Manual para administrar los santos sacramentos conforme al reformado de Paulo V. P. M. mandado sacar. Guatemala, [1665] 1756.

A mayor gloria de Dios novena al Gran Patriarca San Bruno. Guatemala, 1744.

Memorial de Sololá, Anales de los Cakchiqueles, y Título de los Señores de Totonicapán. 2d ed. Trans. Adrián Recinos. Guatemala: Editorial Piedra Santa, 1991.

Modo de hacer los actos de fee, esperanza, y charidad. Guatemala, 1767.

Molina, Antonio de. *Antigua Guatemala: Memorias del M. R. P. Maestro Fray Antonio de*

Molina continuadaσ y marginadaσ por Fray Aguσtín Cano y Fray Franciσco Ximénez, de la orden de Santo Domingo. Transcribed by Jorge del Valle Matheu. Guatemala: Unión Tipográfica, 1943.

Novena a la Seraphica Virgen Santa Catharina de Siena. Guatemala, 1716.

Novena de la Madre Santíσσima de la Luz. Guatemala, 1754.

Novena del Glorioσo doctor de la Ygleσia San Gerónimo. Guatemala, 1746.

Novena prepatoria a la feσtividad del Patrocino de María Santíσσima. Guatemala, 1744.

Novena prepatoria a la feσtividad de la Epiphania en obσequia de loσ Santoσ Reyeσ Magoσ. Guatemala, 1773.

Novena σagrada de el principe de loσ angeleσ wl Señor San Miguel. Guatemala, 1775.

Novenaσ. Hoσpedage amoroσo, que hazen loσ corazoneσ devotoσ a loσ treσ Santíσσimoσ peregrinoσ Jeσúσ, María y Joσeph. Guatemala, 1720.

Patricio, Basilio. *Septema de Eσpíritu Santo, que para alentar la devoción de loσ fieleσ.* Guatemala, 1755.

Philip V El Rey, preσidente, y oidoreσ de mi audiencia real que reσide en la ciudad de Santiago de Guatemala. Guatemala(?), 1711.

Popul Vuh: The Definitive Edition of the Mayan Book of the Dawn of Life and the Glorieσ of Godσ and Kingσ. Trans. Dennis Tedlock. New York: Touchstone, 1985.

Rammillete de mirra electa para laσ Almaσ Devotaσ. Guatemala, 1754.

Recinos, Adrián. *Crónicaσ indígenaσ de Guatemala.* Guatemala: Editorial Universitaria, 1957.

Remesal, Fray Antonio. *Hiσtoria General de laσ Indiaσ Occidentaleσ y particular la gobernación de Chiapa y Guatemala.* Madrid: Francisco de Abarcay Angulo, 1820.

Rivera y Villalón, Pedro de. *Diario y derrotero de lo caminado, viσto, y oσervado en el diσcurσo de la viσita general de precidioσ, σituadoσ en laσ Provinciaσ Ynternaσ de Nueva Eσpaña.* Guatemala, 1736.

Rodríguez, Juan. *Relación del eσpantable terremoto que agora nueuamente ha aconteσido en laσ Yndiaσ en vna ciudad llamada Guatimala.* [Valladolid? Mexico? 1542?]. Boston: Massachusetts Historical Society, 1940.

Septenario y ofrecimiento a la Precioσiσσima σangre de Chriσto Señor Nueσtro. Guatemala, 1762.

Sunzin de Herrera, Francisco. *Conσulta práctica-moral, en que σe pregunta σi loσ fetoσ abortiboσ.* Guatemala, 1756.

Teotamacholozti inyiulilz auk yni . . . o σea tratado de la vida y muerte de Nueσtro Señor Jeσu Chriσto en lengua vulgar Mexicana de Guatemala. Guatemala, 16—.

Til, Jos[eph]. *Silencioσ gemidoσ σangrientoσ lantoσ cordialiσσimoσ . . . que en laσ realeσ exequiaσ de la auguσtiσσima reina catolica, nueσtra S[eño]ra D[oña] María Amalia de Saxonia.* Guatemala, 1761.

Vásquez, Francisco. *Crónica de la provincia del Santíσσimo Nombre de Jeσúσ de Guatemala de la orden de n. σeráfico padre San Franciσco en el reino de la Nueva Eσpaña* [ca. 1714]. 4 vols. 2d ed. Guatemala: Sociedad de Geografía e Historia de Guatemala, 1937–44.

Ximénez, Francisco. *Hiσtoria de la provincia de San Vicente de Chiapa y Guatemala de la orden de Predicadoreσ* [ca. 1700]. 3 vols. Guatemala: Sociedad de Geografia e Historia de Guatemala, 1920–31.

———. *Hiσtoria Natural del Reino de Guatemala.* Guatemala: Editorial "José Pineda Ibarra," [1772] 1967.

————. *Primera parte del Tesorero de las lenguas Cakchiquel, Quiché, y Zutuhil, en que las dichas lenguas se traducen a la nuestra, española.* Ed. Carmelo Sáenz de Santa María. Guatemala: Academia de Geografía e Historia de Guatemala, 1985.

Secondary Sources

Adams, Richard N. *Un análisis de las enfermedades y sus curaciones en una población indígena de Guatemala, con sugerencias relacionadas com la práctica de medicina en el área Maya.* Guatemala: Instituto de Nutrición de Centro América y Panamá, 1951.
Adams, Richard N., and Arthur J. Rubel. "Sickness and Social Relations." In *Handbook of Middle American Indians: Social Anthropology*, vol. 6, 333–55. Austin: University of Texas Press, 1967.
Aguirre Beltrán, Gonzalo. *Medicina y magia: El proceso de aculturación en la estructura colonial.* México, D.F.: Instituto Nacional Indigenista, 1963.
————. *La población negra de México: Estudio etnohistórico.* 3d ed. México, D.F.: Fondo de Cultura Económica, 1990.
Alberro, Solange. *La actividad del Santo Officio de la Inquisición en Nueva España, 1571-1700.* Mexico City: INAH, 1981.
————. *Inquisición y sociedad en México 1571-1700.* México, D.F.: Fondo de Cultura Económica, 1988.
Anderson, Karen. *Changing Woman: The History of Racial Ethnic Women in Modern America.* New York: Oxford University Press, 1996.
————. "Work, Gender, and Power in the American West." *Pacific Historical Review* 61:4 (1992): 481–99.
Anderson, Karen L. *Chain Her by One Foot: The Subjugation of Women in Seventeenth-Century New France.* New York: Routledge, 1991.
Angel, Amanda. "Spanish Women in the New World: The Transmission of a Model Polity to New Spain, 1521–1570." Ph.D. diss., University of California, Davis, 1997.
Annis, Verle Lincoln. *The Architecture of Antigua, Guatemala, 1543-1773.* Guatemala: University of San Carlos of Guatemala, 1968.
Arnold, David. *Colonizing the Body: State Medicine and Epidemic Disease in Nineteenth-Century India.* Berkeley: University of California Press, 1993.
————. "Touching the Body: Perspectives on the Indian Plague, 1896–1900." In *Selected Subaltern Studies*, ed. Ranajit Guha and Gayatri Chakravorty Spivak, foreword by Edward Said. New York: Oxford University Press, 1988.
Arrom, Silvia M. *Containing the Poor: The Mexico City Poorhouse, 1774-1871.* Durham: Duke University Press, 2000.
————. *The Women of Mexico City, 1790-1857.* Stanford: Stanford University Press, 1985.
Bartkey, Sandra Lee. "Foucault, Feminism, and the Modernization of Patriarchal Power." In *Feminism and Foucault: Reflections on Resistance*, ed. Irene Diamond and Lee Quinby. Boston: Northeastern University Press, 1988.
Behar, Ruth. "Sex, Sin, Witchcraft, and the Devil in Late-Colonial Mexico." *American Ethnologist* 14 (1987): 35–55.
————. "Sexual Witchcraft, Colonialism, and Women's Powers: Views from the

Mexican Inquisition." In *Sexuality and Marriage in Colonial Latin America*, ed. Asunción Lavrin. Lincoln: University of Nebraska Press, 1991.

———. "The Visions of a Guachichil Witch in 1599: A Window on the Subjugation of Mexico's Hunter-Gatherers." *Ethnohistory* 34:2 (spring 1987): 115–38.

Behar, Ruth, and Deborah A. Gordon, eds. *Women Writing Culture*. Berkeley: University of California Press, 1995.

Bennet, Herman. "Lovers, Family, and Friends: The Formation of Afro-Mexico, 1580–1810." Ph.D. diss., Duke University, 1993.

Borhegyi, Stephan F. "Culto a la imagen del Señor de Esquipulas en Centro América y Nuevo México." *Anthropología y Historia de Guatemala* 11:1 (1959): 44–49.

Bourque, Susan C., and Kay B. Warren. "Democracy without Peace: The Cultural Politics of Terror in Peru." *Latin American Research Review* 24:1 (1989): 7–34.

———. *Women of the Andes: Patriarchy and Social Change in Two Peruvian Towns*. Ann Arbor: University of Michigan Press, 1981.

Bowser, Frederick P. *The African Slave in Colonial Peru, 1524–1650*. Stanford: Stanford University Press, 1974.

Boyer, Richard E. *Lives of the Bigamists: Marriage, Family, and Community in Colonial Mexico*. Albuquerque: University of New Mexico Press, 1995.

Bozzoli, Belinda. "Marxism, Feminism, and South African Studies." *Journal of South African Studies* 9:2 (April 1983): 139–71.

Brading, David. "Images and Prophets: Indian Religion and the Spanish Conquest." In *The Indian Community in Colonial Mexico: Fifteen Essays on Land Tenure, Corporate Organizations, Ideology, and Village Politics*, ed. Arij Ouweneel and Simon Miller. Amsterdam: CEDLA, 1990.

Breslaw, Elaine G. *Tituba, Reluctant Witch of Salem: Devilish Indians and Puritan Fantasies*. New York: New York University Press, 1996.

Bricker, Victoria R. *The Indian Christ, the Indian King: The Historical Substrate of Maya Myth and Ritual*. Austin: University of Texas Press, 1981.

Briggs, Robin. *Witches and Neighbors: The Social and Cultural Context of European Witchcraft*. New York: Viking, 1996.

Brownmiller, Susan. *Against Our Will: Men, Women and Rape*. New York: Simon and Schuster, 1975.

Burkett, Elinor. "In Dubious Sisterhood: Race and Class in Spanish Colonial South America." *Latin American Perspectives* 4:1–2 (1977): 18–26.

———. "Indian Women and White Society: The Case of Sixteenth Century Peru." In *Latin American Women: Historical Perspectives*, ed. Asunción Lavrin. Wesport, Conn.: Greenwood Press, 1978.

Bynum, Caroline Walker. *Fragmentation and Redemption: Essays on Gender and the Human Body in Medieval Religion*. New York: Zone Books, 1991.

———. *Holy Feast, Holy Fast: The Religious Significance of Food to Medieval Women*. Berkeley: University of California Press, 1987.

Calnek, Edward E. "Highland Chiapas before the Spanish Conquest." Ph.D. diss., University of Chicago, 1962.

Camp, Stephanie M. H. "Viragos: Enslaved Women's Everyday Politics in the Old South." Ph.D. diss., University of Pennsylvania, 1998.

Cardoso, Fernando Henrique, and Enzo Faletto. *Dependency and Development in Latin*

America. Trans. Marjory Mattingly Urquidi. Berkeley: University of California Press, 1979.

Carmack, Robert M. *Quichean Civilization: The Ethnohistoric, Ethnographic, and Archaeological Sources*. Berkeley: University of California Press, 1973.

——. *Rebels of Highland Guatemala: The Quiché-Mayas of Momostenango*. Norman: University of Oklahoma Press, 1995.

Carmack, Robert M., ed. *Harvest of Violence: The Maya Indians and the Guatemalan Crisis*. Norman: University of Oklahoma Press, 1988.

Carmack, Robert M., John Early, and Christopher H. Lutz, eds. *The Historical Demography of Highland Guatemala*. Albany: Institute for Mesoamerican Studies, State University of New York at Albany, 1982.

Carroll, Patrick James. *Blacks in Colonial Veracruz: Race, Ethnicity, and Regional Development*. Austin: University of Texas Press, 1991.

Castaneda Delgado, Paulino. *La Inquisición de Lima*. Madrid: Deimos, 1989.

Cervantes, Fernando. *The Devil in the New World: The Impact of Diabolism in New Spain*. New Haven: Yale University Press, 1994.

Chasteen, John. "Violence for Show: Knife Dueling on a Nineteenth-Century Cattle Frontier." In *The Problem of Order in Changing Societies: Essays on Crime and Policing in Argentina and Uruguay*, ed. Lyman L. Johnson. Albuquerque: University of New Mexico Press, 1990.

Chauncey, George. *Gay New York: Gender, Urban Culture, and the Makings of the Gay Male World, 1890–1940*. New York: Basic Books, 1994.

Chinchilla Aguilar, Ernesto. *La Inquisición en Guatemala*. Guatemala: Editorial del Ministerio de Educación Pública, 1953.

Christian, Barbara. "The Race for Theory." *Feminist Studies* 14:1 (spring 1988): 67–79.

Christian, William A. *Local Religion in Sixteenth-Century Spain*. Princeton: Princeton University Press, 1981.

Clendinnen, Inga. *Ambivalent Conquests: Maya and Spaniard in Yucatán, 1517–1570*. New York: Cambridge University Press, 1987.

——. "Yucatec Maya Women and the Spanish Conquest: Role and Ritual in Historical Reconstruction." *Journal of Social History* 15 (1992): 427–42.

Comaroff, Jean. *Body of Power, Spirit of Resistance: The Culture and History of a South African People*. Chicago: University of Chicago Press, 1985.

——. "Healing and the Cultural Order: The Case of the Barolong boo Ratshidi of Southern Africa." *American Ethnologist* 7:4 (1980): 637–57.

Comaroff, Jean, and John L. Comaroff. *Ethnography and the Historical Imagination*. Boulder: Westview Press, 1992.

Cook, Noble David. *Born to Die: Disease and the New World Conquest, 1492–1650*. New York: Cambridge University Press, 1998.

Cook, Noble David, and W. George Lovell. *Secret Judgements of God: Old World Disease in Colonial Spanish America*. Norman: University of Oklahoma Press, 1992.

Cope, R. Douglas. *The Limits of Racial Domination: Plebeian Society in Colonial Mexico City, 1660–1720*. Madison: University of Wisconsin Press, 1994.

Cosminsky, Sheila. "Childbirth and Change: A Guatemalan Study." In *Ethnography of Fertility and Birth*, ed. Carol P. MacCormack. London: Academic Press, 1982.

——. "Medical Pluralism in Mesoamerica." In *Heritage of Conquest: Thirty Years*

Later, ed. Carl Kendall, John Hawkins, and Laurel Bossen. Foreword by Sol Tax. Albuquerque: University of New Mexico Press, 1983.

Cruz, Anne J., and Mary Elizabeth Perry, eds. *Culture and Control in Counter-Reformation Spain.* Minneapolis: University of Minnesota Press, 1992.

Csordas, Thomas J. "Ritual Healing and the Politics of Identity in Contemporary Navajo Society." *American Ethnologist* 26:1 (1999): 3–23.

Curtin, Philip D. *The Atlantic Slave Trade: A Census.* Madison: University of Wisconsin Press, 1969.

Davis-Floyd, Robbie E., and Carolyn F. Sargent, eds. *Childbirth and Authoritative Knowledge: Cross-Cultural Perspectives.* Berkeley: University of California Press, 1997.

Diamond, Irene, and Lee Quinby, eds. *Feminism and Foucault: Reflections on Resistance.* Boston: Northeastern University Press, 1988.

Dillon, Mary, and Thomas Abercrombie. "The Destroying Christ: An Aymara Myth of Conquest." In *Rethinking History and Myth,* ed. Jonathan D. Hill. Urbana: University of Illinois Press, 1988.

Duden, Barbara. *The Woman Beneath the Skin: A Doctor's Patients in Eighteenth-Century Germany.* Trans. Thomas Dunlap. Cambridge, Mass.: Harvard University Press, 1991.

Dunn, Alvis. "A Cry at Daybreak: Death, Disease, and Defense of Community in a Highland Ixil-Maya Village." *Ethnohistory* 42:4 (1995): 595–606.

Edmunson, Munro. "The Mayan Faith." In *South and Meso-American Native Spirituality: From the Cult of the Feathered Serpent to the Theology of Liberation,* ed. Gary H. Gossen. New York: Crossroad, 1993.

Erice, Ana. "Reconsideración de las creencias Mayas en torno al nahualismo." *Estudios de Cultura Maya* 16 (1985): 255–70.

Espejo-Ponce Hunt, Marta, and Matthew Restall. "Work, Marriage and Status: Maya Women of Colonial Yucatán." In *Indian Women of Early Mexico,* ed. Susan Schroeder, Stephanie Wood, and Robert Haskett. Norman: University of Oklahoma Press, 1997.

Estrada Monroy, Agustín. *Datos para la historia de la iglesia en Guatemala.* Tomo 1. Guatemala: Sociedad de Geografía e Historia de Guatemala, 1973.

Farriss, Nancy M. *Maya Society under Colonial Rule: The Collective Enterprise of Survival.* Princeton: Princeton University Press, 1984.

Few, Martha. "Illness Accusations and the Cultural Politics of Power in Colonial Santiago de Guatemala, 1650–1750." Working Paper 98-10, International Seminar on the History of the Atlantic World, Harvard University, August 1998.

———. "'No es la palabra de Dios': Acusaciones de enfermedad y las políticas culturales de poder en la Guatemala colonial, 1650–1720." *Mesoamérica* 20:38 (December 1999): 33–54.

———. "On Her Deathbed, María de Candelaria Accuses Michaela de Molina of Casting Spells (Guatemala, 1696)." In *Colonial Lives: Documents of Latin American History (1550–1850),* ed. Richard Boyer and Geoffrey Spurling. New York: Oxford University Press, 2000.

———. "Women, Religion, and Power: Gender and Resistance in Daily Life in Late-Seventeenth-Century Santiago de Guatemala." *Ethnohistory* 42:4 (fall 1995): 627–37.

Flax, Jane. "Postmodernism and Gender Relations in Feminist Theory." *Signs: Journal of Women in Culture and Society* 12 (1987): 621–43.

Foster, George. "Nahualism in Mexico and Guatemala." *Acta Americana* 2 (1944): 85–103.

Foucault, Michel. *Discipline and Punish: The Birth of the Prison.* Trans. Alan Sheridan. New York: Pantheon, 1977.

———. *The History of Sexuality: An Introduction.* Vol. 1. Trans. Alan Sheridan. New York: Pantheon, 1978.

Franco, Jean. *Plotting Women: Gender and Representation in Mexico.* New York: Columbia University Press, 1989.

François, Marie. "When Pawnshops Talk: Popular Credit and Material Culture in Mexico City, 1775–1916." Ph.D. diss., University of Arizona, 1998.

Frank, André Gunder. *Capitalism and Underdevelopment in Latin America: Historical Studies of Chile and Brazil.* New York: Monthly Review Press, 1969.

Gates, Henry Louis, Jr., ed. *"Race," Writing, and Difference.* Chicago: University of Chicago Press, 1986.

Geertz, Clifford. *The Interpretation of Cultures.* New York: Basic Books, 1973.

———. *Local Knowledge: Further Essays in Interpretive Anthropology.* New York: Basic Books, 1983.

George, Kenneth M. *Showing Signs of Violence: The Cultural Politics of a Twentieth-Century Headhunting Ritual.* Berkeley: University of California Press, 1996.

Ghidinelli, Azzo. "El sistema de ideas sobre la enfermedad en Mesoamerica." *Tradiciones de Guatemala* 26 (1986): 69–89.

Gibson, Charles. *The Aztecs under Spanish Rule: A History of the Indians of the Valley of Mexico, 1519–1810.* Stanford: Stanford University Press, 1964.

Giffords, Gloria Fraser. *Mexican Folk Retablos.* Rev. ed. Albuquerque: University of New Mexico Press, 1992.

Giles, Mary E., ed. *Women in the Inquisition: Spain and the New World.* Baltimore: Johns Hopkins University Press, 1999.

Ginzburg, Carlo. *The Cheese and the Worms: The Cosmos of a Sixteenth-Century Miller.* Trans. John Tedeschi and Anne Tedeschi. Baltimore: Johns Hopkins University Press, 1980.

———. *Clues, Myths, and Historical Method.* Trans. John Tedeschi and Anne Tedeschi. Baltimore: Johns Hopkins University Press, 1992.

———. *The Night Battles: Witchcraft and Agrarian Cults in the Sixteenth and Seventeenth Centuries.* Trans. John Tedeschi and Anne Tedeschi. Baltimore: Johns Hopkins University Press, 1980.

González Alonso, Julia, and Jude Pasini. "El cuidado médico propio y los trabajadores de las fincas de Guatemala." *Mesoamérica* 32 (December 1996): 315–38.

Gordon, Deborah. "Writing Culture, Writing Feminism: The Poetics and Politics of Experimental Ethnography." *Inscriptions* 3:4 (1988): 7–24.

Gordon, Linda. *Heroes of Their Own Lives: The Politics and History of Family Violence, Boston, 1880–1960.* New York: Viking, 1988.

———. "What's New in Feminist History?" In *Feminist Studies/ Critical Studies,* ed. Teresa de Laurentis. Bloomington: Indiana University Press, 1986.

Gosner, Kevin M. "Caciques and Conversion: Juan Atonal and the Struggle for Legitimacy in Post-conquest Chiapas." *Americas* 49:2 (October 1992): 115–29.

———. *Soldiers of the Virgin: The Moral Economy of a Colonial Maya Rebellion.* Tucson: University of Arizona Press, 1992.

———. "Women, Rebellion, and the Moral Economy of Maya Peasants in Colonial Mexico." In *Indian Women of Early Mexico,* ed. Susan Schroeder, Stephanie Wood, and Robert Haskett. Norman: University of Oklahoma Press, 1997.

Grandin, Greg. *The Blood of Guatemala: A History of Race and Nation.* Durham: Duke University Press, 2000.

Green, Linda. "Fear as a Way of Life." *Cultural Anthropology* 9:2 (1994): 227–56.

———. *Fear as a Way of Life: Mayan Widows in Rural Guatemala.* New York: Columbia University Press, 1999.

Greenleaf, Richard E. "The Inquisition and the Indians of New Spain: A Study in Jurisdictional Confusion." *Americas* 34:3 (1978): 315–44.

———. "The Mexican Inquisition and the Indians: Sources for the Ethnohistorian." *Americas* 34:3 (1978): 315–44.

———. *The Mexican Inquisition of the Sixteenth Century.* Albuquerque: University of New Mexico Press, 1969.

———. *Zumárraga and the Mexican Inquisition, 1536–1543.* Washington, D.C.: Academy of American Franciscan History, 1961.

Griffiths, Nicholas. *The Cross and the Serpent: Religious Repression and Resurgence in Colonial Peru.* Norman: University of Oklahoma Press, 1996.

Griffiths, Nicholas, and Fernando Cervantes, eds. *Spiritual Encounters: Interactions between Christianity and Native Religions in Colonial America.* Birmingham: University of Birmingham Press, 1999.

Groak, Kevin P. "To Warm the Blood, to Warm the Flesh: The Role of the Steambath in Highland Guatemala (Tzeltal-Tzotzil) Ethnomedicine." *Journal of Latin American Lore* 20:1 (1997): 3–96.

Gruzinski, Serge. "Individualization and Acculturation: Confession among the Nahuas of Mexico from the Sixteenth to the Eighteenth Century." In *Sexuality and Marriage in Colonial Latin America,* ed. Asunción Lavrin. Lincoln: University of Nebraska Press, 1989.

———. *Man-Gods in the Mexican Highlands: Indian Power and Colonial Society, 1520–1800.* Trans. Eileen Corrigan. Stanford: Stanford University Press, 1989.

Gutiérrez, Ramón A. *When Jesus Came, the Corn Mothers Went Away: Marriage, Sexuality, and Power in New Mexico, 1500–1846.* Stanford: Stanford University Press, 1991.

Guy, Donna J. "Prostitution and Female Criminality in Buenos Aires, 1875–1937." In *The Problem of Order in Changing Societies: Essays on Crime and Policing in Argentina and Uruguay,* ed. Lyman L. Johnson. Albuquerque: University of New Mexico Press, 1990.

———. *Sex and Danger in Buenos Aires: Prostitution, Family and Nation in Argentina.* Lincoln: University of Nebraska Press, 1991.

Hall, Jacquelyn Dowd. "'The Mind That Burns Each Body': Women, Rape, and Racial Violence." In *Powers of Desire: the Politics of Sexuality,* ed. Ana Snitow, Christine Stansell, and Sharon Thompson. New York: Monthly Review Press, 1983.

Harkin, Michael. "Contested Bodies: Affliction and Power in Heiltsuk Culture and History." *American Ethnologist* 21:3 (1994): 586–605.

Haviland, John Beard. *Gossip, Reputation, and Knowledge in Zinacantán.* Chicago: University of Chicago Press, 1977.

Hernández, Leonardo. "Implicated Spaces, Daily Struggles: Home and Street Life in Late Colonial Guatemala City, 1750–1824." Ph.D. diss., Brown University, 1999.

Herrera, Robinson Antonio. "The People of Santiago: Early Colonial Guatemala, 1538–1587." Ph.D. diss., University of California, Los Angeles, 1997.

Hill II, Robert. "Instances of Maya Witchcraft in the Eighteenth-Century Totonicapán Area." *Estudios de Cultura Maya* 17 (1988): 269–93.

Holler, Jacqueline. "'More Sins than the Queen of England': Marina de San Miguel before the Mexican Inquisition." In *Women in the Inquisition: Spain and the New World,* ed. Mary E. Giles. Baltimore: Johns Hopkins University Press, 1999.

Holmes, Clive. "Women: Witnesses and Witches." *Past and Present* 140 (August 1993): 45–78.

hooks, bell. *Yearning: Race, Gender, and Cultural Politics.* Boston: South End Press, 1990.

Hunt, Nancy Rose. *A Colonial Lexicon of Birth Ritual, Medicalization, and Mobility in the Congo.* Durham: Duke University Press, 1999.

Hutchinson, Sharon E. *Nuer Dilemmas: Coping with Money, War, and the State.* Berkeley: University of California Press, 1996.

Jiménez Rueda, Julio. *Herejías y supersticiones en la Nueva España: Los heterodoxos en México.* México, D.F. City: Imprenta Universitaria, 1946.

Johnson, Lyman L., ed. *The Problem of Order in Changing Societies: Essays on Crime and Policing in Argentina and Uruguay.* Albuquerque: University of New Mexico Press, 1990.

Johnson, Lyman L., and Sonya Lipsett-Rivera, eds. *The Faces of Honor: Sex, Shame, and Violence in Colonial Latin America.* Albuquerque: University of New Mexico Press, 1998.

Jones, Kathleen. "On Authority: Or, Why Women Are Not Entitled to Speak." In *Feminism and Foucault: Reflections on Resistance,* ed. Irene Diamond and Lee Quinby. Boston: Northeastern University Press, 1988.

Jones, Oakah L. *Guatemala in the Spanish Colonial Period.* Norman: University of Oklahoma Press, 1994.

Joseph, Gilbert M., and Daniel Nugent, eds. *Everyday Forms of State Formation: Revolution and the Negotiation of Rule in Modern Mexico.* Foreword by James C. Scott. Durham: Duke University Press, 1994.

Kagan, Richard L. "Politics, Prophecy, and Inquisition in Late-Sixteenth-Century Spain." In *Cultural Encounters: The Impact of the Inquisition in Spain and the New World,* ed. Mary Elizabeth Perry and Anne J. Cruz. Berkeley and Los Angeles: University of California Press, 1991.

Kanter, Deborah. "Hijos del Pueblo: Family, Community, and Gender in Rural Mexico, The Toluca Region 1730–1830." Ph.D. diss., University of Virginia, 1993.

Karasch, Mary C. "Anastacia and the Slave Women of Rio de Janeiro." In *Africans in Bondage: Studies in Slavery and the Slave Trade,* ed. Paul E. Lovejoy. Madison: University of Wisconsin Press, 1986.

————. *Slave Life in Rio de Janeiro, 1808-1850*. Princeton: Princeton University Press, 1987.

Karlsen, Carol F. *The Devil in the Shape of a Woman: Witchcraft in Colonial New England*. New York: Norton, 1987.

Kellogg, Susan. *Law and the Transformation of Aztec Culture, 1500-1700*. Norman: University of Oklahoma Press, 1995.

Kendall, Carl, John Hawkins, and Laurel Bossen, eds. *Heritage of Conquest: Thirty Years Later*. Foreword by Sol Tax. Albuquerque: University of New Mexico Press, 1983.

Kidd, Barbara Ann. "Maya Curing: An Analysis of Ethnohistorical Sources." *Human Mosaic* 2:2 (1977): 31–45.

Klein, Cecilia. "Wild Woman in Colonial Mexico: An Encounter of European and Aztec Concepts of Other." In *Reframing the Renaissance: Visual Culture in Europe and Latin America, 1450-1650*, ed. Claire Farago. New Haven: Yale University Press, 1995.

Klein, Herbert S. "Peasant Communities in Revolt: The Tzeltal Republic of 1712." *Pacific Historical Review* 35 (1966): 247–63.

Klor de Alva, J. Jorge. "Colonizing Souls: The Failure of the Indian Inquisition and the Rise of Penitential Discipline." In *Cultural Encounters: The Impact of the Inquisition in Spain and the New World*, ed. Mary Elizabeth Perry and Anne J. Cruz. Berkeley: University of California Press, 1991.

————. "Martín Ocelotl: Clandestine Cult Leader." In *Struggle and Survival in Colonial America*, ed. David G. Sweet and Gary B. Nash. Berkeley: University of California Press, 1981.

Koehler, Lyle. "The Salem Village Cataclysm: Origins and Impact of a Witch Hunt." In *Women, Families, and Communities: Readings in American History*, ed. Nancy A. Hewitt. Glenview, Ill.: Scott, Foresman, 1990.

Kramer, Wendy. *Encomienda Politics in Colonial Guatemala, 1524-1544: Dividing the Spoils*. Boulder: Westview Press, 1994.

Kuznesof, Elizabeth A. "Ethnic and Gender Influence on 'Spanish' Creole Society in Colonial Spanish America." *Colonial Latin American Historical Review* 4:1 (1995): 153–76.

————. *Household Economy and Urban Development: São Paulo 1765 to 1836*. Boulder: Westview Press, 1986.

Landers, Jane. *Black Society in Spanish Florida*. Urbana: University of Illinois Press, 1999.

Lanning, John Tate. *The Royal Protomedicato: The Regulation of the Medical Professions in the Spanish Empire*. Ed. John TePaske. Durham: Duke University Press, 1985.

Lauderdale Graham, Sandra. *House and Street: The Domestic World of Servants and Masters in Nineteenth-Century Rio de Janeiro*. Austin: University of Texas Press, 1992.

Lavrin, Asunción. "'Lo feminino': Women in Colonial Historical Sources." In *Coded Encounters: Writing, Gender, and Ethnicity in Colonial Latin America*, ed. Francisco Javier Cevallos-Candau, Jeffrey A. Cole, Nina M. Scott, and Nicomedes Suárez-Araúz. Amherst: University of Massachusetts Press, 1994.

————. "In Search of the Colonial Woman in Mexico: The Seventeenth and Eighteenth Centuries." In *Latin American Women: Historical Perspectives*, ed. Asunción Lavrin. Westport, Conn.: Greenwood Press, 1978.

———. "Introduction: The Scenario, the Actors, and the Issues." In *Sexuality and Marriage in Colonial Latin America*, ed. Asunción Lavrin. Lincoln: University of Nebraska Press, 1989.

———. "Sexuality in Colonial Mexico: A Church Dilemma." In *Sexuality and Marriage in Colonial Latin America*, ed. Asunción Lavrin. Lincoln: University of Nebraska Press, 1989.

———. "Women and Religion in Spanish America." In *Women and Religion in America*, vol. 2: *The Colonial and Revolutionary Periods*, ed. Rosemary Radford Reuter and Rosemary Skinner Keller. San Francisco: Harper & Row, 1983.

———. "Women in Spanish American Colonial Society." In *The Cambridge History of Latin America*, ed. Leslie Bethell. Cambridge: Cambridge University Press, 1984.

Lavrin, Asunción, ed. *Latin American Women: Historical Perspectives*. Westport, Conn.: Greenwood Press, 1978.

———. *Sexuality and Marriage in Colonial Latin America*. Lincoln: University of Nebraska Press, 1989.

Lebsock, Susan. "'No Obey': Indian, European, and African Women in Seventeenth-Century Virginia." In *Women, Families, and Communities: Readings in American History*, ed. Nancy A. Hewitt. Glencoe, Ill.: Scott, Foresman, 1990.

di Leonardo, Micaela, ed. *Gender at the Crossroads of Knowledge: Feminist Anthropology in the Postmodern Era*. Berkeley: University of California Press, 1991.

Lewis, Laura. "Blackness, Femaleness, and Self-Representation: Constructing Persons in a Colonial Mexican Court." *Political and Legal Anthropology Review* 18:2 (1995): 81–89.

Lipsett-Rivera, Sonya. "The Intersection of Rape and Marriage in Late-Colonial and Early National Mexico." *Colonial Latin American Historical Review* 6:4 (fall 1997): 559–90.

Lovejoy, Paul E., ed. *Africans in Bondage: Studies in Slavery and the Slave Trade*. Madison: University of Wisconsin Press, 1986.

Lovell, W. George. *Conquest and Survival in Colonial Guatemala: A Historical Geography of the Cuchumatán Highlands, 1500-1821*. Montreal: McGill-Queen's University Press, 1992.

———. "Las enfermedades del Viejo Mundo y la mortalidad indígena: La viruela y el tabardillo en la sierra de los Cuchumatanes, Guatemala (1780–1810)." *Mesoamérica* 9:16 (1988): 239–85.

———. "Surviving Conquest: The Maya of Guatemala in Historical Perspective." *Latin American Research Review* 23:2 (1988): 25–57.

Lovell, W. George, and Christopher H. Lutz, eds. "Conquest and Population: Maya Demography in Historical Perspective." *Latin American Research Review* 29:2 (1994): 133–40.

———. *Demography and Empire: A Guide to the Population History of Spanish Central America, 1500-1821*. Boulder: Westview Press, 1995.

Lovell, W. George, and William Sweezy. "Indian Migration and Community Formation: An Analysis of Congregación in Colonial Guatemala." In *Migration in*

Colonial Spanish America, ed. David J. Robinson. Cambridge: Cambridge University Press, 1990.

Luján Muñoz, Jorge. "El proceso fundacional en el Reino de Guatemala durante los siglos XVII y XVIII: Una primera aproximación." *Anales de la Academia de Geografía e Historia de Guatemala* 53 (1980): 236–56.

Lutz, Christopher H. "Evolución demográfica de la población no indígena." In *Historia general de Guatemala,* Tomo II: *Dominación española: Desde la conquista hasta 1700,* gen. ed. Jorge Luján Muñoz, vol. ed. Ernesto Chinchilla Aguilar. Guatemala: Asociación de Amigos del País, Fundación para la Cultural y el Desarollo, 1993.

———. "Evolución demográfica de la población ladina." In *Historia general de Guatemala,* Tomo III: *Siglo XVIII hasta la independencia,* gen. ed. Jorge Luján Muñoz, vol. ed. Cristina Zilbermann de Luján. Guatemala: Asociación de Amigos del País, Fundación para la Cultural y el Desarollo, 1993.

———. *Historia sociodemográfica de Santiago de Guatemala 1541–1773.* Guatemala: Centro de Investigaciones Regionales de Mesoamérica, 1984.

———. *Santiago de Guatemala, 1541–1773: City, Caste and the Colonial Experience.* Norman: University of Oklahoma Press, 1994.

———. "Santiago de Guatemala, 1541–1773: The Socio-Demographic History of a Spanish American Colonial City." Ph.D. diss., University of Wisconsin, 1976.

———. "Santiago de Guatemala en el Siglo XVII." In *Historia general de Guatemala,* Tomo II: *Dominación española: Desde la conquista hasta 1700,* gen. ed. Jorge Luján Muñoz, vol. ed. Ernesto Chinchilla Aguilar. Guatemala: Asociación de Amigos del País, Fundación para la Cultural y el Desarollo, 1993.

———. "Santiago de Guatemala (1700–1773)." In *Historia general de Guatemala,* Tomo III: *Siglo XVIII hasta la independencia,* gen. ed. Jorge Luján Muñoz, vol. ed. Cristina Zilbermann de Luján. Guatemala: Asociación de Amigos del País, Fundación para la Cultural y el Desarollo, 1993.

———. "La vida cotidiana y la dualidad ladino-indígena." In *Historia general de Guatemala,* Tomo III: *Siglo XVIII hasta la independencia,* gen. ed. Jorge Luján Muñoz, vol. ed. Cristina Zilbermann de Luján. Guatemala: Asociación de Amigos del País, Fundación para la Cultural y el Desarollo, 1993.

McBrien, Richard P., gen. ed. *The HarperCollins Encyclopedia of Catholicism.* San Francisco: HarperCollins, 1995.

MacCormack, Sabine. *Religion in the Andes: Vision and Imagination in Early Colonial Peru.* Princeton: Princeton University Press, 1991.

Macfarlane, Alan. *Witchcraft in Tudor and Stuart England: A Regional and Comparative Study.* New York: Harper & Row, 1970.

McKnight, Kathryn Joy. "Blasphemy as Resistance: An African Slave Woman before the Inquisition." In *Women in the Inquisition: Spain and the New World,* ed. Mary E. Giles. Baltimore: Johns Hopkins University Press, 1999.

MacLeod, Murdo J. "Ethnic Relations and Indian Society in the Province of Guatemala ca. 1620–ca. 1800." In *Spaniards and Indians in Southeast Mesoamerica: Essays on the History of Ethnic Relations,* ed. Murdo J. MacLeod and Robert Wasserstrom. Lincoln: University of Nebraska Press, 1983.

———. "An Outline of Central American Colonial Demographics." In *The Historical Demography of Highland Guatemala,* ed. Robert M. Carmack, John Early, and

Christopher H. Lutz. Albany: Institute for Mesoamerican Studies, State University of New York at Albany, 1982.

———. *Spanish Central America: A Socioeconomic History, 1520-1720.* Berkeley: University of California Press, 1973.

Manarelli, María Emma. *Inquisición y mujeres: Las hechiceras en el Perú durante el siglo XVII.* Lima: Centro de Documentación sobre la Mujer, 1987.

Markman, Sidney David. *Architecture and Urbanization of Colonial Central America: Primary Documentary and Literary Sources.* 2 vols. Tempe: Center for Latin American Studies, Arizona State University, 1993.

———. *Colonial Architecture of Antigua Guatemala.* Philadelphia: American Philosophical Society, 1966.

Martin, Biddy. "Feminism, Criticism, and Foucault." In *Feminism and Foucault: Reflections on Resistance*, ed. Irene Diamond and Lee Quinby. Boston: Northeastern University Press, 1988.

Martínez Peláez, Severo. "Los motines de indios en el período colonial guatemalteco." In *Ensayos de historia Centroamericana*, ed. Germán Romero Vargas et al. San José, Costa Rica: CEDAL, 1974.

———. *La patria del criollo: Ensayo de interpretación de la realidad colonial guatemalteca.* Guatemala: Editorial Universitaria Centroamericana, 1973.

Maza, Sara. "Stories in History: Cultural Narratives in Recent Works in European History." *American Historical Review* 101 (December 1996): 5.

Mello e Souza, Laura de. *O diabo e a Terra de Santa Cruz: Feiticaria e religiosidade popular no Brasil colonial.* São Paulo: Companhia das Letras, 1986.

———. *O Inferno atlântico: Demonologia e colonização, séculos XVI-XVIII.* São Paulo: Companhia das Letras, 1993.

Méndez Domínguez, Alfredo. "Illness and Medical Theory among Guatemalan Indians." In *Heritage of Conquest Thirty Years Later*, ed. Carl Kendall, John Hawkins, and Laurel Bossen. Foreword by Sol Tax. Albuquerque: University of New Mexico Press, 1983.

Mills, Kenneth R. *Idolatry and Its Enemies: Colonial Andean Religion and Extirpation, 1640-1750.* Princeton: Princeton University Press, 1997.

Mohanty, Chandra. "Cartographies of Struggle: Third World Women and the Politics of Feminism." In *Third World Women and the Politics of Feminism*, ed. Chandra Talpade Mohanty, Ann Russo, and Lourdes Torres. Bloomington: Indiana University Press, 1991.

———. "Under Western Eyes: Feminist Scholarship and Colonial Discourses." In *Colonial Discourses and Post-Colonial Theory: A Reader*, ed. Patrick Williams and Laura Chrisman. New York: Columbia University Press, 1994.

Monaghan, John. *The Covenants with Earth and Rain: Exchange, Sacrifice, and Revelation in Mixtec Society.* Norman: University of Oklahoma Press, 1995.

Moreno de los Arcos, Roberto. "New Spain's Inquisition for Indians from the Sixteenth to the Nineteenth Century." In *Cultural Encounters: The Impact of the Inquisition in Spain and the New World*, ed. Mary Elizabeth Perry and Anne J. Cruz. Berkeley: University of California Press, 1991.

Mörner, Magnus. *Race Mixture in the History of Latin America.* Boston: Little, Brown, 1967.

Mott, Luiz R. B. *Escravidão, homossexualidade e demonologia.* São Paulo: Icone, 1988.

———. *Rosa Egipciaca: Uma santa africana no Brasil*. Rio de Janeiro: Bertrand Brasil, 1993.

———. *O sexo prohibido: Virgins, gays e escravos nas garras da Inquisição*. Campinas, São Paulo: Papirus Editora, 1988.

Muir, Edward, and Guido Ruggiero, eds. *Sex and Gender in Historical Perspective*. Trans. Margaret A. Galucci. Baltimore: Johns Hopkins University Press, 1990.

Musgrave-Portilla, L. "The Nahualli or Transforming Wizard in Pre- and Postconquest Mesoamerica." *Journal of Latin American Lore* 8:1 (1982): 13–62.

Nelson, Diane M. *A Finger in the Wound: Body Politics in Quincentennial Guatemala*. Berkeley: University of California Press, 1999.

Ngou-Mve, Nicolás. *El África Bantú en la colonización de México (1595-1650)*. Madrid: Consejo Superior de Investigaciones Científicas, 1994.

———. "El cimarronaje como forma de expresión del África Bantú en la América colonial: El ejemplo de Yangá en México." *América Negra* 14 (1997): 27–51.

Numbers, Ronald L., ed. *Medicine in the New World: New Spain, New France, and New England*. Knoxville: University of Tennessee Press, 1987.

Oakes, Maud. *Beyond the Windy Place: Life in the Guatemalan Highlands*. New York: Farrar, Straus, and Young, 1951.

———. *The Two Crosses of Todos Santos: Survivals of Maya Religious Rituals*. New York: Pantheon Books, 1951.

Orellana, Sandra L. *Indian Medicine in Highland Guatemala: The Pre-Hispanic and Colonial Periods*. Albuquerque: University of New Mexico Press, 1987.

Osorio, Alejandra. "El callejón de la soledad: Vectors of Cultural Hybridity in Seventeenth-Century Lima." In *Spiritual Encounters: Interactions between Christianity and Native Religions in Colonial America*, ed. Nicholas Griffiths and Fernando Cervantes. Birmingham: University of Birmingham Press, 1999.

Ouweneel, Arij, and Simon Miller, eds. *The Indian Community of Colonial Mexico: Fifteen Essays on Land Tenure, Corporate Organizations, Ideology, and Village Politics*. Amsterdam: CEDLA, 1990.

Palmer, Colin A. *Slaves of the White God: Blacks in Mexico, 1570-1650*. Cambridge, Mass.: Harvard University Press, 1976.

Pardo, J. Joaquín. *Efemérides para escribir la historia de la muy noble y muy leal ciudad de Santiago de los Caballeros del Reino de Guatemala*. Guatemala: Tipografía Nacional, 1944.

———. *Miscelanea histórica: Guatemala, siglos 16 a 19: Vida, costumbres, sociedad*. Guatemala: Universidad de San Carlos de Guatemala, 1978.

Pardo, J. Joaquín, Pedro Zamora Castellanos, and Luis Luján Muñoz. *Guía de Antigua Guatemala*. 2d ed. Guatemala: Editorial "José de Pineda Ibarra," 1968.

Parrinder, Edward Geoffrey. *Witchcraft: European and African*. London: Faber and Faber, 1963.

Paul, Benjamin D., and Lois Paul. "The Life Cycle." In *Heritage of Conquest: The Ethnology of Middle America*, ed. Sol Tax. Glencoe, Ill.: Free Press, 1952.

Paul, Lois. "The Mastery of Work and the Mystery of Sex in a Guatemalan Village." In *Woman, Culture, and Society*, ed. Michelle Zimbalist Rosaldo and Louise Lamphere. Stanford: Stanford University Press, 1974.

Perry, Mary Elizabeth. *Gender and Disorder in Early Modern Seville*. Princeton: Princeton University Press, 1990.

Perry, Mary Elizabeth, and Anne J. Cruz, eds. *Cultural Encounters: The Impact of the Inquisition in Spain and the New World.* Berkeley: University of California Press, 1991.

Poole, Stafford. *Our Lady of Guadalupe: The Origins and Sources of a Mexican National Symbol, 1531–1797.* Tucson: University of Arizona Press, 1995.

Purkiss, Diana. *The Witch in History: Early Modern and Twentieth-Century Representations.* New York: Routledge, 1996.

Quezada, Noemí. *Amor y magia amorosa entre los aztecas: Supervivencia en el México colonial.* México, D.F.: UNAM, 1975.

———. *Enfermedad y maleficio: El curandero en el México colonial.* México, D.F.: UNAM, 1989.

———. "The Inquisition's Repression of Curanderos." In *Cultural Encounters: The Impact of the Inquisition in Spain and the New World,* ed. Mary Elizabeth Perry and Anne J. Cruz. Berkeley: University of California Press, 1991.

———. *Sexualidad, amor, y erotismo: México prehispánico y México colonial.* México, D.F.: UNAM, 1996.

Redfield, Robert. *Disease and Its Treatment in Dzitas, Yucatán.* Washington, D.C.: Carnegie Institution of Washington, 1940.

Reis, João José. *Slave Rebellion in Brazil: The Muslim Uprising of 1835 in Bahia.* Trans. Arthur Brakel. Baltimore: Johns Hopkins University Press, 1993.

Restall, Matthew. "He Wished It in Vain: Subordination and Resistance among Maya Women in Post-Conquest Yucatán." *Ethnohistory* 42:4 (fall 1995): 577–94.

———. *Maya Conquistador.* Boston: Beacon Press, 1998.

———. *The Maya World: Yucatec Culture and Society, 1550–1850.* Stanford: Stanford University Press, 1997.

Risse, Guenter B. "Medicine in New Spain." In *Medicine in the New World: New Spain, New France, and New England,* ed. Ronald L. Numbers. Knoxville: University of Tennessee Press, 1987.

Rogers, Susan Carol. "Female Forms of Power and the Myth of Male Dominance: Models of Female/Male Interaction in Peasant Society." *American Ethnologist* 2 (1975): 727–56.

Roper, Lyndal. *Oedipus and the Devil: Witchcraft, Sexuality, and Religion in Early Modern Europe.* New York: Routledge, 1994.

———. "Witchcraft and Fantasy." *History Workshop Journal* 45 (spring 1998): 265–71.

Rowlands, Alison. "Telling Witchcraft Stories: New Perspectives on Witchcraft and Witches in the Early Modern Period." *Gender and History* 10:2 (August 1998): 292–304.

Ruggiero, Guido. *Binding Passions: Tales of Magic, Marriage, and Power at the End of the Renaissance.* New York: Oxford University Press, 1993.

———. *Violence in Early Renaissance Venice.* New Brunswick, N.J.: Rutgers University Press, 1980.

Ruz, Mario Humberto. "Sebastiana de la Cruz, alias 'la Polilla'": Mulata de Petapa y Madre del Hijo de Dios." *Mesoamérica* 13:23 (1992): 55–66.

Sabean, David Warren. *Power in the Blood: Popular Culture and Village Discourse in Early Modern Germany.* New York: Cambridge University Press, 1984.

Sacristán, María Cristina. *Locura e Inquisición en Nueva España, 1571–1760*. México, D.F.: Colegio de Michoacán, Fondo de Cultura Económica, 1992.

———. "Pecadores inocentes: Algunos avances sobre la locura en nueva España (1571–1760)." In *Del dicho al hecho: Transgresiones y partes culturales en la Nueva España*, Seminario de Historia de la Mentalidades, ed. Antonio Guzmán Vázquez and Lourdes Martínez O. México, D.F.: Instituto Nacional de Antropología e Historia, 1989.

Saler, Benson. *Nagual, brujo, y hechicero en un pueblo quiché*. Guatemala: Ministerio de Educación, 1969.

Salomon, Frank. "Ancestor Cults and Resistance to the State in Arequipa, 1748–1754." In *Resistance, Rebellion and Consciousness in the Andean Peasant World, Eighteenth to Twentieth Centuries*, ed. Steve J. Stern. Madison: University of Wisconsin Press, 1987.

———. "Indian Women of Early Colonial Quito as Seen through Their Testaments." *Americas* 44:3 (January 1988): 325–41.

———. "Shamanism and Politics in Late Colonial Ecuador." *American Ethnologist* 10 (1983): 413–28.

Samayoa Guevara, Héctor Humberto. *Los gremios de artesanos en la Ciudad de Guatemala (1524–1821)*. Guatemala: Editorial Universitaria, 1962.

Sánchez Ortega, María Helena. "Sorcery and Eroticism in Love Magic." In *Culture and Control in Counter-Reformation Spain*, ed. Anne J. Cruz and Mary Elizabeth Perry. Minneapolis: University of Minnesota Press, 1992.

Scarry, Elaine. *The Body in Pain: The Making and Unmaking of the World*. New York: Oxford University Press, 1985.

Schele, Linda, and Mary Ellen Miller. *The Blood of Kings: Dynasty and Ritual in Maya Art*. New York: Braziller, 1986.

Schroeder, Susan, Stephanie Wood, and Robert Haskett, eds. *Indian Women of Early Mexico*. Norman: University of Oklahoma Press, 1997.

Schwartz, Stuart B. "Indian Labor and New World Plantations: European Demands and Indian Responses in Northeastern Brazil." *American Historical Review* 83:1 (February 1978): 43–79.

———. "The Manumission of Slaves in Colonial Brazil: Bahia, 1684–1745." *Hispanic American Historical Review* 54:4 (1974): 603–35.

Scott, James C. *Domination and the Arts of Resistance: Hidden Transcripts*. New Haven: Yale University Press, 1990.

———. *Weapons of the Weak: Everyday Forms of Peasant Resistance*. New Haven: Yale University Press, 1985.

Scott, Joan Wallach. "Gender: A Useful Category of Analysis." *American Historical Review* (December 1986): 1053–73.

———. *Gender and the Politics of History*. New York: Columbia University Press, 1988.

Scully, Sally. "Marriage or a Career? Witchcraft as an Alternative in Seventeenth-Century Venice." *Journal of Social History* 28:4 (summer 1995): 857–76.

Seed, Patricia. "Colonial and Postcolonial Discourse." *Latin American Research Review* 26:3 (1991): 181–200.

———. *To Love, Honor, and Obey in Colonial Mexico: Conflicts over Marriage Choice, 1574–1821*. Stanford: Stanford University Press, 1988.

Sharpe, Jenny. "The Unspeakable Limits of Rape: Colonial Violence and Counter-Insurgency." In *Colonial Discourse and Post-Colonial Theory: A Reader,* ed. Patrick Williams and Laura Chrisman. New York: Columbia University Press, 1994.

Sherman, William L. "Abusos contra los indios de Guatemala (1602-1605): Relaciones del Obispo." *Cahiers de Monde Hispanique et Luso-Brésilien Caravelle* 11 (1968): 4-28.

———. *Forced Native Labor in Sixteenth-Century Central America.* Lincoln: University of Nebraska Press, 1979.

———. "Some Aspects of Change in Guatemalan Society." In *Spaniards and Indians in Southeastern Mesoamerica: Essays on the History of Ethnic Relations,* ed. Murdo J. MacLeod and Robert Wasserstrom. Lincoln: University of Nebraska Press, 1983.

Sider, Gerald. "When Parrots Learn to Talk, and Why They Can't: Domination, Deception, and Self-Deception in Indian-White Relations." *Comparative Study of Society and History* 24:1 (January 1987): 3-23.

Silverblatt, Irene. "Interpreting Women in States: New Feminist Ethnohistories." In *Gender at the Crossroads of Knowledge: Feminist Anthropology in the Postmodern Era,* ed. Micaela di Leonardo. Berkeley: University of California Press, 1991.

———. *Moon, Sun, and Witches: Gender Ideologies and Class in Inca and Colonial Peru.* Princeton: Princeton University Press, 1987.

———. "Political Memories and Colonizing Symbols: Santiago and the Mountain Gods of Peru." In *Rethinking History and Myth: Indigenous South American Perspectives on the Past,* ed. Jonathan D. Hill. Urbana: University of Illinois Press, 1988.

Simeon, George. *Illness and Curing in a Guatemalan Village: A Study in Ethnomedicine.* Honolulu: University of Hawaii Press, 1977.

Siquiera, Sonia A. *A Inquisição portuguesa e a sociedade colonial.* São Paulo: Editora Atica, 1978.

Smith, Carol A. "Local History in a Global Context: Social and Economic Transitions in Western Guatemala." *Comparative Studies in Society and History* 26 (1984): 193-228.

Smith, Carol A., ed. *Guatemalan Indians and the State: 1540-1988.* Austin: University of Texas Press, 1990.

Smith-Rosenburg, Carroll. *Disorderly Conduct: Visions of Gender in Victorian America.* Oxford: Oxford University Press, 1985.

Socolow, Susan Midgen. "Women and Crime: Buenos Aires, 1757-97." In *The Problem of Order in Changing Societies: Essays on Crime and Policing in Argentina and Uruguay,* ed. Lyman L. Johnson. Albuquerque: University of New Mexico Press, 1990.

Spalding, Karen. *Huarochirí: An Andean Society under Inca and Spanish Rule.* Stanford: Stanford University Press, 1984.

Stack, Carol B. "Sex Roles and Survival Strategies in an Urban Black Community." In *Woman, Culture, and Society,* ed. Michelle Zimbalist Rosaldo and Louise Lamphere. Stanford: Stanford University Press, 1974.

Stein, Stanley J., and Barbara H. Stein. *The Colonial Heritage of Latin America: Essays on Economic Dependence in Perspective.* New York: Oxford University Press, 1970.

Stern, Steve J. "Approaches to the Study of Peasant Rebellions and Consciousness in the Andean Peasant World." In *Resistance, Rebellion and Consciousness in the*

Andean Peasant World, Eighteenth to Twentieth Centuries, ed. Steve J. Stern. Madison: University of Wisconsin Press, 1987.

———. "Feudalism, Capitalism and the World-System in the Perspective of Latin America and the Caribbean." *American Historical Review* 93 (1988): 829–72.

———. *The Secret History of Gender: Women, Men, and Power in Late Colonial Mexico.* Chapel Hill: University of North Carolina Press, 1995.

Stoler, Ann. "Carnal Knowledge and Imperial Power: Gender, Race, and Morality in Colonial Asia." In *Gender at the Crossroads of Knowledge: Feminist Anthropology in the Postmodern Era,* ed. Micaela di Leonardo. Berkeley: University of California Press, 1991.

Sylvest, Edwin E., Jr. *Nuestra Señora de Guadalupe: Mother of God, Mother of the Americas.* Dallas: Bridewell Library Publications, 1992.

Tax, Sol, ed. *Heritage of Conquest: The Ethnology of Middle America.* Glencoe, Ill.: Free Press, 1952.

Taylor, William B. "Between Global Processes and Local Knowledge: An Inquiry into Early Latin American History, 1500–1900." In *The World of Social History,* ed. Oliver Zunz. Chapel Hill: University of North Carolina Press, 1985.

———. *Drinking, Homicide and Rebellion in Colonial Mexican Villages.* Stanford: Stanford University Press, 1979.

———. *Magistrates of the Sacred: Priests and Parishioners in Eighteenth-Century Mexico.* Stanford: Stanford University Press, 1996.

———. "The Virgin of Guadalupe: An Inquiry into the Social History of Marian Devotion." *American Ethnologist* (1986): 9–33.

Tedlock, Dennis. "Torture in the Archives." *American Anthropologist* 95:1 (1993): 139–52.

Thomas, Keith. *Religion and the Decline of Magic.* New York: Scribner, 1971.

Thompson, E. P. *Customs in Common.* New York: New Press, 1991.

———. "The Moral Economy of the English Crowd in the Eighteenth Century." *Past and Present* 50 (1971): 76–136.

Thornton, John. *Africa and Africans in the Making of the Atlantic World, 1400–1680.* New York: Cambridge University Press, 1992.

Twinam, Ann. *Public Lives, Private Secrets: Gender, Honor, Sexuality and Illegitimacy in Colonial Spanish America.* Stanford: Stanford University Press, 1999.

Vainfas, Ronaldo. *A heresia dos indios: Catolicismo e rebeldia no Brasil colonial.* São Paulo: Companhia das Letras, 1995.

———. *Trópico dos pecados: Moral, sexualidade e Inquisição no Brasil.* Rio de Janeiro: Editora Campus, 1989.

Van Oss, Adriaan C. *Catholic Colonialism: A Parish History of Guatemala, 1524–1821.* New York: Cambridge University Press, 1986.

Van Young, Eric. "Conflict and Solidarity in Indian Village Life: The Guadalajara Region in the Late Colonial Period." *Hispanic American Historical Review* 64:1 (1983): 55–79.

———. "The State as Vampire: Hegemonic Projects, Public Ritual, and Popular Culture in Mexico, 1600–1900." In *Rituals of Rule, Rituals of Resistance,* ed. William Beezley, Cheryl English Martin, and William French. Wilmington, Del.: Scholarly Resources Books, 1994.

Villacorta Calderón, José Antonio. *Historia de la capitanía general de Guatemala.* Guatemala: Tipografía Nacional, 1942.

Villa Rojas, Alfonso. "Kinship and Nagualism in a Tzeltal Community, Southeastern Mexico." *American Anthropologist* 49 (1947): 578–87.

Visweswaran, Kamala. "Defining Feminist Ethnography." *Inscriptions* 3:4 (1988): 27–46.

Wallerstein, Immanuel. *The Modern World System II: Mercantilism and the Consolidation of the European World Economy, 1600–1750.* New York: Academic Press, 1980.

Warren, Kay B. *Indigenous Movements and Their Critics: Pan Maya Activism in Guatemala.* Princeton: Princeton University Press, 1998.

———. "Interpreting *La Violencia* in Guatemala: Shapes of Mayan Silence and Resistance." In *The Violence Within: Cultural and Political Opposition in Divided Nations,* ed. Kay B. Warren. Boulder: Westview Press, 1993.

———. *The Symbolism of Subordination: Indian Identity in a Guatemalan Town.* Austin: University of Texas Press, 1978.

Warren, Kay B., ed. *The Violence Within: Cultural and Political Opposition in Divided Nations.* Boulder: Westview Press, 1993.

Wasserstrom, Robert. "Ethnic Violence and Indigenous Protest: The Tzeltal (Maya) Revolt of 1712." *Journal of Latin American Studies* 12:1 (1980): 1–19.

Watanabe, John M. "From Saints to Shibboleths: Image, Structure, and Identity in Maya Religious Syncretism." *American Ethnologist* 17:1 (1990): 131–50.

———. *Maya Saints and Souls in a Changing World.* Austin: University of Texas Press, 1992.

Weber, Alison. "Santa Teresa, Demonologist." In *Culture and Control in Counter-Reformation Spain,* ed. Anne J. Cruz and Mary Elizabeth Perry. Minneapolis: University of Minnesota Press, 1992.

Wilson, Richard. "Machine Guns and Mountain Spirits: The Cultural Effects of State Repression among the Q'eqchi' of Guatemala." *Critique of Anthropology* 11:1 (1991): 33–61.

Wisdom, Charles. "The Supernatural World and Curing." In *Heritage of Conquest: The Ethnology of Middle America,* ed. Sol Tax. Glencoe, Ill.: Free Press, 1952.

Wolf, Eric R. "Closed Corporate Peasant Communities in Mesoamerica and Central Java." *Southwestern Journal of Anthropology* 13 (1957): 1–18.

———. *Sons of the Shaking Earth.* Chicago: University of Chicago Press, 1959.

Woodward, Ralph Lee, Jr. *Central America: A Nation Divided.* 2d ed. New York: Oxford University Press, 1985.

Wortman, Miles L. *Government and Society in Central America, 1680–1840.* New York: Columbia University Press, 1982.

Zulawski, Ann. "Social Differentiation, Gender, and Ethnicity: Urban Indian Women in Colonial Bolivia, 1640–1725." *Latin American Research Review* 25:2 (1990): 93–113.

Index